Spectacular Realities

Spectacular Realities

Early Mass Culture
in *Fin-de-Siècle* Paris

Vanessa R. Schwartz

UNIVERSITY OF CALIFORNIA PRESS

Berkeley / Los Angeles / London

University of California Press
Berkeley and Los Angeles, California

University of California Press, Ltd.
London, England

First Paperback Printing 1999

Revised versons of the following previously published pieces have
been incorporated into this volume. "Cinematic Spectatorship before
the Apparatus," in *Viewing Positions,* ed. Linda Williams (Rutgers
University Press, 1994). This essay also appeared in *Cinema and the
Invention of Modern Life,* ed. Leo Charney and Vanessa R. Schwartz
(University of California Press, 1995). Copyright 1995 The Regents
of the University of California. "The Morgue and the Musée
Grévin: Understanding the Public Taste for Reality in *Fin-de-Siècle*
Paris," in *Spectacles of Realism,* ed. Margaret Cohen and Christopher
Prendergast (University of Minnesota Press, 1995). Copyright 1995
The Regents of the University of Minnesota. This essay originally
appeared in the *Yale Journal of Criticism* 6, no. 2 (1994). "The
Musée Grévin as Monument of Modern Life," *French Historical
Studies* 19, no. 1 (Spring 1995): 7-26.

Library of Congress Cataloging-in-Publication Data

Schwartz, Vanessa R.
    Spectacular realities: early mass culture in fin-de-siècle Paris /
Vanessa R. Schwartz.
        p.   cm.
    Includes bibliographic references and index
    ISBN 978-0-520-22168-0 (pbk. : alk. paper)
    1. Popular culture—France—Paris—History—19th century.
2. France—Civilization—19th century.   3. Leisure industry—
France—Paris.   4. Spectacular, The—Government policy—
France—Paris.   I. Title.
DC715.S39   1998
944.06—dc21   97-2201

Printed in the United States of America

12   11   10

10   9   8

For my parents and Becky
Who make the everyday spectacular

Contents

Illustrations

Acknowledgments

I would like to thank the Mellon Foundation, the Fulbright Fellowship, and the Townsend Center for the Humanities at the University of California, Berkeley, especially Jean Stone, for financial support of this project when it was a doctoral dissertation for the history department at UC Berkeley. I am grateful to the American University and Dean Betty T. Bennett of the College of Arts and Sciences who have provided the support and time needed to transform a dissertation into a book. I offer thanks to my colleagues in the history department at the American University for welcoming me and my research and for creating an encouraging and supportive workplace. Angela Blake's many hours of research and editorial assistance are only part of the delight of working with a talented graduate student.

Many people have helped this project along the way. In Paris, the direction of the Musée Grévin, especially Chantal Chatelus, Geneviève Morlet of the Bibliothèque historique de la ville de Paris, the staffs of the Police archives and the Arsenal made difficult research easier. Professors Michelle Perrot, Madeleine Rébérioux and especially Alain Corbin were kind enough to allow me to attend their seminars and offered counsel at critical moments when an ocean and a continent separated me from my own advisors. My collaboration with Jean-Jacques Meusy of the Centre national de la recherche scientifique has been a genuine education. I would also like to acknowledge my "Paris friends" for support, intellectual and otherwise: Susan Whitney, Laurie Monahan, Abigail Solomon-Godeau, Carla Hesse, Jann Matlock, Regina Sweeney, Marjorie Beale, Rachel Fuchs, Lenny Berlanstein and Dan Sherman.

In Berkeley, members of Susanna Barrows's dissertation group—David Barnes, Regina Sweeney, Sylvia Schafer, Megan Koreman, Tami Whited, Paul Friedland, Doug Mackaman and Marc Roudebush—read and shaped this project from its initial moments to the last filing rush.

In the process of revising I have relied on a group of scholars for whom I have great respect and who generously read my manuscript. Without the help of Joan Scott, Dan Sherman, Lou Roberts, Cathy Kudlick, Jeannene Przyblyski, Leo Charney and Sharon Marcus this book would still be a dissertation. I have had the privilege to work with the staff of the University of California Press. Ed Dimendberg had faith in my edited book project from the start. Sheila Levine has been of great help and offered much support and counsel. Laura Driussi, Dore Brown and Edith Gladstone have my thanks for the book's production.

Scholars in cinema studies have been especially kind and supportive of my work and I want to thank Annette Michelson, Miriam Hansen, Giuliana Bruno, Linda Williams, Tom Gunning, Richard Abel and especially Mark Sandberg for providing opportunities for scholarly exchange that have enriched me intellectually and have made me feel more like kin than an interloper from French history.

I have had the pleasure and privilege of more than ten years of mentorship from Natalie Z. Davis, Joan W. Scott and Kay B. Warren. They provided the inspiration to pursue academic life, among other things. I have been fortunate to receive additional guidance from Professors Randolph Starn, Carol Clover and Naomi Schor. Susanna Barrows and Tom Laqueur shepherded me through graduate school and made me the historian that I am. Their unbounded enthusiasm and tremendous intellect have inspired me and countless others. Their friendship is the greatest legacy of my years in Berkeley.

Marcus Verhagen, Margaret Cohen, Sarah Farmer and Sharon Marcus offered great friendship and counsel and have sustained an interest in the wax museum that goes beyond the call of duty. Leo Charney is the kind of friend one makes only once in a lifetime. I am grateful that we continue to share our devotion to popular culture (and each other).

Finally, this project was made possible by numerous grants and years of emotional support from the Schwartz family: Ron, Fran and Allison Schwartz and Ruth Haase. They encouraged my intellectual curiosity and sense of the ridiculous. This book, no doubt, reflects that upbringing.

Rebecca Isaacs has been a part of my life for as long as this project has been. Rachel Isaacs Schwartz's arrival overlapped and enhanced its final stages. They, along with E.Z. the dissertation dog, have brought the kind of joy into my life that makes the hours in the archives and at the computer worthwhile. I could not have wished for a more supportive and wonderful family, nor can I imagine any future project without them.

Introduction

"No people in the world are so fond of amusements—or *distractions,* as they term them—as Parisians. Morning, noon, and night, summer and winter, there is always something to be seen and a large portion of the population seems absorbed in the pursuit of pleasure."[1] Cassell's guidebook confirmed that visitors and natives alike expected to find a good time in France's capital. By the last third of the nineteenth century, Paris had become the European center of a burgeoning leisure industry. If Paris seemed a constant source for pleasure, this guidebook also linked that pleasure to the promise of "something to be seen."

"Paris is the real . . . and permanent exposition of all of France," explained Edmond Deschaumes in his book about the city published during the year of the 1889 exposition.[2] The expositions hosted by the city in 1855, 1867, 1878, 1889 and 1900 not only brought millions of visitors (as many as fifty-one million in 1900) to marvel at the temporary displays, but their frequency and success transformed observers' impressions of the city itself. Paris did not merely host exhibitions, it had become one. These impressions of Paris as a place to see captured the defining character of what in the second half of the nineteenth century became known as *Paris nouveau.*

It has become a cliché to speak of the varied means through which representations of the nineteenth-century city and Paris, in particular, attempted to render an increasingly complex and diversified urban space

---

1. *Illustrated Guide to Paris* (London: Cassell, 1884), 111.
2. Edmond Deschaumes, *Pour bien voir Paris* (Paris: Maurice Dreyfous, 1889), 84.

more legible and transparent. Through both words and images, city life became a spectacular realist narrative, and visualizing the city became synonymous with knowing it.

This book looks at the spectacularization of city life and its connection to the emergence of mass culture. It juxtaposes a constellation of distinctly and self-consciously "modern" and "popular" cultural forms: boulevard culture, the mass press, public visits to the Paris Morgue, wax museums, panoramas and dioramas, and film.[3] Aside from their enormous popularity, these forms realistically represented a sensationalized version of contemporary life. Packaged as *actualités*—"current events, news"—this combination of verisimilitude in representation and the thematic display of a press-style version of everyday life are not mere descriptions of urban mass culture. Their consumption became one of the means by which a mass culture and a new urban crowd became a society of spectators.

At the moment that practically universal literacy became a reality in France, so did the saturation of communication forms with images. The development of lithography, photography and technologies that made illustrated books and the illustrated press accessible and cheap led to an unprecedented circulation of mundane visual representations. But they also connected words and images as never before as general readers could for the first time read words and then directly encounter a referenced image.

For ordinary people in the late nineteenth century, the word and the image were linked as never before, yet scholars have tended to treat them as distinct and sometimes even opposed cultural forms. This is nowhere more evident than in the literature about "city texts." Most studies of urban representations have focused on either written or visual materials in their attempts to explain urban legibility or have indiscriminately moved back and forth between written and visual texts, devoting greater attention to thematics than to the specificity of the media.[4]

3. I take "popular culture" to mean "beliefs and practices, and objects through which they are organized, that are widely shared among a population." Chandra Mukerji and Michael Schudson, introduction to *Rethinking Popular Culture* (Berkeley: University of California Press, 1991), 3.

4. For an emphasis on written texts see Peter Fritzsche, *Reading Berlin 1900* (Cambridge, Mass.: Harvard University Press, 1996); and Judith Walkowitz, *City of Dreadful Delight: Narratives of Sexual Danger in Late Victorian London* (Chicago: University of Chicago Press, 1992). T. J. Clark, *The Painting of Modern Life* (Princeton: Princeton University Press, 1984) emphasizes visual culture. Both Priscilla Ferguson, *Paris as Revolution: Writing the Nineteenth-Century City* (Berkeley: University of California Press, 1994); and

As a study of the visuality of urban culture in late nineteenth-century Paris, this book attempts to demonstrate that urban representation relied on the explicit connection between written and visual texts being made by both their producers and consumers. This book advocates a semiotic analysis that moves across different media while paying careful attention to the specificity of each form. More broadly, it argues for the logic of understanding that a culture that became "more literate" also became more visual as word and image generated the spectacular realities described here.[5]

Urban spectacle has been understood as a defining quality of "modernity" generally construed; and Paris toasted as the quintessentially modern city—the "capital of the nineteenth century" in Walter Benjamin's by now classic turn-of-phrase.[6] Modern life seemed urban by definition, yet the social and economic transformations wrought by modernity recast the image of the city in the wake of the eruption of industrial capitalism in the second half of the nineteenth century. In Paris, the city's midcentury redesign, otherwise known as "Haussmannization," was contrived by Napoleon III and his Prefect of the Seine, Baron Georges Haussmann, to "modernize" the city's infrastructure, creating sweeping boulevards for the city's traffic, a new sewer system, and a reconstructed central market.[7] In this formulation, scholars equate modernity with modernization as a set of social historical relations. As an elaboration of modernization, the city's redesign expressed its material fulfillment as a site created by and for the bourgeoisie in its transformation from an industrial to a commercial capital.[8] For others,

Christopher Prendergast, *Paris and the Nineteenth Century* (Manchester: Blackwell, 1992) use different kinds of texts to make general claims about representation rather than specific connections between written and visual cultures.

5. Anne Higonnet also advocates including social and literary history in the analysis of visual culture, in her essay "Real Fashion: Clothes Unmake the Working Woman," in *Spectacles of Realism: Gender, Body, Genre,* ed. Margaret Cohen and Christopher Prendergast (Minneapolis: University of Minnesota Press, 1995). I thank Margaret Cohen for helping me clarify this point.

6. Benjamin's term comes from the prospectus for his arcades project, "Paris, Capital of the Nineteenth Century," in *Charles Baudelaire,* trans. Harry Zohn, 3d ed. (London: Verso, 1989). See also David Harvey, *Consciousness and the Urban Experience* (Baltimore: Johns Hopkins University Press, 1989); and William Sharpe and Leonard Wallock, eds., *Visions of the Modern City* (Baltimore: Johns Hopkins University Press, 1987).

7. See especially David Pinkney's classic study, *Napoleon III and the Rebuilding of Paris* (Princeton: Princeton University Press, 1958).

8. Philip Nord, *Paris Shopkeepers and the Politics of Resentment* (Princeton: Princeton University Press, 1986).

modernity is a set of representational practices that embraces what the poet Charles Baudelaire long ago noted in his seminal essay, "The Painter of Modern Life"—the essential quality of being present, the ephemeral, the fugitive and the contingent.[9]

But modernity's several conceptualizations need not stand in opposition—as T. J. Clark's tour-de-force, *The Painting of Modern Life*, demonstrates. Clark brilliantly recast these divergent definitions, insisting that changes in representation—Impressionism in this case—cannot be understood without recourse to social historical transformation; in particular without primary consideration of the domination of urban life by capitalism that resulted in the city becoming a "sign" of capital.[10] In Clark's book, however, the status of representation is nevertheless derived from, if more than simply reflective of, transformations in the "realities" produced by the rise of capitalism. Extending Clark's argument that no history of culture can be divorced from historical context, this book attempts to show that any history is a history of representation because modes of representation constituted rather than merely characterized modern urban culture.

Clark analyzed the death of the old Paris and the ground preparation for the new "consumer society."[11] Inspired, in part, by Guy Debord's *Society of the Spectacle*, Clark suggests that images replaced social relations in the modern city and led to the atomized, anomic conditions in which the modern urban dweller was seen as alone in a crowd.[12] This alienation, it follows, produced both the failed revolution—the Paris Commune and the bloody week of May 1871—and the decidedly nonrevolutionary nature of social life in Paris for the rest of the century. The anarchist bomb-thrower replaced the revolutionary crowd as the model of fin-de-siècle urban discontents.[13]

This book, in part, asks what happened to the crowd in fin-de-siècle Paris. For, since the Revolution of 1789 forward, whether one's aim was

9. Charles Baudelaire, "The Painter of Modern Life," in *The Painter of Modern Life and Other Essays*, trans. and ed. J. Mayne (London: Phaidon Press, 1964), 13. The most influential articulation of this remains Marshall Berman, *All That Is Solid Melts Into Air* (New York: Simon and Schuster, 1982).

10. Clark, *Painting of Modern Life*, 69.

11. Ibid.

12. See Guy Debord, *The Society of the Spectacle* (Detroit: Black and Red, 1983). As Martin Jay notes, Debord argues that the spectacle is a social relation. Martin Jay, *Downcast Eyes* (Berkeley, University of California Press, 1993), 427.

13. For more on anarchism see Richard D. Sonn, *Anarchism and Cultural Politics in Fin-de-Siècle France* (Lincoln: University of Nebraska Press, 1989).

to tame it, join it, or please it, the crowd became a central player in modern France. If French political culture stood for anything since the end of the Old Regime, it stood for the seemingly limitless powers of the collective action of the urban masses that resulted in the numerous revolutions punctuating French history until the suppression of the Commune. Paris remained a revolutionary space, but in the last third of the nineteenth century, its revolutions were cultural, as the political order of the Third Republic—threatened, challenged, and contested—managed to bend but never break.[14] While the likes of Gabriel Tarde and Gustave Le Bon may have been theorizing the dangers of crowds,[15] this book focuses on the equally potent phenomenon of crowd-pleasing. In particular, this book describes a variety of novel practices and institutions of the visual that sprang up in late nineteenth-century Paris to celebrate the diversity of the Parisian public, as its producers aimed to please this heterogeneous mass through the construction of shared visual experiences.

The use of the term "crowd" has generally implied a sort of urban assembly whose participants derived a collective identity through violent actions. The French term *la foule* also carries the distinctly negative connotations of a term such as "mob." The crowd, and the experience of belonging to an urban collectivity more generally, did not disappear as those who stress the alienation of modern urban life suggest. Rather, their collective violence did. This book argues that there was a new crowd that became the audience of and for urban spectacularity.

In this capacity, this is a book whose depiction of modern urban culture as spectacular questions Foucault's model of interiorization and individuation created by the panoptic machine. For Foucault, the "crowd" disappeared into a "collection of separated individualities" in a disciplinary society.[16] Unlike the model of the Panopticon wherein everyone could be seen, urban spectacle, rather, urged everyone to see. Tony Bennett's formulation of the "exhibitionary complex," which stresses the multiplicity of institutions of exhibition rather than those

---

14. Not all collective political action came to an abrupt halt in Paris after 1871, as social protest such as the Stavisky riots and May 1968 make clear. Yet new uses for city streets and spaces overtook that of home to the revolutionary crowd. See Ferguson, *Paris as Revolution,* on revolution as the primary metaphor for Parisian life.

15. See Susanna I. Barrows, *Distorting Mirrors* (New Haven: Yale University Press, 1981).

16. Michel Foucault, *Discipline and Punish,* trans. Alan Sheridan (New York: Vintage Books, 1979), 201.

of confinement, is a parallel to Foucault's carceral archipelago and makes a good deal of sense when conceptualizing modern urban culture.

Bennett's model offers an important corrective to Foucault's notions of the mechanisms of power in modernity.[17] Bennett returns to the notion that bourgeois governments needed to win their citizens' hearts and minds and enlisted their active support for the values promoted by and for the state.[18] Bennett, however, still employs Foucault's idea of voluntary self-regulation, here instilled by seeing rather than by being seen. His otherwise useful intervention thus ultimately offers only a different means to the same Foucaultian gloomy end.[19] In what follows I attempt to look beyond the state and its institutions as I explain why visual display and exhibition worked best to win the hearts and minds of the urban crowd.

The visual representation of reality as spectacle in late nineteenth-century Paris created a common culture and a sense of shared experiences through which people might begin to imagine themselves as participating in a metropolitan culture because they had visual evidence that such a shared world, of which they were a part, existed.[20] In short, "spectacular realities" in urban culture need to be added to such processes as the democratization of politics, the fruitlessness of mass uprisings, and increased standards of living, as part of the foundations of "mass society."

This book is situated in, but is not primarily conceived as a study of, fin-de-siècle France. It explicitly, self-consciously and exclusively treats Paris as its subject not because Paris was representative of France but because Paris had enormous power to "represent." When it came to "modernity," Paris stood for things French. Further, as a book whose focus is on Parisian and metropolitan culture, it might more fruitfully make connections with city life in London and New York than in Marseilles or Lyons. It favors the term "fin de siècle" over "Belle Epoque," de-emphasizing debates on whether the age that preceded the First

17. Tony Bennett, *The Birth of the Museum: History, Theory, Politics* (New York: Routledge, 1995).

18. Ibid., 87.

19. In *Birth of the Museum*, 229–45, Bennett seems to be pushing for the potential for transgressive uses of Blackpool Pleasure Beach and thus for more than public complicity in their own self-regulation.

20. My argument draws on Benedict Anderson's comments on national community. In *Imagined Communities,* 2d ed. (London: Verso, 1991), 25, he suggests that the representation of the contemporary world through newspapers cultivated nationalism because newspapers provided the "technical means for re-presenting the kind of imagined community that is the nation."

World War was more or less "Belle" or "beleaguered."[21] Rather than examine the way cultural phenomena reflected or constructed the po litical order— and its upheaval—this book explores how cultural phenomena signified and constructed social relations.[22]

The material discussed here was part of a broad transformation in the West known as the rise of consumer culture. Recently, scholars have not only moved analyses of capitalism away from production and work toward consumption and leisure, but also they have been particularly attentive to reconfigurations of public space and to the new publics that appeared freely to inhabit the glitzy, sparkling and seductive spaces of consumption.[23] By describing a constellation of cultural practices in Paris, this book reconfirms the emergence of consumerism as part and parcel of transformations in urban culture. In particular, it delineates the means by which novelty media solicited participation by the broadest and most diverse audience possible. It also attempts to specify what made Paris a particularly interesting site in which to locate these changes.

Beyond the culture of consumption, this book traces the emergence and formation of mass culture in Paris in the late nineteenth-century. Definitions of mass culture are notoriously slippery but have tended to fix on two elements: mass production by industrial techniques and consumption by most of the people, most of the time.[24] The historical study of mass culture has focused primarily on the United States.[25] When mass culture has been discussed in French history, it has been located as part of the history of Americanization.[26] Recent examinations

21. Barrows, *Distorting Mirrors,* 2.

22. This problem plagues Charles Rearick, *Pleasures of the Belle Epoque* (New Haven: Yale University Press, 1985), which understands entertainment as "dancing on the volcano" before the eruption of war.

23. Among the most important works on consumption that relate to this study are Rosalind Williams, *Dream Worlds: Mass Consumption in Late Nineteenth-Century France* (Berkeley: University of California Press, 1982), Rachel Bowlby, *Just Looking: Consumer Culture in Dreiser, Gissing, and Zola* (New York: Methuen, 1985), Michael Miller, *The Bon Marché: Bourgeois Culture and the Department Store, 1869–1920* (Princeton: Princeton University Press, 1981).

24. James Naremore and Patrick Brantlinger, introduction to *Modernity and Mass Culture* (Bloomington: Indiana University Press, 1991), 2.

25. See, for example, John Kasson, *Amusing the Million* ((New York: Hill and Wang, 1978); Kathy Peiss, *Cheap Amusements* (Philadelphia: Temple University Press, 1986); David Nasaw, *Going Out: The Rise and Fall of Public Amusement* (New York: Basic Books, 1993); and Richard Wightman Fox and T. J. Jackson Lears, *The Culture of Consumption* (New York: Pantheon, 1983).

26. See Richard Kuisel, *Seducing the French: The Dilemma of Americanization* (Berkeley: University of California Press, 1993); Victoria de Grazia, "Mass Culture and Sover-

of "Americanism" by such scholars as Jean Baudrillard and Umberto Eco, as well as the hostile French response to American mass culture epitomized in the denunciations of EuroDisney, have blinded scholarship to the fact that, in the late nineteenth century, the French proudly fêted their "modernity"—especially their introduction of novel technologies such as film and their mastery of urban spectacle and modern modes of spectatorship. By focusing on the origins of mass culture in late nineteenth-century Paris, I argue that Paris was an innovator, not a mere imitator, of modern mass cultural forms. Although today Americans and the French themselves like to remark on the capital's quaint cafés and magnificent art museums, it is no coincidence that the Eiffel Tower, an engineering feat of form, designed as spectacle and accomplished for ephemeral consumption at the exposition of 1889, stood as and has remained, a beacon of Parisian life.

One of the key issues in the history of mass culture involves the status of its consumers, now transformed into spectators. Historians have paid scant attention to the transformations in visual culture that constitute the history of mass spectatorship. Instead, their colleagues in cultural studies and cinema studies have explored its many facets.[27] Initially, scholars in these fields studied spectatorship in fundamentally ahistorical ways as a series of idealized models of individual viewing. On the one hand, psychoanalytic frameworks posited a universal and timeless theory of spectatorship in direct relation to a technology such as the cinematic apparatus. On the other hand, scholars adopted a Foucaultian approach that relied on studying the idealized vision of individuals produced through discourses about perception and embodied in technological innovations.[28]

Spectatorship has only just begun to be studied as an historical phenomenon that is produced in a particular cultural moment. Tom

---

eignty: The American Challenge to European Cinemas, 1920–1960," *Journal of Modern History* 61 (March 1989): 53–87; and Kristin Ross, *Fast Cars, Clean Bodies* (Cambridge, Mass.: MIT Press, 1995).

27. Art historians have long been concerned with "viewing" positions, but for a much more limited audience. The most relevant work is Michael Fried, *Absorption and Theatricality* (Berkeley: University of California Press, 1980).

28. See Christian Metz, *The Imaginary Signifier* (Bloomington: University of Indiana Press, 1981); and Laura Mulvey, *Visual and Other Pleasures* (Bloomington: University of Indiana Press, 1989). For the ground-breaking Foucaultian appproach see Jonathan Crary, *Techniques of the Observer* (Cambridge, Mass.: MIT Press, 1990). For a survey of various positions on spectatorship, see Linda Williams, ed., *Viewing Positions* (New Brunswick: Rutgers University Press, 1994).

Gunning, Miriam Hansen, Giuliana Bruno, Mark Sandberg, Leo Charney and I pay more careful attention to specific contexts and conditions of viewing and locate the emergence of film, specifically, in a broader fin-de-siècle visual culture.[29] While previous studies have been technologically driven and media-specific, we argue that spectators participated in a variety of visual entertainments in a given historical moment. Understanding the cues and styles of a variety of visual entertainments enhances what is media-specific while filling out a richer, more historically embedded experience. To contribute to the history of spectatorship, this study locates the emergence of film in a diverse culture of visual habits and activities in late nineteenth-century Paris.

Scholars attempting to historicize spectatorship have turned to *flânerie* and its location in the historically specific conditions of the new consumer-oriented city.[30] *Flânerie* in this context is a shorthand for the mode of modern urban spectatorship that emphasizes mobility and fluid subjectivity.[31] My conceit is that *flânerie* dominated commercial cultural spectating for and by the masses. *Flânerie*'s delights unlock the pleasures of modern urban spectatorship.

As a Parisian "type" the *flâneur* has been taken to exemplify the masculine and bourgeois privilege of modern public life in Paris.[32] The *flâneur* delighted in the sight of the city and its tumultuous crowd, while allegedly remaining aloof and detached from it. His sentiments about life in the city could be found in Baudelaire's pronouncement that "The life of our city is rich in poetic and marvellous subjects."[33] An inveterate stroller, the *flâneur* "goes botanizing on the asphalt" according to Walter Benjamin, who also noted that his original home was

---

29. See Tom Gunning, "The Aesthetic of Astonishment: The Cinema of Attractions," in *Viewing Positions,* ed. Linda Williams (New Brunswick: Rutgers University Press, 1994); Miriam Hansen, *Babel and Babylon* (Cambridge, Mass.: Harvard University Press, 1991); Giuliana Bruno, *Street-Walking on a Ruined Map* (Princeton: Princeton University Press, 1993); and Mark Sandberg, "Missing Persons: Spectacle and Narrative in Late Nineteenth-Century Scandinavia" (Ph.D. diss., University of California, Berkeley, 1991). See also Leo Charney and Vanessa R. Schwartz, eds., *Cinema and the Invention of Modern Life* (Berkeley, University of California Press, 1995).

30. *Flânerie,* like "modernity," has inspired much discussion and debate. On its interpretations and uses see Keith Tester, ed., *The Flâneur* (New York: Routledge, 1994).

31. See Anne Friedberg, *Window Shopping* (Berkeley. University of California Press, 1993), 16–17.

32. See Janet Wolff, "The Invisible *Flâneuse*," in *Feminine Sentences* (Berkeley, University of California Press, 1990), 5. See also Tester, ed., *The Flâneur.*

33. Charles Baudelaire, *The Salon of 1846,* cited in Wolff, *Feminine Sentences,* 37.

the arcade before Haussmann's transformations made the streets themselves comfortable places in which to walk.[34]

According to the cultural critic Janet Wolff, he had no female counterpart: "There is no question of inventing the *flâneuse:* the essential point is that such a character was rendered impossible by the sexual divisions of the nineteenth century."[35] Nineteenth-century writers and artists reinforced this notion through their obsessive depiction of prostitutes.[36] Anne Friedberg, among others, argues there was a *flâneuse* and traces her origins to women's legitimate occupation of urban space through the rise of consumer culture.[37] I would like to suggest that debate over the existence of the *flâneuse* or the working-class *flâneur*, for that matter, misses the point. The *flâneur* is not so much a person as *flânerie* is a positionality of power—one through which the spectator assumes the position of being able to be part of the spectacle and yet command it at the same time.[38]

But there was more to viewing than the "viewing positions" it offered spectators. One of the pleasures of modern life, this book argues, was the collective participation in a culture in which representations proliferated to such an extent that they became interchangeable with reality. As I have already remarked, and as the first chapter will explore in greater detail, life in Paris became so powerfully identified with spectacle that reality seemed to be experienced as a show—an object to be looked at rather than experienced in an unmediated form. At the same time, shows featured modern life, represented as realistically as possible.

Realism has already been well studied in art and literature in nineteenth-century France.[39] As a mode of representation, it worked to con-

34. Benjamin, *Charles Baudelaire*, 37.

35. Wolff, *Feminine Sentences*, 47.

36. See Charles Bernheimer, *Figures of Ill Repute* (Cambridge, Mass.: Harvard University Press, 1989); and Jann Matlock, *Scenes of Seduction: Prostitution, Hysteria, and Reading Difference in Nineteenth-Century France* (New York: Columbia University Press, 1993) for insights on the representation of prostitutes.

37. Friedberg, *Window Shopping*, 32–37. See also Bowlby, *Just Looking*; Walkowitz, *City of Dreadful Delight*; Erika Rappaport, *The West End and Women's Pleasure: Gender and Commercial Culture in London, 1860–1914* (forthcoming, Princeton University Press) on women in the city; and my paper, "Gender and Boulevard Culture: Were the Only Women in Public, Public Women?" delivered at the annual meeting of the American Historical Association, San Francisco, 1994.

38. I thank Jeannene Przyblyski for helping me rethink *flânerie*.

39. See Linda Nochlin, *Realism* (London: Penguin, 1971); T. J. Clark, *Image of the People* (Greenwich, Conn.: New York Graphic Society, 1973); Michael Fried, *Courbet's Realism* (Chicago, University of Chicago Press, 1990); Georg Lukács, *Studies in European Realism,* introduction by Alfred Kazin (New York: Grosset and Dunlop, 1964); Eric Auerbach, *Mimesis,* trans. Willard Trask (Princeton: Princeton University Press, 1974); Fredric

struct standards of the real to which it then referred. The real is thus only an effect although it seems to precede its representation.[40] This book explores its effect on forms of mainstream commercial culture designed for a mass audience using texts and images that have, for the most part, gone unexamined. In particular, it attempts to explain the appeal of the category of reality as an object of consumption and delineates the way that experiences were configured into moments and events.[41] This study also shows how sensationalizing and literally spectacularizing became the means through which reality was commodified.

The cultural forms described in this book represented, captured and "produced" reality in a variety of ways. Some forms, such as the panorama, existed as early as the beginning of the nineteenth century; others, such as film, arrived at the century's end. Haussmannization occurred at midcentury. But it was in the fin de siècle—which in this project denotes Paris after the Commune, and mostly in the 1880s and 1890s—that the phenomena examined in this book first coexisted in an urban frenzy out of which a culture "for the masses" emerged.

Each of the five chapters of this book approaches the construction of spectacular realities through different but allied material. The first sets the stage by examining the visuality of modern boulevard culture and its connection to the way the mass press used sensationalism to frame and re-present the everyday as spectacle. The second chapter concerns the popularity of public visits to the Paris Morgue, where bodies were laid out behind a large display window for consideration by anyone who stopped by. As a free theater for the masses, the morgue fit into a modern Parisian landscape in which the banal and the everyday were embedded in sensational narratives.

If the first two chapters elaborate the way that modern urban life was re-presented as spectacle, the next three chapters focus on novel entertainments whose form and content attempted to be as realistic as possible. Chapter three examines the wildly successful wax museum

Jameson, *The Political Unconscious* (Ithaca: Cornell University Press, 1981); George Levine, ed., *Realism and Representation* (Madison: University of Wisconsin Press, 1993); Naomi Schor, *Reading in Detail* (New York: Methuen, 1987); and Cohen and Prendergast, eds., *Spectacles of Realism.*

40. Roland Barthes describes the notion in "The Reality Effect," in *The Rustle of Language,* trans. Richard Howard (New York: Hill and Wang, 1986).

41. Joel Fineman suggests that because the narration of a singular event uniquely refers to the real, it has a privileged status among forms of historical narrative. I think the depiction of urban life as a series of singular news items also shored up their status as real. See Joel Fineman, "The History of the Anecdote: Fiction and Fiction," in *The New Historicism,* ed. H. Aram Veeser (New York: Routledge, 1989).

opened in 1882—the Musée Grévin—and asks why a wax museum captured the public imagination in fin-de-siècle France. In the course of
my research in France, I gained access to the museum's private and un-
cataloged papers, which also provide a rare glimpse into the daily work-
ings of this institution belonging to the nascent entertainment industry. Chapter four examines the contemporaneous "o-rama" craze of the
1880s and 1890s. Chapter five details the history of early cinema at the
Musée Grévin as a prism through which to see cinema's origins as part
of a broader cultural climate that demanded "the real thing."

This book takes popular behavior and entertainments seriously in
order to explain what might be appealing about such things as the
morgue and the wax museum to rather diverse groups of people. It is
not merely that these phenomena were the best "sold"—although they
had to be sold well to succeed. Anyone who has mulled through the
bankruptcy files at the Paris Archives knows that for every successful
type of novelty there were infinitely more failures. Mass culture works
through a dialogue between its producers and consumers—a dialogue
that disrupts the fixed notions of production and consumption. This
book attempts to illuminate the possible spaces between manipulation
and enjoyment that Michel de Certeau introduced in recognition that
culture is more "poached" than it is produced and consumed.[42]

The perhaps seemingly eclectic juxtaposition of these different cultural practices identifies a newly forming Parisian mass culture characterized by a shared visual experience of seeing reality represented. This
project delineates the popularity of seeing "reality" as a set of refer-
ents—people, places, incidents—that Parisians shared, whatever their
social origins or gender identities. Nowhere do I claim that these different sets of eyes experienced this culture of realist spectacle in the
same way. No doubt, they did not. Rather, by studying the realistic
re-presentation and visualization of modern life, this book shows that
what appears to the historian like disparate phenomena formed a shared
culture in late nineteenth-century Paris. This culture produced a new
crowd as individuals joined together to delight in the transformation
of everyday life into spectacle while avidly consuming spectacles of a
sensationalized everyday life. In this way, Paris not only earned its label
as the "capital of the nineteenth century," it brilliantly anticipated the
twentieth.

42. Michel de Certeau, *The Practice of Everyday Life,* trans. Steven Rendall (Berkeley:
University of California Press, 1984), xxiv.

CHAPTER I

Setting the Stage

*The Boulevard, The Press
and the Framing of Everyday Life*

Gustave Fraipont, in a book whose very title, *Paris, à vol d'oiseau,* suggested that the city should be observed from above, boasted, "It's the freedom of gazes that rules in Paris and rules here alone . . . and that turns the big city into a spectacle that is always lively, animated and joyous."[1] Although the connection of city life to visuality was not new in the nineteenth century, the identification of Paris as a place where everyday life was elevated to a spectacle for mass consumption was. These qualities, along with the redesign of the city known as Haussmannization, became markers of the city's modernity whereby Paris became the metropolis *par excellence* (fig. 1).

Contemporaries celebrated and lionized Paris precisely for its modernity, which of course served as the very means of rhetorically constructing it. Although it is essential to account for transformations in the actual Parisian landscape, most notably the results of Haussmannization and the explosion of commercial capitalism that it denotes— what I will call "boulevard culture"—Paris also became powerfully identified as an object by being widely disseminated as a spectacle in the new mass press; in guidebooks, serial novels, and most importantly, in the daily newspaper. Simply put, Paris was transformed into spectacle in these texts through the invention of an "everyday" that was then framed as textual representation and subsequently re-presented as sen-

1. Gustave Fraipont, *Paris, à vol d'oiseau* (Paris: Librairie illustrée, 1889), 5.

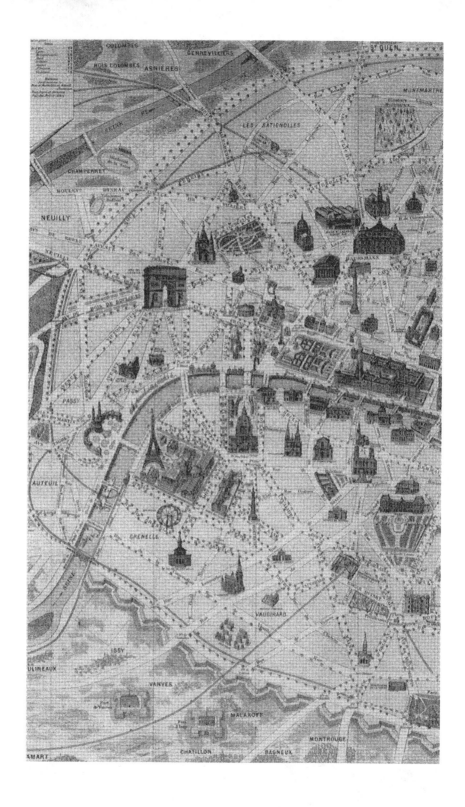

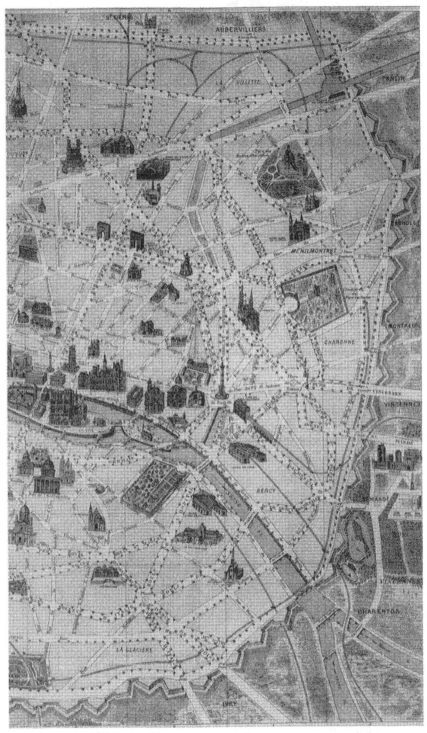

1. Map of central Paris, ca. 1900. Geography and Map Division, Library of Congress, Washington, D.C.

sational. For it was not the seemingly quotidian elements of Parisian life that served as the measure of the modern, but rather the implication and the possibility that the everyday could be transformed into the spectacular and the sensational.

Georg Simmel, the early urban sociologist, noted that "the interpersonal relationships of people in big cities are characterized by a markedly greater emphasis on the use of the eyes than that of the ears," as if to say that what marked modern urban life was its flamboyant visuality.[2] More recently, scholars have associated this pleasure strictly with the bourgeois male known as the *flâneur*. I suggest, instead, the many ways in which *flânerie* became a cultural activity for a generalized Parisian public.

In a discursive feat of centralization that mimicked the city's administration and reorganization, the mass press incessantly conjured a never-ending festival of modern life that unfolded in and around the *grands boulevards*. The new mass press provided a printed digest of the *flâneur*'s roving eye. The printed word provided access to modern Paris for an increasingly literate population by constructing Paris as an image. The interlocking relation between the boulevards and the press fostered a new curiosity among a large and diverse population to first read and then see things for themselves and created a culture in which individuals from different classes and of both sexes were expected to derive pleasure from the same sights and experiences.[3] The spectacular and sensational urban life promoted on the boulevards and in the mass press offered the means through which a new collectivity was constituted—one that was distinctly urban and quintessentially "modern."

Haussmannization

"Haussmannization," which vastly altered the city's topography, is often used as a shorthand for the profound economic and cultural changes associated with the ascension of the bourgeois social order in the Paris of the 1850s and 1860s. Haussmann opened up the

2. Georg Simmel, "Mélanges de philosophie rélativiste," cited in Benjamin, *Charles Baudelaire*, 151.

3. Fritzsche's book *Reading Berlin 1900* addresses similar issues but appeared too late for me to take full account of his contribution.

city's center, leading one English guidebook to remark that "in Paris everything is so large and so broad, that the pedestrian can move with perfect freedom."[4] The old streets had rarely been wider than fifteen feet. As one observer looking back, put it: "The inner streets were narrow, crooked, crowded, ill built, and very unsavoury."[5] The city had practically no thoroughfares going north-south except from the rue St-Denis to the rue de la Harpe and from the rue St-Martin to the rue St-Jacques. No street went through from east to west.

In an effort to facilitate the movement of traffic through the city, Baron Haussmann, Napoleon III's prefect of the Seine, built boulevards. The boulevard Sébastopol, the first boulevard work of the Second Empire, formed an extension south of the Gare de l'Est and crossed the city north-south, running through the Ile de la Cité as the boulevard du Palais and across the left bank as the boulevard St-Michel (see fig. 1). Because the boulevard pierced through a populous area, many working-class dwellings were destroyed, setting the pace of the displacement of workers from the city's center that has been associated as both a goal and by-product of the city's redesign. Haussmann built still other boulevards: the boulevard Malesherbes, the boulevard de la Madeleine, and the boulevard Haussmann in the center of town; the boulevards Magenta, Richard Lenoir and Prince Eugène further east; and those that radiated from the place de l'Etoile in the west of the city.

Both during and since their construction, these boulevards have sparked much debate. Scholars have considered them to epitomize the counterrevolutionary tactics of social control enforced by Haussmannization because of their displacement of workers from the city's center and because they effectively separated working-class neighborhoods from each other. The new straight thoroughfares were thought to be barricade-proof (barricades had been crucial to the success of the revolution of 1848 that, ironically, led to Napoleon III's rise to the presidency) and would facilitate the rapid deployment of troops and provide unbroken lines of fire for artillery. Yet the *grands boulevards* that stretched in a semicircle from the Bastille in the east to La Madeleine in the west—those boulevards that came to stand for "modern Paris"— actually predate the midcentury transformation of the nation's capital.

4. *Illustrated Guide to Paris*, 64.
5. *The Morning Post*, 1862, cited in Donald J. Olsen, *The City as a Work of Art* (New Haven: Yale University Press, 1986), 35.

The *grands boulevards* stood as the city's original ramparts until the late seventeenth century when Louis XIV transformed them into an open throughway and built great arches to commemorate his military victories. The *grands boulevards* were neither designed nor built during Hausssmann's vast reconstruction of the city.[6] "Boulevard culture" during the second half of the nineteenth century, instead, was an amalgamation of long-term urban practices that were recast in light of Haussmannization.

Historians of the eighteenth century have argued that the boulevards offered the greatest show in prerevolutionary Paris.[7] Robert Isherwood has described an animated culture of café-goers, musicians, prostitutes and workers; what Louis Sébastien Mercier, in his *Tableau de Paris* of the 1780s called the place "most open to every estate."[8] The boulevards, but especially the boulevard du Temple, became celebrated for the popular theater that played there. At a time when almost all theater in Paris was a highly restricted and state-supported monopoly venture among the Opéra, the Comédie-Française and the Comédie-Italienne, the boulevard du Temple featured the Théâtre Nicolet and that of his rival Audinot, the Ambigu-Comique.[9] Other entertainments abounded on the boulevards: marionettes, acrobats, menageries, wax cabinets. One contemporary observer noted:

An infinite crowd of people, an amazing quantity of carriages, street merchants darting in and out amongst . . . the horses with all sorts of merchandise, chairs set on the sidewalks for those who want to watch and for those who want to be watched, cafés fitted up with an orchestra and French and Italian singers, pastry-cooks, restaurant-keepers . . . marionettes, acrobats . . . giants, dwarfs, ferocious beasts, sea monsters, wax figures, automatons, ventriloquists.[10]

The eighteenth-century commercial culture associated with the boulevards "cracked the social stratification separating the highborn and the lowborn," concluded Isherwood, creating a unified counterculture to the officially sanctioned culture of the court. He argued for a common

---

6. *Les grands boulevards* (Paris: Réunion des musées de Paris, 1985), 5.

7. Robert Isherwood, *Farce and Fantasy: Popular Entertainment in Eighteenth-Century Paris* (New York: Oxford University Press, 1986), 161.

8. Ibid, 163.

9. For a history of Parisian theaters see Michèle Root-Bernstein, *Boulevard Theater and Revolution in Eighteenth-Century Paris* (Ann Arbor: UMI Research Press, 1984).

10. Memoirs of Carlo Goldoni, from 1780s, cited in ibid., 42.

culture of entertainment, what Michèle Root-Bernstein in her history of boulevard theater dubbed "an urban popular culture."[11]

Social life continued to parade on the *grands boulevards* during the first half of the nineteenth century. At the same time, the newly built *passages* or arcades, located either directly off the boulevards or just slightly to the south of the boulevard Montmartre, attracted fashionable society. Early mini-malls of the luxury trade, the arcades were described as "a city, indeed a world in miniature."[12]

Cafés, theaters and newspapers also rallied Parisians to the boulevards. Despite a proliferation of sites of entertainment and amusement throughout the city, the boulevards continued to draw a dense and diverse crowd as they had during before the French Revolution. In fact, their theaters, such as the Théâtre des Funambules, remained one of the few places where workers and ladies mixed under the same roof. Some scholars such as Philip Nord have stressed the semiaristocratic flavor of boulevard life before Haussmannization, followed by a post-Haussmann "democratization" and commercialization of space.[13] I suggest that what changed were the values attributed to a boulevard culture that had existed, more or less continuously, since the late eighteenth century. By the mid-nineteenth century, life on the boulevard was no longer represented as cross-class Parisian counterculture as Isherwood characterized it in the Old Regime. The *grands boulevards* had come to stand not only for "the heart and the head of Paris" but also "the soul of the entire world."[14] In the eighteenth century, cross-class culture was counterculture; in the nineteenth it came to epitomize the pleasures of modern urban life.

When Parisians in the second half of the nineteenth century spoke of *les grands boulevards*, they usually meant the area west of the newly refurbished place du Château-d'Eau and more specifically the area between the Théâtre du Gymnase at the porte St-Martin and the Madeleine.[15] The easternmost portion of the boulevards lay squarely within

11. Ibid., 107. Aside from the boulevards, the Palais-Royal was an important site of popular entertainment, especially around the turn of the nineteenth century.

12. Unidentified guidebook cited in Benjamin, *Charles Baudelaire,* 158.

13. See Philip Nord, paper delivered at the conference "Paris in the time of Manet" in San Francisco, March 1992, 5. I thank the author for sharing the paper with me and for our discussions about Parisian culture.

14. *Paris en poche: guide Conty* (Paris: Maison Conty, 1883), 147.

15. In 1862 Haussmann razed most of what had been the boulevard du Temple (also known as "the boulevard du crime") to allow for the extension of the place du Château d'Eau (now place de la République) despite objections to the loss of many by-then historic theaters.

one of the few areas not "Haussmannized"; there workers remained and dwellings had not been rebuilt. Not part of "modern" Paris, their exclusion reveals what has been called the westward shift of the city. As one observer noted, "one has to reach the place de la République [changed from the place du Château d'Eau in 1879] itself to find this liveliness, this noise, this intensity of life that is the distinctive characteristic of the boulevard."[16] Some observers, such as Emile Goudeau, pushed the boundaries further west, arguing that the center of town could be identified as the several blocks on the boulevards between the rue de Richelieu (the boulevard Montmartre) and the Madeleine.[17]

A new social geography contributed to the perception of the boulevards as the "center" of Paris. This center was north of the actual city-center that Haussmann had erected—the *grande croisée*—the intersection at the place du Châtelet of the rue de Rivoli and the boulevard Sébastopol. The location of the boulevards directly south of three of the city's six train stations, however, meant they were often the first large commercial thoroughfares reached by visitors to Paris.[18] While Haussmann's new boulevards may have served as by-ways, as a means by which to reach one's ultimate destination rapidly, the older *grands boulevards* had always been and remained a destination in and of themselves. Beyond their actual proximity to the train stations that had been recently built, the boulevards were imagined as the center of the city precisely because of their association as a theater of modern life.

Commentators represented the boulevards as a festive space in which everyday life was rendered spectacular. Gustave Fraipont presented the boulevards as offering "the spectacle of the street."[19] To Georges Montorgeuil, the boulevards were a "feast for the eyes," and he echoed Fraipont in his assurance that "the real Parisian spectacle is where we found it: in the street."[20] What made this a spectacle worth seeing, observers agreed, was the sense that any and all observers might gather to watch there. As one commentator noted, "the whole of the gay capital may be said to be concentrated" on the boulevards.[21]

16. Fraipont, *Paris, à vol d'oiseau,* 38.

17. Emile Goudeau, *Paris qui consomme* (Paris: Henri Beraldi, 1893), 99.

18. These were the Gare du Nord, the Gare de l'Est and closest was the Gare St-Lazare; 62 percent of all the city's train traffic passed through the Gare St-Lazare.

19. Fraipont, *Paris, à vol d'oiseau,* 115.

20. Georges Montorgeuil, *La vie des boulevards* (Paris: Librairies Imprimeries réunies, 1896), iii and 141.

21. H. Sutherland Edwards, *Old and New Paris* (London: Cassell, 1893), 43.

Yet the boulevards were considered to be not only the center of Paris, even the center of France, but also quite explicitly the center of the universe because of the diversity of things and people that could be found there. As a newspaper article boasted, "On the boulevard, one can say everything, hear everything and imagine everything. It's the ideal forum of the free city."[22] Alfred Delvau proclaimed that "the boulevards are not only the heart and the head of Paris, but also the soul of the entire world."[23]

The boulevards were thought of as the "distributive centre of all the flitting fancies of France."[24] Luxury stores flourished on the boulevards that finally replaced the Palais-Royal as the shopping center. The new *grands magasins* did not, however, open on the older boulevards but rather sprang up on many of Haussmann's new streets. As Philip Nord has insightfully argued, the old boulevards and the new department stores became conflated as part of *Paris nouveau*. The department store interiors mimicked not only the architectural style of the rebuilt Paris, but also the "boulevards of the *grand magasin* interior were so many extensions of the *grands boulevards* that stretched from the Madeleine to the Bastille."[25]

Department stores traded in spectacle, which linked them to the boulevards in the Parisian imagination. Improved glass technology facilitated vast window displays that were increasingly aided by better lighting (culminating in the use of electricity in the 1880s), thereby putting a premium on visibility. The introduction of new shopping styles—among them fixed prices and the *entrée libre*—meant customers could wander around by themselves and did not have to interact with clerks, thus emulating a stroll on the boulevards. As a woman visiting Paris remarked, "It is as good as a play to stand at the window of this shop and watch the people inside!"[26]

If these institutions offered a certain theatricality through their visuality, genuine theatrical performances also abounded on the boulevards beginning in the eighteenth century. Although the 1862 enlargement of the place du Château-d'Eau did away with the "boulevard du crime," the boulevards to the west of the boulevard du Temple remained the site

22. Emile Bergerat, "Le boulevard," *L'Echo de la Semaine,* October 9, 1892.

23. Alfred Delvau, *Les plaisirs de Paris* (Paris, 1867), 17–18.

24. Richard Whiteing, *The Life of Paris* (Leipzig: Tauchnitz, 1901), 196–97.

25. Nord, *Paris Shopkeepers,* 133. See also Miller, *The Bon Marché;* Rosalind Williams, *Dream Worlds;* and Bowlby, *Just Looking.*

26. Maude Annesley, *My Parisian Year* (London: Mills and Boon, 1912), 80.

of an increasingly diverse array of entertainments such as the Théâtre des Folies-Dramatiques, the rebuilt Ambigu-Comique, the Théâtre de la porte St-Martin, and the Théâtre de la Renaissance on the boulevard St-Martin; the Gymnase Dramatique on the boulevard Bonne-Nouvelle; and the Parisiana music hall on the boulevard Poissonnière. The boulevard Montmartre featured the Théâtre des Variétés, one of the oldest self-supporting theaters in Paris, and the Musée Grévin, the wax museum that opened in 1882. The Théâtre Robert-Houdin, a magic show eventually run by the early filmmaker Georges Méliès, could be found on the boulevard des Italiens as could the Opéra-Comique, the Théâtre des Nouveautés and the Vaudeville. The Olympia music hall replaced the *montagnes russes* (early roller coasters) on the boulevard des Capucines, where one could also find the Théâtre de la Salle des Capucines, run by the Isola brothers, a pair of Algerian magicians who later went on to direct the Parisiana, the Olympia and the Folies-Bergères. Finally, of course, the expensive new Opera house stood practically at the end of the line, a symbol of the new Paris. This partial list, which does not begin to enumerate the many *cafés-concerts* that sprang up on and around the boulevards in the eighties and nineties should serve as ample evidence that on the boulevards, Parisians and visitors could find a variety of entertainments that were increasingly grand and glitzy but at the same time offered seats affordable to a socially diverse audience.[27]

Cafés all over the nation served as "the primary theater[s] of everyday life in nineteenth-century France," according to Susanna Barrows.[28] Yet the boulevard café, like the boulevard theater, offered large-scale spectacle. The café's setting literally in the streets poised the viewer for a transient and constantly renewed spectacle of an ever-changing crowd. The boulevard café that served as a central observation point from which to watch the world turned into a show at the same time that the line between the show and its audience blurred.[29] One guidebook described café seats as theater seats and suggested to its readers that "the best way to attend this spectacle . . . is to take your stall at the door of one of the many cafés on the boulevard Montmartre or the boulevard

27. See Concetta Condemi, *Les cafés-concerts* (Paris: Quai Voltaire, 1992); and Rearick, *Pleasures of the Belle Epoque.*

28. Susanna I. Barrows, "Nineteenth-Century Cafés: Arenas of Everyday Life," in *Pleasures of Paris: Daumier to Picasso,* ed. Barbara Stern Shapiro (Boston: Museum of Fine Arts, 1991), 17.

29. On the increased thematic and kitschy elements of cafés, where service became a show, see Susanna I. Barrows, "Eros in the Age of Mechanical Reproduction."

des Italiens, and while savoring your coffee or your grog, look with your own two eyes."[30] A Danish visitor noted that "the café is a reserved seat in the street, a sort of comfortable sofa-corner in the great common parlor."[31] Cafés provided theater seats "of a great common parlor" as opposed to the selectivity of a theater.

The café was not the only observation point for the new Paris. The hotel lobby served as an important place from which to watch the *va et vient* of modern life. Starting in the 1860s, no lobby seemed a better place than that of the Grand Hôtel, a large triangular edifice on the boulevard des Capucines between the rues Scribe and Auber, with 750 rooms and all the "modern comforts" such as bathrooms, escalators, telegraphs and translation services. Like the boulevards outside, the lobby offered the image of the world in microcosm. Georges Montorgeuil described "the mingling fez and turbans, Scotch plaid, and Spanish cloak"[32] that someone seated in the lobby might see parade by. Edmond Deschaumes remarked on the lobby's bright lights and described it as a world stage: "At midnight, seated on a large arm-chair in the middle of this blaze, the spectator watches the members of the African embassy and some wife of a rich industrialist covered in a bone-ash opera cloak with a swan decoration."[33]

Like the new city itself, the institutions it gave birth to were always conceived as *grand: grands boulevards, grands magasins, le Grand Hôtel.* In his description of *Paris nouveau,* Fraipont could not keep away from a language of scale: "This place de l'Opéra, with its big ways that open onto everything, with these vast luxury stores, these gigantic cafés, the Grand Hôtel and the Opéra. This is modern Paris."[34] The meaning of *grand* here also implied a certain encyclopedic range, as found, for example, in department store fare. As a young provincial girl living in Paris for the year explained about the department stores, "They are splendid bazaars where one finds practically everything one can desire, and merchandise at all prices . . . objects for a few centimes up to several thousand francs."[35] She celebrates the possible fulfillment of any and everybody's desire through the range of fare found in a department

30. *Paris en poche: guide Conty,* 148.
31. Richard Kaufman, *Paris of To Day,* cited in Shapiro, ed., *Pleasures of Paris,* 49.
32. Montorgeuil, *Vie des boulevards,* 109.
33. Deschaumes, *Pour bien voir Paris,* 13.
34. Fraipont, *Paris, à vol d'oiseau,* 52.
35. Rose Eméry, *Une année à Paris* (Paris: Chez l'auteur, 1886), 17.

store. And like the department stores it spawned, Parisian spectacle seemed utterly encompassing and inviting to all.

These boulevard institutions stood as emblems of the new city and, in different ways, loci of audience and spectacle. The *grands boulevards* were made into monuments of modern life; their monumental status in fact served to highlight the fleeting nature of urban life. Rather than permanent structures in stone, the sight worth seeing was the flow of traffic on the boulevards; the people who came and went. The site was not merely architectural and spatial but social as well. One came as much to see and be a part of the crowd as to visit a particular place. And crowds did frequent the boulevards. For example, omnibuses traveled the semicircle of boulevards more frequently than on any other line— more than ten thousand cars in a twenty-four-hour period by 1880— according to one source.[36]

The urban crowd was celebrated by Parisian chroniclers and the popular press as one of the distinctive features of the *grands boulevards.* Fraipont explained, "One has to have lived in the provinces to feel the joy one experiences when one finds oneself mixed into a constantly changing crowd . . . well, the Parisian is a man of crowds, he is happy about the racket that is one of the signs of life."[37]

Many sources represented a socially and sexually diverse crowd occupying the boulevards of the new city. As a guidebook in English explained, "This promenade is full of people of all ranks, from the laborer to the peer, in search of entertainment and pleasure."[38] Even the Communard Jules Vallès, who might be expected to be suspicious of the celebration of the new Paris, remarked on the wonder of the boulevard's diversity:

What characterizes this Parisian boulevard [the boulevard Montmartre], distinguishes it, constitutes its genius, is that its *flânerie* is active and abundant. . . . Open to all, invaded by businessmen or men of leisure, furrowed by all the city's passions, the boulevard watches on its sidewalks the mingling of all of the classes and all the prejudices and hates evaporate in the dust.[39]

An Englishman described the boulevard as "a pageant" and one with no privileged view because "it does not depend for its effect on the

36. *Les grands boulevards,* 199.
37. Fraipont, *Paris, à vol d'oiseau,* 47.
38. *Paris in Four Days* (Paris: Charles Moonen, 1886–87), 70.
39. Jules Vallès, *Le tableau de Paris* (1882; Paris: Messidor, 1989), 55–56.

consideration whether you see it from a bench on the *trottoir* or from a *fauteuil* under the awning."[40] The spectacle of the crowd was evoked in the *Guide Conty* as a "camera obscura where all the objects and the characters, differently but always picturesquely colored, change with every step and in every moment. All of Parisian society and its representatives, from the duchess to the flirt, and from the millionaire stockbroker to the beggar."[41] Guidebooks promised a kaleidoscopic and infinitely transforming spectacle defined by its substantial breadth and its status as visible.

A diverse crowd that might now legitimately "take to the streets" occupied the boulevards and spaces of commercial culture. Cassell's guide remarked, as if to warn its non-French readers about the phenomenon, that "one thing that will strike the stranger is the immense proportion of women in the streets as compared with men."[42] Georges Montorgeuil attested to the variety of women on the boulevards, explaining that public transport "brought and returned . . . in feminine humanity . . . the *grande dame* to the errand girl."[43] It appears that to contemporaries, at least, urban gazing was hardly the privileged domain of the bourgeois male.

Part of the boulevard crowd's modern diversity was a sort of democratic cosmopolitanism. An English guidebook noted that "representatives from nearly every country on the globe may be seen here, as it is the grand meeting-place for all peoples, nations and tongues."[44] All forms of life seemed to burst forth on the boulevard; there one found "a mob, an indescribable vitality" that defined "this Parisian existence."[45]

Yet the framing of life in the streets was not only perceived from such places as café seats. In particular, café-goers could also read about the spectacle of the street in the newspaper, the product that fin-de-siècle curmudgeon Maurice Talmeyr called "the leitmotiv of the street."[46] Indeed, the information they could gather by sitting at a café read like

40. Whiteing, *The Life of Paris*, 155.
41. *Paris en poche: guide Conty*, 147.
42. *Illustrated Guide to Paris*, 65.
43. Montorgeuil, *Vie des boulevards*, 9.
44. *Pleasure Guide to Paris for Bachelors* (London: Nilsson, n.d.), 165.
45. Edmond Benjamin and P. Desachy, *Le boulevard: croquis parisien* (Paris: Flammarion, 1893.), 6.
46. Maurice Talmeyr, "Le roman-feuilleton et l'esprit populaire," *Revue des deux mondes*, September 1903, 204.

advertising copy for the contents of a daily newspaper: "At café terraces, listen to the spirit with which the small and the big happenings of the day are recounted; *mondain* scandal, artistic productions, legislative discussions, financial disasters, all this happens in this sieve of this inimitable Parisian spirit."[47]

The popular press during the second half of the nineteenth century featured a written scenario of life on the boulevards—a sort of literary voyeurism. Modern journalism, especially in the mass-circulation dailies (*presse à grand tirage*), functioned as a major source for legitimating the experience of the city as a spectacle and of looking as a pastime. Like the boulevards, the press—especially in its sensationalization of the everyday—promoted the shared pleasures and identification of individual city dwellers that transformed them into "Parisians."

The *Presse à Grand Tirage*

"To read one's newspaper is to live the universal life, the life of the whole capital, of the entire city, of all France, of all nations. . . . It is thus that in a great country like France, the same thought, at one and the same time, animates the whole population . . . It is the newspaper that establishes this sublime communion of souls across distances."[48] This quote from an 1893 editorial in *Le Petit Parisien* elaborates the newspaper's status as a mechanically reproduced form that represented the standardized quality of mass production.[49] But this editorial (admittedly one written from an interested position) also celebrates the newspaper's ability to enact a "sublime communion of souls across distances." A newspaper created an "imagined community," to borrow Benedict Anderson's phrase, through which its otherwise unconnected readers were able to participate in a shared community—evoked and constructed in the newspaper.[50]

Many scholars have pointed to the mass newspaper as the quintes-

---

47. Alexis Martin, *Paris: promenades des 20 arrondissements* (Paris, 1890), 167.

48. Editorial from *Le Petit Parisien,* 1893, cited in Richard Terdiman, *Discourse/Counter-Discourse* (Ithaca: Cornell University Press, 1985), 131.

49. In his analysis of the mass press, Terdiman also sees it as a dominant discourse that homogenized social life through commodification and shifted readers' views of relations of power. Terdiman, *Discourse/Counter-Discourse,* esp. 118–38.

50. See Anderson, *Imagined Communities,* esp. ch. 2.

sential modern and urban form. After all, it in many ways can be considered one of the first commodities devised for mass consumption; it even included built-in obsolescence since its contents were designed to be replaced daily.[51] Aside from its embeddedness in capitalist exchange, however, the newspaper has also been examined as a great engine and purveyor of the transformation from "tradition" to "modernity," an analysis originally championed by American sociologist Robert Park. Park argued that the newspaper replaced the gossip that otherwise traveled in face-to-face communities.[52] Walter Benjamin had another perception of the newspaper's effect. He wrote that the alienation and fragmentation of the individual in modernity could be seen in the mass newspaper's form and content.[53] Although it is problematic to frame a discussion around social needs (community/communication) as though they are an essential structural element in human interaction as Park did, his interpretation seems to summarize at least how the mass newspaper was represented in its own time. Building on Park's framework, I suggest that the newspaper served as one of the most powerful forms of modern mass cultural urban entertainments in the sense that it constituted a collective and then aimed to please it through newspaper reading.[54]

The new press aimed to reach as broad and diverse a constituency as possible and was designed to address an imagined "universal" reader. The newspaper, along with several very popular novel forms of commercial entertainment (and the Paris Morgue, all to be discussed in subsequent chapters) and the Parisian boulevard culture described above, framed, represented and sensationalized the "real thing" as the essence of modern Parisian spectacle.

The late nineteenth century in France has been justifiably called the "golden age of the press."[55] Between 1880 and 1914, the overall circu-

51. See Terdiman, *Discourse/Counter-Discourse*, 120; and Anderson, *Imagined Communities*, ch. 2.

52. See Robert Park, "The Natural History of the Newspaper," *American Journal of Sociology* 29 (November 1923): 273–89. See also Michael Schudson's analysis of the history of American journalism, *Discovering the News: A Social History of American Newspapers* (New York: Basic Books, 1978), 40–42 for a discussion of Park.

53. See Benjamin, "Some Motifs in Baudelaire," in *Charles Baudelaire*, 112; and see also Terdiman, *Discourse/Counter-Discourse*, 127–28 and throughout, on Benjamin and issues of alienation.

54. Stressing the collective elements of newspaper reading, Anderson called it an "extraordinary mass ceremony" and Hegel noted that the newspapers substituted for morning prayers for the modern man. See Anderson, *Imagined Communities*, 35.

55. Jacques Wolgensinger, *L'histoire à la une: la grande aventure de la presse* (Paris: Decouvertes Gallimard, 1989)

lation of Parisian dailies increased 250 percent.[56] But beyond mere circulation figures, the newspaper became an emblem of Parisian culture as its sensational reality came to stand for the best translation of the urban experience. In fact, it created the terms through which people might order and make sense of their experiences. Like the city, the newspaper celebrated speed, spontaneity, the unpredictable and the ephemeral. This was a press whose production Emile Zola described as "steam-powered journalism, polished off in twenty minutes, edited on the fly, written at full gallop at a café table."[57]

The longer history of the mass press stretches back to 1836, when Emile de Girardin founded *La Presse*, whose forty-franc subscription price was half the usual cost.[58] As Léo Claretie bemoaned in a chapter dedicated to the press in his 1909 history of French literature, "The literary press is no more than a memory. Emile de Girardin killed it."[59] Girardin planned to generate the lost subscription revenue through an increase in readers and advertising revenue. Until that time, newspapers were sold by subscription only and the circulation of the largest dailies peaked at fewer than ten thousand Parisian subscribers. There were, of course, more readers who rented the paper at various *cabinets de lecture* and cafés, but the newspaper remained outside the cultural world of the majority of even the bourgeoisie. Girardin's *La Presse* also revolutionized the content of newspapers by introducing the *feuilleton*—the serial novel. Balzac's *La vieille fille* debuted there, and the *feuilleton* soon emerged as the sine qua non of every Parisian daily.

La Presse, along with Armand Dutacq's daily *Le Siècle*, which also lowered subscription rates, broadened the newspaper's audience, but the greatest emblem of the popular press became *Le Petit Journal*, founded in 1863. It was not only one of the first newspapers that could

---

56. Anne-Marie Thiesse, *Le roman du quotidien* (Paris: Le Chemin Vert, 1984), 17.

57. Zola interviewed by Henri Leyrat, "M. Emile Zola, interviewé sur l'interview," *Le Figaro*, January 12, 1893.

58. On the history of the mass press in France, see Theodore Zeldin, *France, 1848–1945: Taste and Corruption* (Oxford: Oxford Univeristy Press, 1979); Claude Bellanger, *Histoire générale de la presse française*, vol. 3 (Paris: Presses universitaires de France, 1972); Roger Bellet, *Presse et journalisme sous le Second Empire* (Paris: Armand Colin, 1967); and Michael Palmer, *Des petits journaux aux grandes agences* (Paris: Aubier, 1983). For publishing more generally, see Roger Chartier and Henri-Jean Martin, eds., *Histoire de l'édition française: le temps des éditeurs*, vol. 3, 2d ed. (Paris: Fayard, 1990); and James Smith Allen, *In the Public Eye: A History of Reading in Modern France, 1800–1940* (Princeton: Princeton University Press, 1991).

59. Léo Claretie, *Histoire de la littérature française: le XIXe siècle* (Paris: Société d'Editions littéraires et artistiques, 1909), 4:760.

be purchased for a sou, but it also could be bought by the issue at kiosks and from street criers.[60] An explicitly nonpolitical newspaper, its founder Moïse "Polydore" Millaud, the "father of the cheap press," thus avoided the heavy security deposit to the government and the *droit de timbre* of six centimes an issue that "opinion" newspapers were forced to pay during the Second Empire.[61] A great success, *Le Petit Journal* reached a circulation of one million in 1886 and had far out-paced its competition—in 1880 its circulation was four times higher than its nearest rival, *La Petite République française*.[62] Among *Le Petit Journal*'s readers were many of the increasing population of the newly literate. Emile Zola even credited the paper with the rise in literacy, "It has been said, and not without reason, that it created a new class of readers."[63] Millaud's system of sending papers out to major railroad stations and hiring thousands of ambulant criers who roamed both Paris and the provinces help us understand Zola's conclusion.

If *Le Petit Journal* contributed to the drive for literacy, the law of July 29, 1881, fomented a revolution in print and image. Called simply the "freedom of the press law," it reversed the course of almost a century's limitations on freedom of expression following the French Revolution. "Printing and book selling are free" it simply declared, rendering obsolete the stamp duty, the government-required security deposit, arbitrary trials and censorship.[64] The law, described as "a freedom law the likes of which the press has never seen in any moment,"[65] can be held partially responsible for the explosion in the number of periodicals available. In 1882, 3,800 periodical titles were printed in France. Ten years later, that number had expanded to 6,000.[66]

Newspapers for a sou made up the greatest number of new titles. Whereas in 1881, Paris had twenty-three such newspapers, in 1899 city

60. While *Le Petit Journal* is generally referred to as the first newspaper sold for a sou, René Livois asserts that *Le Journal du peuple* in 1848 and Dutacq's *La Liberté* preceded *Le Petit Journal*. See René Livois, *Histoire de la presse française* (Paris: Les Temps de la Presse, 1965), 1:274.

61. Arthur Meyer, *Ce que mes yeux ont vu*, 3d ed. (Paris: Plon, 1911), 187.

62. Allen, *In the Public Eye*, 42.

63. Palmer, *Des petits journaux*, 24.

64. Yet libel laws against citizens were far-reaching, and various amendments to the law introduced restrictions through the Great War. Censorship of the theater was maintained. See Bellanger, *La presse française*, 7–60; Zeldin, *France, 1848–1945*, 547–51; and Allen, *In the Public Eye*, 88–89.

65. Chartier and Martin, eds., *Histoire de l'édition française*, 48.

66. Raymond Manévy, *La presse de la Troisième République* (Paris: J. Forêt, 1955), 9.

dwellers might choose among sixty such publications.[67] Four newspapers, *Le Journal, Le Matin, Le Petit Journal* and *Le Petit Parisien*, accounted for 75 percent of the Parisian market by 1900.[68] While the new press law, not to mention the increase in literacy among the French and especially among urban populations, may help explain the growing number of publications and readers, social practices and desires associated with *Paris nouveau* shaped the novel genres of the modern mass press. As Eugène Dubief, former secretary of the press division of the Ministry of the Interior noted in 1892, newspapers had become "department stores where the shelves need to be stocked daily."[69]

As much as display windows, hotels and cafés, the newspaper became a fixture of and transmitter for boulevard culture. One observer noted, "The movement . . . of newspapers toward the boulevard was inevitable. Is it not fitting that journalism should place itself in the center of activity? Where better than the boulevard to feel the pulse of the city?"[70] Newspapers could be found all over the *grands boulevards,* at the many kiosks located along them.[71] A visitor marveled, "The kiosk is, above all things, a Parisian institution."[72] In 1855, the city inaugurated the "lighted kiosks," seven on the boulevard Montmartre alone—more than any one place in Paris.[73] Newspapers were available in racks to patrons of sidewalk cafés, where they could be read free with the purchase of a drink.

The association of the newspapers with the boulevards is also a reference to the location of the newspaper offices—most of which were on and around the boulevards—despite the high cost of the vast space they required (fig. 2).[74] *Le Petit Journal* moved from the well-known Maison Frascati on the boulevard Montmartre in 1869, where the ground floor sported a bazaar, aquarium and art gallery, to a building

67. Ibid., 19. Other sources list slightly different numbers but indicate the same overall growth pattern. Bellanger lists the number of Parisian papers for a sou at four in 1871, thirty in 1882 and fifty-one in 1892. See Claude Bellanger, *La presse française,* 140.

68. Jean-Pierre Rioux, *Frissons fin-de-siècle* (Paris: Le Monde, 1990), 8.

69. Eugène Dubief, *Le journalisme* (Paris: Hachette, 1892), 245–6.

70. Montorgueil, *Vie des boulevards,* 42.

71. Almost all kiosks on the boulevards were run by women, usually veterans' widows. See Archives de la Préfecture de police (hereafter APP), DB 198.

72. Whiteing, *The Life of Paris,* 217.

73. APP, DB 198.

74. To name just a few, *Le Gaulois* was located at 9, boulevard des Italiens, *L'Evènement* across the street at number 10. *Le Figaro* was at the corner of the boulevard Montmartre and the rue Druot, *Le Gil Blas* at 10, boulevard des Capucines.

ASPECT DE L'ANGLE DU BOULEVARD MONTMARTRE ET DE LA RUE RICHELIEU LE JOUR DE L'APPARITION D'UN NUMÉRO DU *Journal illustré*. Dessin d'H. DE HEM.

2. *Le Journal illustré* and *Le Petit Journal* on the boulevard Montmartre, 1864. Musée Carnavalet. © Photothèque des musées de la Ville de Paris.

nearby at the corner of the rue Lafayette and the rue Cadet. There an enormous five-centime piece, lighted all night long, decorated the front of the building, which also featured a ground-floor bazaar.

Newspapers integrated themselves into the fabric of boulevard spectacle by turning not just their products, but also their offices into centers for the immediate consumption of news, even before it hit the papers. For example, the *salle des dépêches* (telegram room), first opened at *Le Figaro* in 1877, opened onto the street and news items would be posted in the window. Dubief noted that this became a brilliant form of publicity, whose goal was to transform curiosity seekers into "clients."[75]

But the new press did not simply take its place on the boulevards in

75. Dubief, *Le journalisme*, 187.

geographic terms. Rather, the paper's content, which offered a sensationalized reality and an emphasis on novelty, matched and re-presented the framing of everyday life that came to define boulevard culture. In the mass press, coverage of political life took a back seat to theater openings, horse races, fairground descriptions and initially to the *roman-feuilleton* and the *faits divers* and eventually to what was called *reportage* and such new press genres as the interview.

Le Petit Journal's attempts to avoid paying the *caution* that opinion newspapers needed to pay inadvertently inaugurated a new journalistic philosophy in France. In the words of its most successful columnist Timothée Trimm (whose real name was Napoléon Lespès): "I tell of the recent event, current events that are still hot, the latest anecdote, the play review the day after, the polite and sincere critique of yesterday's book."[76] Rather than attempt to influence opinion, this newspaper would deliver information in the form of *actualités* or current events.

The newspaper was supposed to be a mirror that reflected the broadest possible spectrum of contemporary life. As its founder Millaud advised his reporters:

You should spend your time in buses, in trains, in theatres, in the street. Find out what the average man is thinking. Then let yourself be guided by this. At the same time keep up with all the latest discoveries, all the latest inventions. Publish all the knowledge that gets buried away in the serious heavies . . . Your job is to report what most men are thinking and to speak of everything as if you know far more about it than anybody else.[77]

Millaud instructed reporters to draw their material from the common spaces of urban life, the places where Parisians gathered, while cultivating novelty all the while. At the same time that reporters were supposed to be guided by the thoughts of the average Parisian, they were also then to assume the role of expert, guiding readers through everyday life in which they would instruct the masses on urban spectatorship.

By the late nineteenth century, however, almost all newspapers also offered fiction in the form of the serial novel, clearly demarcated from the rest of the newspaper by a bar across the bottom of the page. Yet these popular narratives were often derived from the stories above the line of demarcation, and their literary conventions placed them squarely within a realist frame. The newspaper's form was "anti-organicist" as

76. *Le Petit Journal,* June 25, 1866, cited in Palmer, *Des petits journaux,* 24.
77. Zeldin, *France, 1848–1945,* 527.

Richard Terdiman has noted, because "its form denies form."[78] It offered up a fragmented reality that was paired with a fragmented so-called fiction in the form of the *roman-feuilleton*.

Michael Palmer has argued that in the *presse à grand tirage* "the successful elements of the . . . serial novel are those of the *faits divers* and other events taken from the real world."[79] Both the newspaper and the serial novel blurred the boundaries between reality and representation. The newspaper claimed to tell the truth, to present a nonfictive drama of contemporary life. Articles purported to be "nonfiction"; their relation to each other was entirely non-narrative.

Yet, as Palmer has suggested, the narratives of the serial novels were often based on what its authors and readers consumed above this line of demarcation. This overflow of the categories "reality" and "representation" can be seen in a variety of cultural forms in the second half of the nineteenth century, but the newspaper's popular pairing of the serial novel and the *faits divers* arguably set the standard for many other forms.

In 1903 Maurice Talmeyr lamented in the pages of *La Revue des deux mondes* the formidable power of the newspapers' *feuilletons:*

Let's imagine that we are returning from the ball. It is between six and seven in the morning, and we notice, from the back of our carriage, the spectacle of a Paris street. Workers going to their work, carriage-men pass with their cartloads, concierges open their doors. We pass milkmen and bread deliverers. And what do we notice? That all these people, or almost all, are reading the newspaper. And what are they reading? The serial novel![80]

He also remarked that later in the day, the butcher's apprentice could be found reading the paper while running his errands, the coachman became mesmerized by it while waiting for clients, and the women in Les Halles fell silent, entranced by the *feuilleton*. As a veritable *manne quotidienne des foules* (daily manna of the crowds), he explained that there was not a newspaper without its *feuilleton* and some even offered two or three at a time.[81]

Talmeyr dated the unfortunate introduction of the genre to the early 1840s and explored it in order to understand what havoc it had wreaked

78. Terdiman, *Discourse/Counter-Discourse*, 122.
79. Palmer, *Des petits journaux*, 27.
80. Talmeyr, "Le roman-feuilleton," 203.
81. Ibid., 204.

on the popular imagination. Some sources point to Balzac's *La vieille fille,* which appeared in *La Presse* in October 1836, as the first serial novel, others to *La Presse*'s publication of *Le Rhin* by Victor Hugo.[82] Regardless, even before newspapers had a massive audience and were sold by the issue, the *feuilleton* was seen as a way to augment subscriptions. For example, Eugène Sue's *Mystères de Paris* published in *Le Journal des débats* boosted subscriptions by several thousand; his *Le juif errant* raised the circulation of *Le Constitutionnel* from 3,600 to an exceptional figure of 20,000.[83] As one contemporary noted in 1845, "One no longer subscribes to a newspaper because it has an opinion similar to one's own; one subscribes, without paying attention to political colors, instead determining which serial novel is more or less amusing."[84]

Launching a *feuilleton* became an event in which the newspaper could barrage the city with publicity (fig. 3). It involved a "veritable capture of the city streets," and as such "the serial novels of popular newspapers . . . become public events."[85] Newspapers employed men and women to plaster posters all over the city and as many as four hundred peddlers went shouting through the city streets, distributing illustrated handbills containing the beginning of a novel.

If fiction in installments drew public attention, the *faits divers* improved on the formula by creating sensation out of the quotidian. "Future historians of Paris will only need the *faits divers* recounted day by day in the newspaper to write the history of the customs of the capital,"[86] noted the Parisian writer Charles Virmaître. Technically, the *fait divers* was a newspaper rubric. Yet the term denoted a certain kind of story and a particular style of reporting. The genre included an enormous range in subject matter, but all *faits divers* represented contemporary and real-life events. As Georges Montorgeuil asked rhetorically, "At bottom, is the *fait divers* not life, all of life?"[87] Its definition, which

82. Anne-Marie Thiesse, "Le roman populaire," in *Histoire de l'édition française,* ed. Roger Chartier and Henri-Jean Martin (Paris: Fayard, 1990). 3:511; and Wolgensinger, *Histoire à la une,* 80, respectively.

83. Charles Brun, *Le roman social en France au XIXe siècle,* cited in Walter Benjamin, *Paris, capitale du XIXe siècle,* ed. Rolf Tiedmann, trans. Jean Lacoste (Paris: Editions du Cerf, 1989), 760.

84. Montlaville, before the Chamber of Deputies, March 14, 1845, cited in Palmer, *Des petits journaux,* 26.

85. Anne-Marie Thiesse, *Le roman du quotidien* (Paris: Le Chemin Vert, 1984), 90.

86. Charles Virmaître, *Les curiosités de Paris* (Paris: Lebigre-Duquesne, 1868), 87.

87. *Le Paris,* August 6, 1886.

3. Ad leaflet for Emile Zola, *La bête humaine,* in serial novel form. Musée Carnavalet. © Photothèque des musées de la Ville de Paris.

appeared for the first time in the 1872 edition of *Le Grand Larousse universel,* seemed to include an incredibly broad range of subjects:

Under this rubric, the newspapers artfully group and regularly publish stories of all kinds that circulate around the world: small scandals, carriage accidents, horrible crimes, lovers' suicides, roofers falling from the fifth floor, armed robbery, showers of locusts or toads, storms, fires, floods, comical tales, mysterious kidnappings, executions, cases of hydrophobia, cannibalism.[88]

The term came into use only in the last third of the nineteenth century to denote a particular kind of newspaper fare. In many ways, the *faits divers* can be understood as the modern equivalent of the *occasionnels* (pamphlets) and *canards* (tall tales), which had been part of the repertoire of *colportage* (printed material peddling). Early one-sheet "broadsides," they most often featured a simple woodcut image accompanied by text in prose or in verse, full of "blood and lies."[89] As Gérard de Nerval explained, the *canard* was "sometimes true, always exaggerated and often false."[90] Criers paraded through towns and lured their populace with parts of the story and then sold them the rest. Due to technological limitations, the *canard's* image was a summary one, attempting to capture the entire story or perhaps its critical moment in one image. A single image appeared over and over, suggesting both the standard repertoire of tales and a lack of demand for precision and detail.

The *fait divers,* by contrast, reproduced in extraordinary detail, both written and visual, stories that might have seemed unbelievable but were actually true—as opposed to the earlier genre's tall tale. The genre consisted of exceptional events that happened to ordinary people. The newspaper *faits divers* implied that the everyday might be transformed into the shocking and sensational and ordinary people lifted from the anonymity of urban life and into the realm of spectacle.

88. In Alain Monestier, *Le fait divers* (Paris: Editions de la Réunion des musées nationaux, 1982), 50–51.

89. Robert Simon, "Cézanne and the Subject of Violence," *Art in America,* May 1991, 125.

90. Jean-Pierre Séguin, *Nouvelles à sensation* (Paris: Armand Colin, 1959), 194. A significant departure from the structuralist analysis of the *faits divers* (such as Georges Auclair, *Le mana quotidien* [Paris: Editions Anthropos, 1970]) is Michelle Perrot, "Fait divers et histoire au XIXe siècle: note critique (deux expositions)," *Annales: économies, sociétés, civilisations* 38, no. 4 (July–August 1983): 911–19.

Stylistically, graphic detail filled *faits divers* newspaper columns in support of the veracity of the story whose visual specificity lent credence to its truth. As Dubief noted in his book on journalism, "The need to see is no less universal than the need to understand."[91] The illustrated press became the ideal venue for the *faits divers*. Illustration in this case meant an attempt at nearly exact reproduction as opposed to the caricatures that could be found in much of the *mondain* or radical press before the advent of the mass press.[92] The first of the illustrated popular newspapers was *Le Journal illustré* founded in 1864, but it was not until the nineties that both *Le Petit Journal* and *Le Petit Parisien* published weekly illustrated supplements with color engravings that often featured the latest *faits divers* (fig. 4).

Technological limitations prevented the widespread use of photography until the turn of the century, although it became the metaphor for what newspapers hoped to achieve.[93] As Georges Montorgueil noted, "The impression made on the senses by a photograph of a human nude cannot be compared to that made by a photograph of a drawn nude. The *fait divers* is photography drawn from life; ugly, stupid, brutal, but cynically sincere in its stupid reality."[94] The attraction of the newspaper's *fait divers* was its representation of reality, no matter how base or brutal.

The centrality of *faits divers* in the mass press stemmed in part from historical circumstance. Because *Le Petit Journal* was a nonpolitical newspaper, it turned to "daily life" for its material. It was not until 1869, however, with the explosion of "l'affaire Troppmann" that the *fait divers* sealed its success by exploiting the murder of the entire famille Kinck in late September of that year.[95] From start to finish, this case

91. Dubief, *Le journalisme*, 235.

92. For more on caricature, see Philippe Roberts-Jones, *De Daumier à Lautrec: essai sur l'histoire de la caricature française entre 1860 et 1890* (Paris: Beaux-Arts, 1960); Jacques Lethève, *La caricature et la presses sous la IIIe République* (Paris: Armand Colin, 1961); Chartier and Martin, eds., *Histoire de l'édition française*, part 3; Terdiman, *Discourse/Counter-Discourse*, ch. 3.

93. For a precise history of the use of photography in the illustrated press, see Anne-Claude Ambroise-Rendu, "Du dessin de presse à la photographie (1878–1914): histoire d'une mutation technique et culturelle," *Revue d'histoire moderne et contemporaine* 39 (January–March 1992): 6–28.

94. *Le Paris*, August 6, 1886.

95. For an interesting account of the Troppman affair and the public who attended trials, see Katherine Fischer Taylor, *In the Theater of Criminal Justice: The Palais de Justice in Second Empire Paris* (Princeton: Princeton University Press, 1993).

4. The "crime de Pecq," from *Le Journal illustré*, June 18, 1882.

was its newspaper coverage as the press investigated alongside the po-lice.[96] The press, in fact, became so associated with the story that rumors circulated that one of the *Petit Journal* reporters actually helped with Troppmann's execution.[97]

The affair also cemented the real power of the new mass press to construct a shared culture of daily life. *La Chronique illustrée* captured this quality in 1869 when it explained, "The emperor, who keeps himself informed of the inquiry, hour by hour, worries from his imperial resi-dence about Troppmann as the worker worries about it in the cabaret and as the bourgeois docs, calm in his house."[98] The emphasis here on the different locations of the affair's public only serves to underscore how the newspaper constructed common ground. Through represen-tation, the newspaper drew these separate audiences together and en-dowed them with a common frame of reference.

The historian Michelle Perrot explained the genre's function by sug-gesting that the *fait divers* valorized the private and asserted the "tri-umph of the subject."[99] Yet more than anything else, the *fait divers* constructed a new kind of public life by thrusting ordinary people, even innocent victims and murderous transients, onto a vast stage for inspec-tion by the "universalized" eye of the newspaper reader. The *fait divers* indicated that all life, no matter how banal, could be rendered spectacu-lar through sensational narrative. In addition, the *faits divers'* precise location in contemporary and ordinary Paris meant that readers could identify with the narrative. At any moment they might find themselves the subject of a notorious *fait divers*.

The *fait divers* also embodied a genuinely commercial logic. For such columns did not always report such extraordinary tales as the Tropp-mann affair. Even as small an item as a three-line statement reporting an accident, a lost pet, or a theater opening, could count as news in the *fait divers* rubric. After all, in "the big city" something was always hap-pening. The daily newspaper was a commercial form that had to entice

---

96. On the press's role in creating, pathologizing and normalizing "criminals," see Marie-Christine Leps, *Apprehending the Criminal: The Production of Deviance in Nine-teenth-Century Discourse* (Durham, N.C.: Duke University Press, 1992).

97. Edward Berenson, *The Trial of Madame Caillaux* (Berkeley: University of Cali-fornia Press, 1992), 230. See also Michelle Perrot, "L'affaire Troppmann," *L'Histoire,* January 30, 1981.

98. *La Chronique illustrée,* October 1869, cited in Pierre Drachline, *Le fait divers au XIXe siècle* (Paris: Editions Hermé, 1991), 149.

99. Perrot, "Fait divers," 916.

readers daily by creating interest in and stimulating desire for their product. By taking everyday life and transforming it into sensation, the press guaranteed a constantly renewable "news" source.

The sensationalized banality of the *faits divers* spawned what by the 1880s and 1890s became known as the *presse d'information;* new titles such as *Le Matin* (1883), *L'Eclair* (1888) and *Le Journal* (1892) began to rival the popularity of such standards as *Le Petit Journal.*[100] *Chroniqueurs* such as *Le Petit Journal*'s Timothée Trimm were surpassed in popularity by reporters such as Charles Chincholle and Fernand Xau, who were thought to better serve "the recently developed taste for precise information."[101]

In particular, contemporaries pointed to the novelty of the interview in the *presse d'information.* Anatole France simply declared that "the interview is the order of the day."[102] Emile Zola called it "the public's favorite plaything."[103] *L'Actualité* had become the *soupe du jour*—and papers served up *l'homme du jour* as an essential ingredient. In fact, the newspaper *L'Eclair* had a column called *L'homme du jour,* through which newsworthy individuals were commodified and turned into news. Like the popular *fait divers,* the interview became an indispensable press rubric because it was a perfect vehicle through which to fabricate news in a press that was driven by the requirements of daily purchase. The *fait divers* banked on sensationalizing the banal events of everyday life, and the "interview" could attest to the range of newsworthy individuals roaming the city streets. Additionally, the interview form mimicked elements that were vaunted as the value of the *presse d'information:* speed, spontaneity and a kaleidoscopic range of facts and information transformed into "news" by the press.

"Interview," as is fairly apparent, is not a French word. It first turned up in the pages of *Le Petit Journal* in 1884, according to the *Grande Encyclopédie* of the same year. The term made its way into the second supplement of Larousse's *Grand Dictionnaire universel* of 1890, where it was explained as American in origin. In fact, most histories of the modern press point to the conversation in 1836 between James Gordon

100. Henri Avenel, *Histoire de la presse française: depuis 1789 à nos jours* (Paris: Flammarion, 1900), 816

101. "L'interview," *Le Temps,* October 21, 1894.

102. Anatole France, "A propos de l'interview," *Annales politiques et littéraires,* August 26, 1894, 131–32.

103. Henry Leyret, "M. Emile Zola, interviewé sur l'interview," *Le Figaro,* January 12, 1893.

Bennett, publisher of *The New York Herald*, and the mother of a murder victim as the first press interview.[104] But interviews did not catch on. The American press did not return to the genre until the late 1860s.[105] The French press only used it when it moved to *reportage*. Yet the popularity of the interview prompted Henry Fouquier to urge a French name, given the form's popularity: "It's a banality to note that the interview—which I would like to see have a French name since it has become very French—has triumphantly entered the ways of the press."[106]

So what exactly was the interview and its value, as discussed by contemporaries? Anatole France defined it as "a meeting in which a well-known person, M. Coquelin cadet or M. Pasteur, confers with a journalist, particularly a reporter, a Chincholle, regarding a recent event."[107] This seemingly economical definition says quite a bit because it sets up the essential elements of the interview: audience (by whom the interviewed is already "well known"), the celebrity, the interviewer and some recent event as the point of departure. In his definition, France further specified that written responses were not sufficient: "Written response has neither the spontaneity of dialogue, nor the charm of words that trip off the tongue, nor the revelatory truth of intimate talk."[108] Maurice Barrès explained that the advantage of the interview "seems to me to give an exact impression of a well-known fellow as he really is in flesh and blood."[109] The interview thus used the spoken word to provide what the mass press offered in spades—the unpredictable, the spontaneous, the unresolved and the true.

Spontaneity and truth were meant to guide the interview and thus became the subjects of scrutiny in discussions concerning the popularity of the form. For example, Léon Say complained that the interview was dangerous "because it encourages politicians to improvise their opinions," and that it was better to use the rostrum than take "the whole world, by way of the journalist, as their interlocutor."[110] Victorien Sardou complained that reporters exaggerated and made a travesty of

104. See Schudson, *Discovering the News;* and Helen Hughes, *News and the Human Interest Story* (New York: Greenwood, 1968) for more on Gordon and the press in the United States.

105. Schudson, *Discovering the News*, 66.

106. *Le XIXe Siècle*, October 1, 1891.

107. France, "A propos de l'interview," 131.

108. Ibid., 132.

109. Maurice Barrès, "Les beautés de l'interview," *Le Figaro*, August 22, 1890.

110. Léon Say, cited in France, "A propos de l'interview."

what was said and made the interviewee responsible for their faulty memory.[111]

The interview became the means through which journalists, supposedly relegated to the background by the "facts," maintained their roles as guides. In particular, reporters circulated in more open and apparently democratic space than did the earlier columnists. As Hughes Leroux explained in *Le Temps*, "chroniqueurs belonged to the salon, the theater, the boudoir, and the back rooms, [while] the reporter was 'the man of the street.'" Whereas the *chroniqueurs* had "remembrances," the reporter was supposed to have legs.[112] Those legs gave them and newspaper readers through them, access and proximity to a host of city people. The big interviewers such as Fernand Xau, Pierre Griffard, Paul Ginisty, Hughes Leroux, Gaston Calmette, Charles Chincholle, Séverine (the only woman) and Adolphe Brisson became the readers' stand-ins.[113] Rather than encourage readers to feel as though they had witnessed a conversation between the reporter and his source, interviews were set up to encourage the reader to identify with the interviewer. In this way, the interview was as much about the heroism and shamelessness of the reporter (and the public) as it was about those interviewed.

Cynics, in fact, mocked the foppery of reporters desperate for an interview. The columnist for the Courrier de Paris section of *L'Illustration*, who wrote as Rastignac, often took aim at the excesses of reporters. As he explained, a reporter presents himself at the home of a general during mealtime. The annoyed prospective interviewee says that the reporter has interrupted his dinner and, besides, he has nothing to say. The reporter insists: "What kind of soup had you just finished when I had the bad fortune to interrupt you? A consommé? A bisque? That'll be enough for my article." The next day the general opens the paper and to his surprise reads four columns "containing a description of his furniture, his living room, his table setting, his noodle soup."[114]

In his discussion of the new press, Eugène Dubief pointed to the pushiness of interviewers. He recounts that a ship transporting a celebrity on a transatlantic voyage found a small boat coming up along its side. "It's not pirates, it's the interviewers. . . . They throw them-

---

111. Ibid.

112. *Le Temps*, February 22, 1889.

113. For more on Séverine, see Marie Louise Roberts, "Subversive Copy: Feminist Journalism in fin-de-siècle France," paper delivered at the Western Society for French History, Las Vegas, November 1995.

114. *L'Illustration*, May 15, 1886.

selves on the stranger . . . ask whether he is married or single, if he pre-
fers his meat well done or rare."[115] The cartoonist Caran d'Ache took
his own swipe at journalists. In a series of illustrations, César Beau-
crayon is refused entry to a private club, denied a seat at the theater, a
table at a café, a place in a coach. He throws himself into the Seine,
which promptly regurgitates him. At the morgue, the other corpses
insist on his removal. Finally at the gates of heaven, Saint Peter tells
him he has no place in heaven, purgatory or hell. "So, come over here,
mumbled Saint Peter, seizing the soul by the collar: Over there is the
court to decide on journalists."[116]

Pirates, opportunists, liars—interviewers perfectly negotiated the
demands of modern urban life. Dubief again: "He entered like a breeze,
he speaks like a train whistle, with staccato, panting words. Dressed in
the latest fashions, he's restless, he draws attention to his own importance. It's he that visits all the lively characters, big and small: just as
you see him, if he's not leaving the Ministry, he's coming out from
visiting a diva, if not the assassin of the moment."[117] But the interviewer did not merely negotiate the challenges of the city, the adjectives
used to describe him double as descriptions of the urban context.

Beyond their often shared subjects, the *roman-feuilleton* and the *fait
divers* and *reportage* promised narrative suspense, novelty and a faithful
representation of a city that seemed both remote and yet strangely familiar to the vast majority of Parisian readers. This familiarity became
the measure of the readers' sense of participation and belonging to a
broader urban collective. By promoting a sensationalized reality, the
mass press offered its readers evidence of Paris as a community—as a
community they, or any newspaper reader for that matter, might join.

In a letter from Paris to his future sister-in-law, Minna Bernays, Sigmund
Freud wrote in 1885,

I don't think they know the meaning of shame or fear; the women no less
than the men crowd round nudities as much as they do round corpses in
the morgue or the ghastly posters in the streets announcing a new novel
in this or that newspaper and simultaneously showing a sample of its content. . . . If you do come here you will probably first of all be attracted by
what captivates most people exclusively—the brilliant exterior, the swarm-

115. Dubief, *Le journalisme*, 96.
116. *L'Illustration*, January 14, 1888.
117. Dubief, *Le journalisme*, 95.

ing crowds, the infinite variety of attractively displayed goods, the streets stretching for miles, the flood of light in the evening, the overall gaiety and politeness of the people.[118]

Freud's letter suggests that he was dazzled by the surfaces and exteriors of Paris—by everything that could be seen. Parisians, he noted, were shameless because life in the city was neither hidden nor remote, it transpired in "the swarming crowds" and in the "brilliant exterior." In the new Paris, life was thought of as something to be seen as well as lived. Lived experience or "reality," whether on the boulevard or in the newspaper, became the matter represented. In the capital's newly organized spaces in and around the old *grands boulevards* and through the modern mass press, viewing became an essential means of participating in Parisian life.

The boulevard and the press are no doubt most obviously linked through their blatant ties to a burgeoning consumer culture. As Guy Debord theorized and as many historians of consumerism have argued, the spectacularization of everyday life epitomizes its saturation by capital.[119] Yet to tie them to consumerism does not explain the particular forms they took and why these forms and not others were popular with the urban masses whose support and participation was essential to their success.

In the chapters that follow, the reader will recognize large and socially diverse crowds gathered as spectators, clamoring to see "the real thing." At the city morgue, dead bodies displayed behind a large glass window drew as many as a million visitors a year. In a number of commercial entertainments—wax museums, panoramas, dioramas and cinema—crowds delighted to see "real life" realistically represented. Through the spectacularization of reality, urban dwellers could assume the pleasures of looking as the very means of constructing a new collectivity. Rather than subsist as alienated and detached individuals lost in the crowd, the urban mob happily assembled as a new collective in front of the spectacle of the real. In, and thus as, the audience, they became "Parisians."

118. *The Letters of Sigmund Freud*, ed. Ernst L. Freud, trans. Tania and James Stern (New York: McGraw Hill, 1964), letter 87, December 3, 1885. I thank Toby Gelfand for drawing my attention to this letter.

119. See Debord, *Society of the Spectacle;* Alice Kaplan and Kristin Ross, eds., *Everyday Life,* Yale French Studies no. 73 (New Haven: Yale University Press, 1987); and especially, T. J. Clark, *Painting of Modern Life,* for Paris.

CHAPTER 2

Public Visits to the Morgue

Flânerie in the Service of the State

On April 3, 1895, *Le Petit Journal* reported that "an enormous crowd went to the morgue yesterday" to view the corpse of an eighteen-month-old girl found in the Seine at Suresnes. The next day the newspaper reported that another corpse, that of a three-year-old girl, had been fished out of the river near St-Cloud. An article appearing on April 4 asked, "Are these two sisters?"[1] Hordes continued to gather to see the two little bodies displayed at the Paris Morgue, eager to participate in—or perhaps even solve—what newspapers called "le mystère de Suresnes."[2] On April 5, *Le Petit Journal* reported that "an enormous crowd has not stopped gathering" and explained that the police had set up a special service to keep visitors lined up in an orderly fashion and corral them through the morgue's *salle d'exposition* (exhibit room), no more than ten at a time.[3] *L'Intransigeant* remarked, "The crowd was so large that it was difficult to keep the curious visitors lined up."[4] *Le XIXe Siècle* estimated that ten thousand people had visited the morgue during the first four days that these little corpses were on display.

What did they see? Visitors entered the exhibit room where, along with some ten dead bodies laid out on black marble slabs, they saw

1. *Le Petit Journal*, April 4, 1895.
2. The story was also reported under other equally dramatic headlines: "Les bébés de la morgue," *Le XIXe Siècle*, April 10, 1895; and "Les petites noyées de Suresnes," *L'Intransigeant*, April 6, 1895.
3. *Le XIXe Siècle*, April 7, 1895.
4. *L'Intransigeant*, April 6, 1895.

Les petites noyées de Suresnes
Gravure de Navellier — Voir l'article, page 13.

5. The "mystère de Suresnes," from *Le Journal illustré,* April 21, 1895.

the two little girls, "on chairs covered in gray material" (fig. 5).[5] The "fillettes de Suresnes" were not the first to draw crowds to the Paris Morgue, however. Listed in almost every guidebook to Paris, the morgue even merited a stop on the Thomas Cook tour of the city.[6] As Parisian man-about-town Hughes Leroux remarked, "There are few people having visited Paris who do not know the morgue."[7] One newspaper plainly proclaimed, "It would be difficult to find a Parisian, native or transplanted, who does not make his pilgrimage."[8]

As a depository for anonymous corpses found in the public domain, the morgue represented the quintessentially urban experience of anonymity with its potential for both increased freedom and alienation. After all, only in a city might a woman or man or child die alone and go unrecognized. Other European cities also had their morgues, but only in Paris were corpses displayed behind a large glass window through which the public might freely pass, seven days a week, from dawn to dusk. At the Paris Morgue city and state officials, in conjunc-

5. *Le Petit Journal,* April 5, 1895.

6. See Paul Veyriras, "Visiteurs britanniques à la morgue de Paris au dix-neuvième siècle," *Cahiers victoriens et édouardiens,* no. 15 (April 1982): 51–61. Veyriras argues that visitors' interest resided in the fact that no English morgue received the public at large.

7. Hughes Leroux, *L'enfer parisien* (Paris, 1888), 353.

8. *Le XIXe Siècle,* April 20, 1892.

tion with the popular press, turned the allegedly serious business of identifying anonymous corpses into a spectacle—one eagerly attended by a large and diverse crowd. The popularity of public visits to the Paris Morgue during the nineteenth century was part of the spectacular "real life" that chroniclers, visitors and inhabitants alike had come to associate with Parisian culture.

The Paris Morgue cannot help but fit into a landscape of representations of death in nineteenth-century Paris despite the fact that contemporary observers would literally stare death in the face and then talk instead about theater and mystery. This very public nature of the display, however, seems to contradict Philippe Ariès's important thesis that death became invisible in the nineteenth century. It also highlights his overreliance on the bourgeois experience of death, in which he paid scant attention to death and dying among the poor during this period.[9] Although the morgue display and its representation in the press clearly drew on contemporary conventions for representing death, especially in gripping tales of women and children who wound up in the window, they functioned as a Parisian attraction, whose draw was the display of "real" dead bodies.[10]

Although neither Ariès nor the historian Thomas Kselman in his book about death in modern France mentions the Paris Morgue, the morgue has received some attention from scholars interested in science and positivism, most notably Alan Mitchell.[11] He described the morgue as a "shrine of positivism" whose "social function was inseparable from the growing prestige of nineteenth-century science."[12] Elaborating

9. Although he wrote extensively about death, Ariès's most synthetic work is *The Hour of Our Death,* trans. Helen Weaver (New York: Vintage Books, 1982). In *Death and the Afterlife in Modern France* (Princeton: Princeton University Press, 1993), Thomas Kselman also takes Ariès to task for this weakness. See 3–4. For an interesting focus on death and the poor in England, see Thomas Laqueur, "Bodies, Death, and Pauper Funerals," *Representations* 1 (1983): 109–31.

10. For more on representing death, see Ariès, *The Hour of Our Death;* Linda Nochlin, *Realism* (London: Penguin, 1971); Elizabeth Bronfen, *Over Her Dead Body* (London: Routledge, 1993); Stanley Burns, *Sleeping Beauty: Memorial Photography in America* (Altadena: Twelvetrees Press, 1990); and Jay Ruby, *Secure the Shadow: Death and Photography in America* (Cambridge, Mass.: MIT Press, 1995). In their essay about Paris, Anne, Margaret and Patrice Higonnet tie the display of corpses to bourgeois fetishism. "Façades: Walter Benjamin's Paris," *Critical Inquiry* 10 (March 1984): 391–419, esp. 408–13.

11. Alan Mitchell, "The Paris Morgue as a Social Institution in the Nineteenth Century" *Francia* 4 (1976): 581–96. Mitchell's article inspired this chapter on the morgue.

12. Ibid., 596.

further on Mitchell's work, Bruno Bertherat cast the institution in a Foucaultian framework that includes the prison and the clinic, arguing that the morgue participated "in the enormous regulatory function" of nineteenth-century science.[13]

These interpretations are fruitful and certainly explain the enormous interest in the morgue and help contextualize the bureaucracy that was elaborated at the morgue from its foundation in 1804 to its transformation into the Institut medico-légal in the twentieth century. But what about the crucial relation between the administration and the crowds who visited in numbers of sometimes as many as forty thousand in a day? If we consider the morgue as a public exhibition, represented in the popular press and even by its administration as a Parisian attraction, then it is crucial to examine and explore its crowd and their relation to the display of corpses. The so-called forces of positivism, the police and forensic doctors in charge of the morgue, in addition to the popular press, spectacularized and theatricalized dead bodies and offered them up to what they hoped would be a large and diverse public. The question remains: why, in a city that did not lack attractions, did large numbers of people gather to see the corpses in the morgue's window?

The morgue's administrative director answered this question by explaining that "the morgue is considered in Paris like a museum that is much more fascinating than even a wax museum because the people displayed are real flesh and blood."[14] The morgue, in short, was a spectacle of the real. In particular, the morgue fit into a modern Parisian landscape in which the banal and the everyday developed in sensational narratives, in which life—and even death—turned into the spectacular. As Linda Nochlin has noted, nineteenth-century critics berated realism for transforming representations of death from a transcendental state to "a banal level of mere commonplace, everyday actuality."[15] And the discourse about the morgue suggests that public fascination with its display may have resided in the complex mix of its desacralization of death and its insistence that a corpse be observed in relation to a particular narrative context—in its transformation of the corpse from its association with the eternal to its affiliation with the newspaper's *plat*

13. Bruno Bertherat, "La morgue et la visite de la morgue à Paris au XIXe siècle, 1804–1907" (Master's thesis, Université de Paris I, 1990).

14. *La Presse,* March 22, 1907.

15. Nochlin, *Realism,* 58.

du jour. Aided by the growth of the mass-circulated press and organized tourism, the spectacle of the corpse in the morgue's display window transformed the formerly eternal corpse into something ephemeral: current events. The corpse was thereby considered in the context of the ultimate ephemeral object—the wax figure. Yet the morgue's corpses were even better than wax, the morgue director noted, because these ephemeral bodies were "real flesh and blood."

From *Basse-Géôle* to Morgue

The morgue that housed the corpses of the two young girls described earlier was built in 1864 behind Notre-Dame on the quai de l'Archevêché (now the site of the Mémorial à la Déportation) (see fig. 1). The history of the morgue proper covers a period of just over two hundred years, from its first entry into the dictionary of the Académie in 1718 to its transfer in 1921 to its current site at the place de Mazas by the quai de la Rapée, where it ceased being called the "morgue" and became instead the Institut médico-légal, signifying the changes in the morgue's conceptualization during the twentieth century from an institution that relied heavily on public visits to one run by medical experts.

Throughout its history, the morgue's principal goal was to serve as a depository for the anonymous dead, "found in the domain of the prefecture of police."[16] Their public display, it was believed, might help determine their identities. An 1800 police decree explained the value of the public display at the morgue. Establishing the identity of a missing person, it argued, was essential to "the social order."[17]

The morgue can be seen in the context of growing state interest in and responsibility for the dead and as part of an ever-increasing reliance on the "expert knowledge" of a professionalized corps of doctors of forensic medicine.[18] By the end of the nineteenth century, the former

16. Arrêté réglementaire du service intérieur de la morgue de Paris, January 1, 1836, reprinted in Firmin Maillard, *Recherches historiques et critiques sur la morgue* (Paris: Delahays, 1860), 50

17. Arrêté concernant la levée des cadavres trouvés dans la rivière ou ailleurs, April 29, 1800, reprinted in ibid., 42–43.

18. On death see Kselman, *Death and the Afterlife.* For expert knowledge and specialization, see Michel Foucault, especially *Discipline and Punish;* and Robert Nye, *Crime,*

basse-géôle had witnessed the growth of a large bureaucracy with multiple administrations, all interested in regulating deaths here as much as bureaucrats tracked births elsewhere.[19]

From the start, the morgue institutionalized the public viewing of corpses. According to Adolphe Guillot, moralist, jurist and author of a full-length work on the morgue, as early as the fourteenth century, the order of Sainte Catherine oversaw a depository for unidentified bodies found in the public domain.[20] Firmin Maillard, the institution's other chronicler, noted the 1718 definition from the *Dictionnaire de l'Académie,* which defined the morgue as "a place at the Châtelet [prison] where dead bodies that have been found are open to the public view, in order that they be recognized."[21] The term morgue itself incorporates visuality as the institution's defining quality since it is derived from the archaic verb *morguer*—to stare, to have a "fixed and questioning gaze."[22]

The *basse-géôle* at the Châtelet, as it was called in the eighteenth century, was geographically as well as institutionally attached to the prison through the Cour du Châtelet.[23] According to Alphonse Devergie, the morgue's first medical inspector, the room in the basement of the prison was small, dark, dank and housed bodies strewn one on top of another. There "relatives, with a lantern in hand, go . . . to identify their kin."[24] Devergie, like many of the later nineteenth-century ob-

Madness, and Politics in Modern France (Princeton: Princeton University Press, 1984); and Ruth Harris, *Murders and Madness: Medicine, Law, and Society in the Fin de Siècle* (Oxford: Clarendon Press, 1989).

19. The morgue's administration was labyrinthine. As a municipal institution, it displayed anonymous corpses found within the city and outlying suburbs. Yet it operated at the departmental level, doing scientific and police work to determine criminal involvement in deaths, and at the national level, offering instruction in forensic medicine. It was administered by three different agencies: the Prefecture of the Seine maintained the building, the Prefecture of Police was in charge of hygiene and daily administration, including the varied expert services, and finally, the Ministry of Public Instruction was responsible for the courses in forensic medicine taught at the morgue starting in 1877.

20. Adolphe Guillot, *Paris qui souffre: la basse-géôle du Grand-Châtelet et les morgues modernes,* 2d ed. (Paris: Chez Rouquette, 1888), 25.

21. Maillard, *Recherches sur la morgue,* 7.

22. Guillot, *Paris qui souffre,* 33.

23. In his book *Death in Paris* (Oxford: Oxford University Press, 1978), Richard Cobb creatively used the records from the Basse-Géôle for the years 1795–1801 to write a brief social history of suicide. The institution offered no public display.

24. Alphonse Devergie, *Notions générales sur la morgue de Paris* (Paris: Félix Malteste, 1877), 4.

servers, described the old *basse-géôle* in order to highlight the improvements in management and hygiene made at the morgue over the course of the nineteenth century. Guillot went on at length:

It was a stinking pestilent place with little of the respect that death deserves . . . , where corpses were randomly thrown on the ground, without being covered, until the moment when they were returned to the community of Sainte Catherine. . . . Visitors could only present themselves one at a time; in order to look into the horrible and somber cave they were forced to breathe the poisoned air of this grotto and put their faces against a narrow opening.[25]

Henri Brochin complained of the inefficiency of the old morgue in *Paris pittoresque,* saying that the cadavers "could only be seen by the public through a grill-covered skylight, which opened out onto the ground floor of a small interior courtyard of the monument."[26]

Given the inadequacy of the *basse-géôle* and the destruction of the Châtelet prison, a police ordinance on August 17, 1804, ordered its transfer to a specially designed building in the shape of a Greek temple at the well-frequented place du Marché-Neuf, on the Ile-de-la-Cité, historic and administrative heart of Paris. Not far from the Palais de Justice and bordering the Seine, the new location facilitated the arrival of corpses, many of which were transported by boat. Now officially called *la morgue,* the new building was celebrated as a great improvement over the *basse-géôle* and its design reveals both a rationalization of space and an emphasis on the display of the dead bodies.

The exhibit room of the 1804 morgue made it possible for large crowds to gather and gaze at the neatly arranged corpses. Beyond the single entrance of double doors lay the exhibit room, measuring two hundred and ten square meters. As the Parisian chronicler Jean-Henri Marlet described it in his *Nouveau tableau de Paris,* "Everything seems to have been thought of in terms of the interior setup of this dismal building. The big high windows perfectly light the marble ramps on which the corpses are placed. Vast closed-off glass windows permit people to examine the corpses without being exposed to their fumes, as many of them are in a decaying state."[27] The new morgue offered a

25. Guillot, *Paris qui souffre,* 43.

26. H. Brochin, "La morgue," in *Paris pittoresque,* ed. G. Sarrut and B. Saint-Edmé (Paris: D'Urtubie, 1837), 2:261.

27. Jean-Henri Marlet, *Le nouveau tableau de Paris* (Paris, 1821–24).

6. Morgue interior, from Léopold Flameng, *Paris qui s'en va et qui vient* (1860). Musée Carnavalet. © Photothèque des musées de la Ville de Paris.

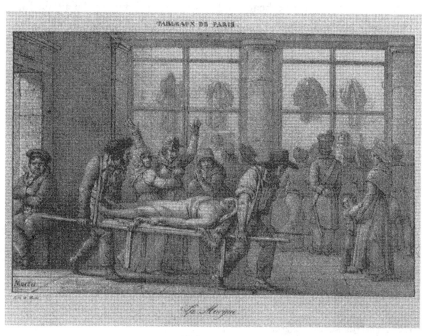

7. Morgue interior, from Jean-Henri Marlet, *Le nouveau tableau de Paris* (1821–24). Musée Carnavalet. © Photothèque des musées de la Ville de Paris.

display at the same time that it separated the dead from the living, in keeping with contemporary concern about the toxicity of the dead.[28]

The small Greek temple on the quai du Marché-Neuf became so associated with Parisian life that it was included in such compendiums as the *Livre des cent et un* (1831), Marlet's *Nouveau tableau de Paris* (1821–24), and Texier's *Tableau de Paris* (1852). Léon Gozlan even described the morgue as a "central neighborhood spot." He explained, "The morgue, is the Luxembourg, the Place Royale of the Cité. One goes there to see the latest fashions, orange trees blooming, chestnut trees that rustle in the autumn winds, in spring, and in winter."[29] Gozlan imagined the morgue as a permanent display that would bear witness to things ephemeral, if perennial: fashion and the seasons.

Early images depict the morgue as a neighborhood gathering spot, drawing on normal foot traffic that passed by the busy marketplace locale. Men, women and even children, bourgeois and worker alike (figs. 6–7), gaped at the bodies that were normally displayed nude, except for a cloth covering their genitals. A corpse's clothing was hung nearby to aid identification. Despite the glass window that separated the living from the dead and their fumes, the 1804 morgue did not entirely succeed in segregating the two. Jean-Henri Marlet's image (see fig. 7) dramatizes the possible mingling of the living and the dead, suggesting that the framing of corpses in this early nineteenth-century morgue was not quite fixed. The morgue as yet contained no clearly delimited "backstage."

The Morgue Haussmannized

Like many well known sites, the morgue at the Marché-Neuf was forced to close its doors as part of the reorganization of the city directed by Napoleon III's prefect of the Seine, Baron Georges Haussmann. Haussmann's wreckers razed the old morgue at the place du Marché-Neuf because it blocked the line of the new boulevard Sébastopol, designed as one of the thoroughfares built to disembowel me-

28. See Philippe Ariès, *L'homme devant la mort* (Paris: Editions du Seuil, 1977); and Kselman, *Death and the Afterlife*, 165–221.

29. Léon Gozlan, "La morgue," in *Le livre des cent et un* (Paris: Chez Ladvocat, 1831), 1:303.

dieval Paris, epitomized by the crowded Ile-de-la Cité. Condemned with the rest of "old Paris," the morgue would have to find a new home.

The relocation of the morgue sparked renewed discussion concerning the proper location for the dead. As Philippe Ariès and others have demonstrated, the separation of the living from the dead began in the late eighteenth century and was most vividly typified by the relocation of the *cimetière des innocents* in 1780.[30] By the mid-nineteenth century, however, the separation had already begun to be eroded by the mere growth of the city limits that engulfed the cemeteries originally located outside the city limits. Despite the perceived health hazard of mixing the living and the dead, the belief in surrounding death "by a sacred atmosphere" and Napoleon's decree of 23 Prairial in the year XII (1804) locating cemeteries outside the city limits, the annexation of the suburbs—including the communes of Belleville, Montmartre and Montrouge in 1860—effectively reintroduced the cemeteries of Père-Lachaise, Montmartre and Montparnasse within the city limits.[31] Although Haussmann initiated a project to close these cemeteries in 1864, objections were raised in the municipal council and the Senate that this plan showed "indifference to Catholic piety."[32] The dead, it seemed, needed to be at some distance from daily life, but not so far as to remove them entirely from social rhythms.

In 1857, as work progressed on the boulevard Sébastopol, the prefect of the Seine invited the police and the Conseil d'hygiène et salubrité to determine a site and plan for the reconstruction of the morgue.[33] While they and the general council of the Seine voted to move it far from city dwellings, Haussmann decided that it should remain centrally located. After all, the morgue's location in a busy place was thought to be essential to its function. If it were moved to a site where it was not easily accessible to random visitors, fewer bodies would be identified, he reasoned.[34] Thus, despite the alleged "sanitation" of the city center and

30. See Ariès, *Homme devant la mort;* and Kselman, *Death and the Afterlife.*

31. Kselman, *Death and the Afterlife,* 302.

32. Michel Ragon, *The Space of Death,* trans. Alan Sheridan (Charlottesville: University of Virginia Press, 1983), 269.

33. Louis Dausset and Georges Lemarchand, *Rapport sur la reconstruction de la morgue et la création d'un Institut médico-légal* (Paris: Imprimerie municipale, 1908), 12. See also *Rapport général sur les travaux du Conseil d'hygiène du département de la Seine* (Paris: Imprimerie municipale, 1849–1861), 284–86.

34. Alphonse Devergie, "La morgue de Paris: sa description, son service, son système hygiènique—de l'autopsie judiciaire, comparée à l'autopsie pathologique," *Annales d'hygiène publique et de médecine légale,* 2d s., 4 (1878): 44–79, 53–54.

the waning of bloody sights (the slaughterhouses were relocated in the 1830s; in 1832 public executions were moved from the place du Grève to the barrière St-Jacques; in 1850 the loi Grammont prevented the beating of animals in public),[35] the cemeteries remained within the city limits and the new morgue was to be even more visible and accessible than the old one at the Marché-Neuf.

In the end, all groups settled on a location owned by the city of Paris called *le terrain,* the area behind Notre-Dame at the eastern tip of the Ile de la Cité. Félix Gilbert, a member of the Académie des Beaux-Arts, winner of the Grand Prix de Rome, architect for the renovated police prefecture and the Hôtel-Dieu and chief architect of Paris during much of Haussmannization, designed the new morgue. At the cost of 400,000 francs, Gilbert, according to Haussmann, "had to hide this lugubrious institution under a simple form."[36] No longer shaped like a Greek temple, the new morgue that opened in February 1864 looked like a generic administrative building—symmetrical, made of stone and supported by heavy pillars, with *Liberté, Egalité, Fraternité* written across the front (figs. 8–9).

Touted for its "modernity," the 1864 morgue was celebrated as a model institution by public health experts. Ambroise Tardieu, a leading doctor of forensic medicine and attending medical inspector at the morgue during the 1860s and 1870s, ended his description of the morgue in the *Paris-Guide* with a flurry of positivist bravado: "It can be considered the model of what these establishments, which are of primary necessity in populous cities, which are never useless, which respond to highly decent feelings and to an undoubted interest in public order and cleanliness, should be."[37]

Indeed, developments at the morgue on the quai de l'Archevêché reveal a rationalizing impulse based on increasingly specified and technical knowledge. With a surface of eight hundred and thirty-five square meters, the new morgue was almost quadruple the size of the old one.[38] The building contained many more rooms for increasingly specialized functions: more space for autopsies, a special rear entrance for receiving

35. See Alain Corbin, *Le village des cannibales* (Paris: Aubier, 1990); and Corbin, "Le sang de Paris, réflexions sur la généalogie de l'image de la capitale," in *Ecrire Paris,* ed. Daniel Oster and Jean-Marie Goulemot (Paris: Editions Seesam, 1990).

36. Haussmann, *Mémoires* (1890–93; reprint, Paris: Guy Durier, 1979), 2:268.

37. Ambroise Tardieu, "La morgue," in *Paris-Guide* (Paris: A. Lacroix, 1867), 2:2005.

38. "La nouvelle morgue de Paris," *Revue générale de l'architecture et des travaux publics* 22 (1864): 229–30, plans 33 to 39; 230.

8. Exterior of the morgue, quai de L'Archevêché, 1905. Bibliothèque nationale, cabinet des estampes.

9. Exterior of the morgue, from the Left Bank, 1904. Bibliothèque nationale, cabinet des estampes.

corpses, a laundry for washing and drying the corpses' clothing, more space for the registrar and his growing staff. This room, the *salle du public*, in which the public actually stood and the exhibit room that faced it through a glass window, were the most frequented locations at the morgue, and remained at the center of the new building, but with a few modifications. Instead of two rows of five corpses, there were now two rows of six in the bigger exhibit room. Of the three large doors in the front of the building, the middle one remained closed while the one to the left served as the entrance and the one to the right as an exit through which the public filed. This led Clovis Pierre, the morgue registrar from 1878–1892, to refer to the morgue as nothing more than an *entresort* (a fair attraction in which one paid and walked through to see a display).[39]

Tardieu described the new morgue as an institution dedicated to the accessibility of public viewing:

The main entrance leads to a large display room that occupies the center of the building and that, separated from the sidewalk by only a barrier intended to stop the penetration of gazes from the outside inside, is always open to visitors and invites them in a way, to come in; an essential setup for the prompt and easy recognition of the displayed individuals. The room is separated along its entire width into two by a window that can by design be shut-off behind curtains, but that usually remains open and allows people to see into the other half. Lighted directly from above, it has twelve stone slabs in two rows on which corpses, stripped of their clothes, are protected by a loincloth that alone guards against stares.[40]

The wooden barrier between the doorway and the display room partially screened the sight inside from passersby on the street. In effect, the screen turned the display into a peep show at which passersby actually had to make an effort to come and look. Once around the screen, visitors saw a large glass window, split into three sections by two columns.[41] Among the other innovations that announced the new building's spectacular qualities was a green curtain that hung at the display window's sides. Morgue staffers would use the curtain to close off the

39. Clovis Pierre, *Les gaietés de la morgue* (Paris: Gallimard, 1895).
40. Tardieu, "La morgue," 2:1998.
41. When he retired in 1893, the morgue registrar Clovis Pierre described the exhibit room as having no window: "the corpses were displayed before the public who could see them without the separation of a window." From *Le Figaro*, September 9, 1893. All other reports contradict his.

display when a change of scene took place; which is to say when they either removed a body from display or added one to those already in the window.

The administrators employed other changes in display techniques with an eye to prolonging the period a corpse might be seen by the public. For example, in 1877 the morgue staff began photographing all its inhabitants and posted the photos of corpses that had been buried but remained unidentified on the wooden barrier at the entrance, thus prolonging the display of any unidentified corpse long after the usual three days of display.[42] In 1882 the administration installed a system for the refrigeration of the corpses—a system that slowed their decay and thus extended display time.[43] Previously, the only "preservative" used on the bodies, some of which had been in the Seine for days, was a continuous trickle of cold water over the corpses. The conservation of corpses had been complicated by the fact that doctors of forensic medicine were prohibited from using any material on the corpse that might falsify the results of an autopsy. The new refrigeration system, modeled on one developed for the transport of meat to markets, "has served as a model for all the large European cities."[44] It was especially important in cases in which the police suspected foul play. This new preservation system sparked much interest (during the 1880s people were witnessing the Pasteurian revolution all around them) and even became the object of some amusement. For example, a joke invitation was printed for "an evening of music and dance" in the refrigerated room, signed by the "président de la Ch. Syndicale des Figurants [extras]: Reffroidy [re-chilled]."[45]

Yet the morgue's so-called positivist improvements in the visual ease of its display do not sufficiently explain such theatrical elements as the green curtain, nor do they explain its popularity among Parisians and tourists—a million visitors a year, according to *L'Eclair*[46]—a popularity

42. *The Morning Journal,* July 19, 1891. Hoping for leads, police officers often carried around photos of victims (especially useful before the morgue was able to refrigerate corpses). A photograph was also placed next to each entry in the morgue records, where many remain today.

43. Dr. Paul Brouardel, medical director, arranged the system. In 1877 he gave the first seminars in forensic medicine on the quai de l'Archevêché.

44. *Le Figaro,* September 9, 1893.

45. APP, DB 210. Morgue folklore includes stories of vagrants begging to serve as "extras" in the exhibit room and thus get a place to sleep on one of the slabs.

46. *L'Eclair,* August 29, 1892.

that indicates that many people who visited had no hope of identifying a body; a popularity that led most commentators about the morgue to begin with some version of "Everyone in Paris knows the morgue . . . "[47]

The Morgue as Spectacle

Especially after the opening of the new morgue in 1864, commentators described the institution as a site of pleasure and entertainment—a "spectacle"—in the French double sense of theater and grand display. The morgue administration may have needed people to come and see the bodies in order to identify them, but could it possibly have needed hundreds of thousands of people? While the display's defenders claimed that the spectacle existed in the name of science, the public knew what the morgue administration might have known but certainly would not admit: they offered the best free theater in town.

"It is nothing but a *spectacle à sensation,* permanent and free, where the playbill changes every day," wrote Ernest Cherbuliez.[48] Many observers compared the exhibit room to various nineteenth-century displays that dotted the Parisian landscape. Guillot described it as "an enormous window similar to a store front;"[49] Gourdon de Genouillac wrote, "Picture a large department store window when the merchandise has been removed on a Saturday night."[50] Cherbuliez described the exhibit room as a department store window in recounting an anecdote concerning a man walking down the boulevard Sébastopol. He stopped in front of a department store window to ask the window dressers for work; they suggested he ask at the morgue.[51]

Most often, however, commentators described the experience of visits to the morgue as theatrical entertainment. Its administrator Gaud noted that, "The morgue is a theater of dramas and comedies; but once in a while vaudevilles play there."[52] In his *Chansons de la morgue,* An-

47. Jacques Clavel, "La morgue," *Le Paris,* August 31, 1886.
48. Ernest Cherbuliez, "La morgue," *Revue des deux mondes,* January 1891, 344.
49. Guillot, *Paris qui souffre,* 213.
50. H. Gourdon de Genouillac, *Paris, à travers les siècles* (Paris. Roy, 1882–89), 5:262–63.
51. Cherbuliez, "La morgue," 360.
52. *Le Journal,* February 16, 1908.

gelin Ruelle described the crowd's objectifying and eager gaze in a poem called "The Drowned":

> They are lined up on the slabs,
> In front of the crowd that pushes forward,
> With the look of drunks, raided by a last drunkenness . . .
> But in front of these horrible corpses,
> In front of whose terror you freeze
> The crowd, content and without remorse,
> Takes their place as though at the theater.[53]

Ruelle hastens here to question the "moral standing" of the pathetic corpses who have been found dead and in the public domain (who else would wind up there?) and seems to distinguish between the individual viewer's "terror" and the eager and unfazed spectatorship of the theater crowd.

Commentators often evoked conversations between viewers to bear witness to their experience of the morgue as "real-life" theater. Guillot described a conversation in the exhibit room in which a woman reassured her companion that "it will be better soon, they are installing electric lighting, it's been posted."[54] In addition, popular rhetoric referred to a *relâche* (an intermission) when, on rare occasions, no bodies were exhibited.[55] And, according to the head of the Sûreté, Gustave Macé, when the registrar had to evacuate the exhibit room, he "closed the curtain and the disappointed public insulted him, threatened him with punches, because he ventured to cancel their show without warning."[56] Victor Fournel also noted the crowd's ire "when the slabs are empty and there is no show to see, they are apt to complain that death allowed itself an intermission that day, without thinking of their good pleasure."[57]

To many observers, the morgue simply satisfied and reinforced the desire to look that seemed to permeate so much of their culture in the late nineteenth-century. "They came to see, just to see, just as they read a serial novel or go to the Ambigu; at the door, calling out to each other and demanding the program: 'What have they got in there?' "[58]

---

53. Angelin Ruelle, *Les chansons de la morgue* (Paris: Léon Varnier, 1890).
54. Guillot, *Paris qui souffre,* 190.
55. Maxime Du Camp, *Paris, ses organes, ses fonctions et sa vie* (Paris: Hachette, 1869), 1:431.
56. Gustave Macé, *Mon musée criminel* (Paris: Charpentier, 1890), 119.
57. Victor Fournel, *Ce qu'on voit dans les rues de Paris* (Paris, 1858), 351–52.
58. Georges Montorgueil, "La morgue fermée," *L'Eclair,* September 7, 1892.

The display window's framing of the corpses identified the site as a spectacle. One newspaper put it simply: "people go the morgue 'to see.' "[59] "La Vitrine," a poem from the collection *Les gaietés de la morgue,* written by Clovis Pierre, exploits the crowd's voyeurism. He wrote that "in Paris, they are curious," and thus "each visitor comes to exercise his retina at the window."[60]

The display was so integrated into Parisian public spectacle that observers noted, perhaps with a hint of irony, the crowd's resentment at having their gaze disciplined. In the Parisian melodrama *Casse-Museau,* the guards shout "Move along, move along." In response, a visitor, with an annoyed air of someone entitled, complains of being rushed through: "Move along, move along, you'd think we were in a museum . . . we don't even have enough time to see."[61] In an almost poised counter-distinction to a museum, where the public was represented as experiencing itself as "rushed through" this playwright seems to be hinting that the theater at the morgue belonged "to the people" who thus refused to be corralled through.

In a time of increasingly private and commercial entertainment (which was, however, rendered more accessible because it was inexpensive), the morgue was open and free. Although an English traveler to Paris called the morgue a "forlorn side-show of the great entertainment we now call Paris," it was generally celebrated as free public theater.[62] As one newspaper pointed out, it was the only "free theater in Paris with the exception of July 14 and Sunday at the salon."[63] In *Thérèse Raquin,* Zola described it as "a show that was affordable to all. . . . The door is open. Enter those who will."[64] Another observer noted, "The vast majority go there as though to a theater, which has the advantage over others of costing nothing."[65]

The fact that the morgue was free theater seemed to enhance its status as an institution of and for the public. When the morgue was finally closed to the public in March 1907, one journalist protested this way:

59. *Le Cri du Peuple,* July 6, 1885.
60. Pierre, *Gaietés de la morgue.*
61. Gaston de Marot, et al , *Casse-Museau* (Paris: Tresse, 1882), 70.
62. E. V. Lucas, *A Wanderer in Paris* (London: Methuen, 1909), 54–55.
63. *Le Paris,* August 31, 1891.
64. Emile Zola, *Thérèse Raquin* (1867; Paris: Flammarion, 1970), 131.
65. *Le Voleur illustré,* October 27, 1882; article originally from *Le Français.*

The morgue has been the first this year among theaters to announce its closing. . . . As for the spectators, they have no right to say anything because they didn't pay. The show being always free, there were no subscribers, only regulars. It was the first free theater for the people. And they tell us it's being canceled. People, the hour of social justice has not yet arrived.[66]

He also noted the never-changing decor, compared it to classical Greek theater, remarked that the actors always "just turned up," and that the crowd represented a genuine social mix since the institution offered only a *parterre*. In the scene at the morgue from *Casse-Museau* when the attendant tries to clear the room, one of the characters objects, protesting, "What do you mean leave! It's public here! It's the temple of equality."[67] Not only does this boulevard melodrama reflect the status of the display at the morgue as essentially public, but also the use of the term "temple of equality" implies an equality among spectators in life as much as among the corpses in death.

The morgue offered an active and participatory kind of spectatorship—one through which the public looked and then could be called on to act in the name of civic duty by identifying a corpse. As an article in *Le Petit Parisien* noted, "It is of the highest social interest that everyone go in there. . . . The citizens of a large democracy must be convinced that for both the public interest and their private interest, they [the police] need their cooperation in the shared work of justice."[68] Senator Paul Strauss commented that the passerby is solicited to enter and "take a look at these corpses."[69] Dr. J. C. Gavinzel, who promoted the utility of the morgue, urged his readers thus, "Sympathetic reader! When you go past this somber building over there . . . no longer shiver while turning your head away; enter boldly, and if any object strikes you or jogs your memory, go to the registrar, make a declaration."[70] Rather than shy away from looking at corpses, Gavinzel regarded it as a civic duty. The display at the morgue encouraged the crowd to scrutinize the corpses and thus reason along with the experts about the causes of death. In the end though, the public gaze was solicited for identification of a body and not to determine how the individual died. No doubt, however, the vast majority of visitors probably did not go

66. Pierre Véron, "La morgue," *Le Magasin pittoresque,* March 1907, 171–72.
67. Marot, *Casse-Museau,* 72.
68. *Le Petit Parisien,* December 3, 1900.
69. Paul Strauss, *Paris ignoré* (Paris: Librairies Imprimeries réunies, 1892), 248.
70. Dr. J. C. Gavinzel, *Etude sur la morgue au point de vue administratif et médical* (Paris: Baillière et fils, 1882), 46.

to the morgue thinking that they actually might recognize a corpse. The "duties" of urban life were thus transformed into spectacular entertainment.

The Morgue and Its Public

If the morgue administration turned the serious business of identifying anonymous corpses into a show, the new morgue also witnessed a surge in the numbers of visitors that attended. By the second half of the nineteenth century, descriptions of the institution inevitably pointed to its popularity. "Whether we like it or not, the fact remains that the morgue is one of the most popular sights in Paris."[71] The morgue became part of the landscape of leisure: "it is incontestable that Parisians consider a visit to the morgue as a sort of pastime. The exhibit room is never empty; there are many more people than we might imagine who go deliberately out of their way to go there."[72] Despite its location in the shadows of a great religious institution, its deliberately undramatic facade and its seemingly somber subject-matter, the new morgue became more than a lively neighborhood spot. As Guillot, who wrote his history of the morgue in order to incite an end to public exhibitions, despaired, "One enters there as one enters a carnival barrack . . . it is a place of distraction and of gatherings; the children who play on the sidewalk or in the pretty garden of the quai de l'Archevêché interrupt . . . their games to come and see whether a new corpse has been brought in."[73] In fact, the location was so well frequented that vendors lined the sidewalk outside. As Leroux wrote, "All along the sidewalk, vendors sell oranges, apples and popular pastries."[74] Guillot detailed, "an old woman had authorization to sell oranges and cakes by the entrance; an honest fellow, very well known on the Ile St-Louis, has a stall next to the door through which the dead are brought in, where he sells a topical ointment nicknamed in the neighborhood *la pâte de la morgue*."[75] These descriptions were not mere rhetoric. For example, when the

71. E. A. Reynolds-Ball, *Paris in Its Splendours* (London: Gay and Bird, 1901), 2:312.
72. *Le Voleur illustré,* October 27, 1882.
73. Guillot, *Paris qui souffre,* 186–87.
74. Leroux, *L'enfer parisien,* 353.
75. Guillot, *Paris qui souffre,* 177.

morgue was closed to the public in March 1907, forty merchants from the quartier Notre-Dame petitioned the second commission of the municipal council, claiming the closure had damaged their businesses:

Sirs, the undersigned, licensed merchants established in the area around the morgue, are honored to reveal to you the losses they have had to incur since the new regime related to the recent closing of this establishment.

In effect, since this closing, not only the tourist buses have canceled the visit from their schedule, but also Parisians themselves, who used to make a detour from their path to take a quick look at the unfortunates whom luck had landed in failure on the slabs, don't stop any longer; and thus for the neighboring local commerce—restaurants, bakers, butchers, grocers, wine merchants and so on—there has been a significant decline in receipts, and we are therefore obligated to ask the city for compensation through a tax break.[76]

The local merchants who relied on the morgue's large public for business echoed the newspapers in underscoring the popularity of the morgue as an attraction.

Representations of the morgue characterized its visitors, which included "regulars" and tourists alike, as a diverse crowd. According to Tardieu, "All day long a multitude of the curious, of the most diverse ages, elbow and jostle one another from eight in the morning until nightfall in the public gallery."[77] The stage directions for *Casse-Museau*, whose third act transpired at the morgue, elaborated that "the vestibule is crowded with curious people, men, women and children."[78] In an article in *Les annales littéraires et politiques,* Georges d'Esparbès listed "three or four workers, an old bourgeois man, about ten women, most of whom were young, some of whom were pretty and children from eight to twelve years of age" among those looking at the corpses in the exhibit room.[79]

Descriptions of the morgue's public often read as though they were a catalog of Parisian social types. The accounts, whether written by natives or foreigners, seemed to invoke the diverse crowd as somehow typifying the city, suggesting that the crowd, like the morgue itself, stood for the peculiarly Parisian. An American newspaper observed:

76. *Bulletin municipal officiel,* July 11, 1907.
77. Tardieu, "La morgue," 2:1997.
78. Marot, *Casse-Museau,* 70.
79. Georges d'Esparbès, "La morgue," *Annales littéraires et politiques,* March 31, 1907, 196.

An old woman with two empty baskets enters by one side door as a well-dressed man emerges from the other. A workman, hands deep in his ample corduroys, his patched and well-worn blouse hanging loosely from his shoulders, leans lazily against a pillar, bleary-eyed and smoking, while a little girl helps her baby sister to climb the steps.

An omnibus—Square des Batignolles, Jardin des Plantes—passes with glittering wheels. . . . A woman, in a Breton cap, stands as if in thought. Two workmen, picturesque in the clay-smeared corduroy, shovels and spades thrown over their shoulders, suddenly halt and exchange a word; then cross the street and enter. A woman in black, without a bonnet, lingers on the pavement; hesitates; goes in. English tourists, newly married, evidently, arrive en masse with a guide.[80]

This description paints the morgue as a gathering place for all Parisians, who, despite the obvious markers that signify their social class and even nationality, could share the sight at the morgue. In fact, of all the visitors described above, perhaps only the woman in black who hesitates to enter might actually have been in mourning and thus be more likely to have a particular, as opposed to a general, reason for visiting the morgue. The Parisian chronicler Georges Montorgeuil matched the American representation in his depiction of a "crowd [that] constantly renews itself: errand girls, Englishmen, female peasants, prostitutes, street urchins, *flâneurs*, gentlemen, old women, young women, one following another."[81] Further, the familiarity of the morgue and its crowd among Parisians is echoed in Zola's *Thérèse Raquin* when Laurent visits the morgue daily for over two weeks, looking for the corpse of Camille, his murder victim:

Laurent quickly recognized the site's public, a mixed and disparate public that pities and sneers together. Workers entered, on their way to work. . . . Then came the *petits rentiers*, thin and dried-up men, *flâneurs* who entered out of idleness who looked at the bodies with stupid eyes, and pouty, peaceful and delicate men. Women were to be found in large numbers; there were pink young working girls, with white linen, clean skirts, who slowly went from one end of the window to the other, with big attentive eyes, as though standing in front of a department store window display; there were also *femmes du peuple*, who stared with dazed and mournful looks, and well-dressed women nonchalantly wearing silk dresses.[82]

80. *The Free Review*, October, 1893.
81. *L'Eclair*, September 7, 1892.
82. Zola, *Thérèse Raquin*, 132.

Here Zola constructs a representative contemporary Parisian crowd, which is to say, one diverse in class, mixed in gender and nationality.

The presence of a diverse crowd did not necessarily erase class and gender distinctions, at least for some of the morgue's portrayers. Authors often show us their intended audiences by the constituencies they single out from among the crowd. Guidebooks, directed toward a primarily bourgeois audience, sometimes highlighted the attendance of the working classes. Joanne's *Paris illustré* remarked that "a more or less compact crowd of men, women and children from the inferior classes" swelled the ranks of visitors.[83] English guidebooks portrayed the morgue as a double attraction: one where both dead bodies and genuine live workers could be observed at once. "The lower classes smoke and chat, and laugh with the greatest gusto over the horrible sights which may any day be seen here" noted one such book, while another remarked that "This chamber of horrors is an irresistible sight to the lower orders, who never pass by without looking in."[84] The tone of these remarks seems to offer rationalizations for middle-class visitors by in effect offering the spectacle of the decadence of lower-class tastes.

The Parisian press also labeled the morgue as a stopping point for workers. For example, several newspapers remarked on the large Monday crowds, explaining that "every day, above-all every Saint Monday [workers' day off] . . . the worker goes there while on a stroll to see if by chance his pal who's at loose ends hasn't gone there to press his nose to the glass."[85]

Descriptions of morgue visitors sometimes dwelled on the women who went to see the corpses. Most frequently, depictions of women among the crowd were intended to stand as evidence of its diversity. When commentators did single women out among the visitors, they portrayed their voyeurism as particularly illicit. Women went, some observers believed, as thrill-seekers. Edmond Deschaumes, in a guide to Paris, remarked on the "lines of one thousand to fifteen hundred persons, where women, intrepid with curiosity—are in the majority"—at least on days when a sensational crime had been announced in the newspapers.[86]

Although the spectacle at the morgue did draw criticism in the name

83. *Paris illustré: guide Joanne* (Paris: Hachette, 1885), 924.

84. W. Edwin Gaze, *Paris and How to See It* (London: Gaze and Son, 1884), 85; and *Paris in Four Days*, 118.

85. *Le Soir*, September 1, 1895; see also *Le XIXe Siècle*, April 20, 1892.

86. Deschaumes, *Pour bien voir Paris*, 81–82.

of decency, the discussion of women spectators suggests a level of discomfort with women's participation in public spectacles at the same time that it acknowledges that they probably gaped as much as, if not more, than men. In his long tirade against the public exhibition of corpses, the jurist Guillot carped on the presence of women as one of the display's dangers. The spectacle at the morgue rendered women even more suggestible than they naturally were, he reasoned, arguing that "they will fall prey to all that degrades." He complained of their thrill-seeking and noted that he overheard a working-class woman complain, "It's boring, it's still the same ones."[87]

Observers seemed to enjoy being shocked at what they constructed as overly enthusiastic interest on the part of the morgue's women visitors. One newspaper reported,

Women were foremost in pushing to the front. The horrid fascination which the morgue has for the female mind, both foreign and native, is one of those phenomena which observers note in going through life, but cannot understand. Many a young and sensitive creature . . . begs her father, husband or brother to take her to the morgue and although she lingers on the threshold a bit, and looks whiter than usual, she always finds nerve enough to enter and go through the ordeal.[88]

Although this comment suggests that women would not amble into such a space unaccompanied by male companions, by almost all accounts, written and visual, women arrived in the company not of men, but of other women and children. Despite a rhetoric in which critics bemoaned women's participation in such public viewing, the morgue's administration encouraged such visits and women seemed to attend in great numbers.

The sexual nature of the morgue display did not go unnoticed and served as grounds on which to object to women's voyeurism and even to a perceived necrophilia.[89] While Zola described Laurent's viewing of the corpse of a twenty-year-old girl as erotic—"Laurent looked at her for a long time, his eyes wandering on her flesh, absorbed by a frightening desire"[90]—it is important to note that over two-thirds of the bodies displayed at the morgue were male.[91] Visitors, and women in

87. Guillot, *Paris qui souffre*, 188–90.

88. *The Morning Advertiser* (London), January 14, 1893.

89. For more on necrophilia see Ariès, 374–81; and Bronfen, *Over Her Dead Body*.

90. Zola, *Thérèse Raquin*, 131.

91. APP, morgue registers.

particular, could come here to see male "nakedness." As a newspaper article noted, "a girl on her mother's arm . . . formulates thoughts that hardly match the age of innocence."[92] Zola also described a woman's inspection of the corpse of a mason of whom "death has made a marble statue." He wrote, "The woman examined him, looked back at him, pondered him, absorbed by the spectacle of this man. She raised the corner of her veil, looked again and then left."[93] The boundaries for the female voyeur were murky. Unlike Laurent, whose look was direct, hers was represented as a veiled, almost uncomfortable peek. In this way, women's voyeurism and the thrill-seeking of necrophilia became the markers of the institution's spectacularity—one whose unashamed display raised concern in certain quarters.

If the morgue on the quai de l'Archevêché managed to draw a large and diverse crowd that extended beyond those who lived in the neighborhood, it was in no small part owing to the institution's relation to the sensationalism of the Parisian press. Because the morgue exhibited unidentified dead bodies, the institution was inextricably linked to revolutions, accidents, crimes and suicides.[94] The litany of *causes célèbres de la morgue* is long, but in every case the Parisian public knew that such dead bodies were sent to the morgue where they could be found on display.[95]

The bodies at the morgue were therefore not mere corpses. As Cherbuliez explained, "To the attraction of the spectacle of death is added the interest of drama . . . all the displayed corpses almost always have a dramatic story, often noisy and whose final word often remains a mystery."[96] Behind each corpse's mysterious identity lay an untold story that readers searched out in a press that offered them up for wide-scale consumption.

Comments about the sight at the morgue suggest that rather than mere inanimate, lifeless objects, the corpses were embedded in particular and sensational narratives that encouraged viewer identification with

---

92. *L'Evènement*, September 2, 1892.

93. Zola, *Thérèse Raquin*, 132.

94. Durkheim used the morgue registers to calculate suicide rates for his book *Suicide*, and Cobb used the Basse-Géôle records in the same way. I assert that it would be wrong to read the morgue as exclusively about suicide: mysterious death—whether self-inflicted, accidental or the result of foul play—is a better label to describe the bodies at the morgue.

95. A title for displays that drew unusually large audiences, *Causes célèbres de la morgue* was also one section in a report published by the Conseil général de la Seine, see, Dausset and Lemarchand, *Reconstruction de la morgue*.

96. Cherbuliez, "La morgue," 344.

the corpses because they revealed a "sad equality of all sorts of lives and social stations," as Senator Paul Strauss noted.[97] Guillot stressed that anyone might wind up at the morgue: "You don't need to be a misunderstood genius or a seduced woman to end at the morgue; the most unforeseen accidents that interrupt the most calm and bourgeois existence may lead you there."[98] In this way, the corpses became a sort of everyman and everywoman on whom the unpredictable dangers of Parisian life might fall. Visitors might identify with, as well as identify, the corpses displayed. Yet the stories that lurked behind the anonymity of the corpses rendered them particular corpses, grounded in the sensationalized circumstances that seemed essentially Parisian.[99]

The burgeoning mass press served as both engine and bearer of the corpses' sensationalism. As Devergie explained, "Once the newspapers announce the commission of a crime, one sees a large number of the curious flock to the morgue."[100] And, of course, once a large crowd gathered at the morgue, *it* then became the subject of further news reports, which in turn kept the corpse, the unsolved crime and the morgue in the public eye, and kept people going to the morgue. Such occasions became known as the morgue's *jours d'affluence*.

While the new morgue seemed to attract enough visitors on a daily basis by 1866 for a new job to be created—a guard whose function was to "watch the front of the exhibit room"[101]—the morgue records do not provide consistent information about the numbers of visitors.[102] In addition, since the archival records concerning attendance are scant, press accounts become the sole means of determining the morgue's *jours d'affluence*. The press seemed to favor reporting tales from the morgue that involved the corpses of women and children, especially those cases that involved foul play or remained "unsolved mysteries." Not only did these cases offer the greatest potential to exploit a sensational narrative since women and children were less likely to be in pub-

---

97. Strauss, *Paris ignoré*, 252.

98. Guillot, *Paris qui souffre*, 9.

99. The display and press engravings of corpses at the morgue differ in this way from mortuary photography, which was not designed to convey something about the deceased as an individual. See Ruby, *Secure the Shadow*, 69.

100. Devergie, "La morgue de Paris," 11.

101. APP, DB 210, letter from the police prefect to the municipal commissioner, December 21, 1866.

102. The records at the APP are the registers of the morgue, which list information about the bodies and could serve as a wonderful source for a social history of death but give no information about visitors.

lic, let alone die in the public domain. But popular descriptions and illustrations also relied and drew on a set of conventions for representing death in literature and mortuary portraiture—and eventually photography—in which women and children seemed to have a privileged position.[103]

The two little girls around whom the newspapers created the "mystère de Suresnes" filled newspaper columns daily for approximately three weeks. The authorities, the papers reported, did not suspect foul play but rather misery: "we presume that the mother wanted to commit suicide and wanted to take her children with her."[104] Visitors clamored to see the two children who were displayed on chairs. L'Intransigeant reported that "placed on chairs, the two children seem to be sleeping."[105] The next day, the same paper reported that among the large numbers of visitors, women formed the majority. On April 8, after four days of display, Le XIXe Siècle estimated that thirty thousand people had filed by the two cadavers and yet no declaration of recognition had been made. On April 9, the papers commented that "Despite the bad weather, several thousand curious people crowded to the morgue."[106] The next day, however, the papers reported that M. Masselot, who had saved a Madame Rousseau from suicide, recognized the children's corpses as Rousseau's children. Then Madame Duval, who had at one time fed and lodged them, also made a positive identification. Others came forward, all claiming these were the children of Madame Rousseau. The police even found the children's aunts, who also identified the bodies. "All over, the testimonies were the same. It was absolutely the two Rousseau girls that were fished out of the Seine."[107] The morgue staff removed the bodies from the exhibit room. Dr. Brouardel performed an autopsy and the corpses awaited their burial, when on April 11 the papers reported that Madame Rousseau and her two children had been found—alive and well and living in Paris. Le Petit Journal estimated that fifty people had wrongly identified the bodies. The paper sarcastically queried, "Who will recognize them tomorrow when they will be displayed?" The bodies, which had been defrosted for the autopsy, were refrozen and displayed once more to the delight of the

103. See Bronfen, *Over Her Dead Body;* and Ruby, *Secure the Shadow.*
104. *Le Petit Journal,* April 3, 1895.
105. *L'Intransigeant,* April 6, 1895. For more on the association of death, sleep and the notion of a beautiful death, see Bronfen, *Over Her Dead Body,* esp. 59–95.
106. *Le XIXe Siècle,* April 9, 1895.
107. *Le Journal illustré,* April 21, 1895. My thanks to Bruno Bertherat for a copy of the article, which was unavailable for consultation at the Bibliothèque nationale.

crowd that now came to see the unidentified and misidentified little corpses: "A large crowd invaded the lugubrious establishment all day long, and the guardians of the peace charged with maintaining order had a great deal of difficulty avoiding skirmishes. At five in the afternoon, more than three hundred people stood outside waiting for the moment when they could enter and see the two children."[108]

By April 15, the bodies were rapidly decaying yet the authorities decided that the show must go on "because of the two Easter vacation days, which will lead to a large crowd of visitors to the morgue."[109] Makeup was applied, to cover up the decay that was making the bodies even more difficult to identify. After the long weekend, the bodies were returned to the refrigerated cases although their clothes remained on display. *L'Eclair* reported that "they had to be removed, but the curiosity had hardly been satisfied. Meanwhile, no one has the right to complain. Before [the introduction of refrigeration], the display lasted only three days."[110]

The discovery on April 18 of a female corpse that had been in the Seine for three weeks renewed hopes for an identification. Berthillon, the police expert, even claimed that the corpse had the same kind of ears as the children. The promise of a connection between the woman and the children were dashed when a relative claimed the drowned victim. With the display finished, and no identification made, the story disappeared from the papers after April 26.

While the newspaper narratives incited interest, the morgue administration was integrally involved in spectacularizing the display that people came in droves to see. While the mise-en-scène of putting the two little corpses on chairs drew on such conventions of representing death as mortuary photography, the effect of putting them on chairs instead of slabs pulled them out of the context of the display of the other ten bodies that were already framed by their very placement in the exhibit room. The public responded by attending in even larger numbers.

Not all the *causes célèbres* of the morgue remained unsolved mysteries, however. The historian Alan Mitchell has described what became known as "l'affaire Billoir:" the case of a provincial drifter, Joseph Billoir, who killed his lover in November of 1876, cut her body into two pieces that he packaged and threw into the Seine.[111] Mitchell's study

108. *Le Petit Parisien,* April 13, 1895.

109. *Le XIXe Siècle,* April 15, 1895.

110. *L'Eclair,* April 21, 1895.

111. See Alan Mitchell, "The Paris Morgue as a Social Institution." The information on the case exists because Billoir was found, charged and guillotined. As far as I have been

focuses on the battle between the doctors of forensic medicine and Billoir over what weapon he used to kill the victim. The experts insisted that he had bludgeoned his victim to death with a heavy weapon. Billoir countered, insisting, "I respect science but (a gasp in the audience) . . . I used a razor."[112] Whether with a hammer or a razor, Billoir was convicted and executed for premeditated murder on April 27, 1877. Mitchell concluded: "L'affaire Billoir deserves to be recorded not as an exceptional melodrama of passionate crime but as a characteristic illustration of the positivist spirit in the public domain."[113]

But before the trial, the display of the dismembered corpse of Billoir's victim served as an occasion for drawing enormous crowds to the morgue. The case reveals just how the public, the morgue administration and the popular press transformed this real-life crime into a spectacle. Visitors went to the morgue where they and the morgue administration hoped that the body might reveal its story.

On November 8, 1876, a report of the police prefect to the Minister of the Interior indicated that a corpse split into two packages had been found in the Seine just outside Paris in Saint-Ouen and had been sent to the morgue to be put on display.[114] Three days later a special security force at the morgue controlled the crowd of four thousand to five thousand people, who had already come to see the "woman cut into two pieces," as the case became known.[115] The newspaper Le XIXe Siècle noted that the body was laid on one of the slabs closest to the glass "to be seen better" and that a cloth smock of the material in which the body had been wrapped was thrown over it so that only the head and feet were exposed.[116]

During the next few days, "from the opening of the doors [in the morning], the movements of the public have not stopped," the police noted. They estimated that in the morning, one person went by the window each second and that in the afternoon between five and six thousand people filed through in one hour.[117] By nightfall of November 13, three thousand people still remained in line, so the administration

---

able to ascertain, these files are the only ones that contain police reports about the numbers at the morgue.

112. Ibid, 594.
113. Ibid, 596.
114. APP, BA 87, November 8, 1876.
115. Ibid., BA 81, November 11, 1876.
116. Le XIXe Siècle, November 12, 1876.
117. APP, BA 87 and BA 81, November 12, 1876; BA 81, November 13, 1876.

put two candles next to the face and continued the exhibition until 5:10 P.M., when everyone present had filed through the exhibit room. Anywhere from ten thousand to twenty thousand people a day visited the morgue during the next two weeks, leading the popular crime newspaper *L'Audience* to remark, "There is perhaps at this time not as well visited a place in all Paris as this sad museum."[118]

By November 20, no positive identification of the corpse had been made in what was perceived as an obvious case of foul play (as a popular song about the case concluded, "For one cannot commit suicide and then cut oneself up afterward"),[119] but authorities bent on identifying the corpse and finding her murderer wanted to "hold over" the display despite the rapid decomposition of the head. The morgue administrators removed the corpse from the exhibit room and replaced it with a wax reproduction of the head, sculpted by Jules Talrich, the anatomical sculptor at the Paris Medical School. The head was then placed on a mannequin covered with a white sheet.[120] The police prefect reported that "this reproduction whose resemblance is striking. . . . has already attracted a considerable crowd."[121] The morgue guard reported that the bust "is a perfect resemblance" and the newspaper echoed the police by saying that "the effect is thrilling and the resemblance to the victim of the mysterious crime is striking. . . . Everyone was struck by the 'truth of the cast.' "[122] Now visitors were lining up to see two spectacles in one: the corpse of an apparently murdered woman and the wax bust that "seemed so real." In this way, reality as a spectacle was transformed into realist spectacle. After all, how different was this display from the museum that Talrich, the anatomical sculptor, opened the next week at 5, rue Rougemont?[123]

The story of the "woman cut into pieces" gripped the public. Police reports indicated that among the working classes rumors circulated that the entire affair had been plotted by the government to deflect public attention from "the affairs in the East and serious matters being discussed in the National Assembly."[124] Another note elaborated:

---

118. *L'Audience,* November 26, 1876.

119. Complainte de la femme coupée en deux morceaux, APP, BA 81.

120. *L'Audience,* November 26, 1876.

121. APP, BA 87, November 20, 1876.

122. *L'Audience,* November 26, 1876.

123. *Le XIXe Siècle,* November 24, 1876. On Talrich and wax sculpture see Michel Lemire, *Artistes et mortels* (Paris: Chabaud, 1990).

124. APP, BA 81, note dated November 28, 1876.

Many people in my district claim that it is an affair arranged by the police in order to entertain the public in connection with the talk of war that is circulating. This opinion is based on the Troppmann affair, that preceded the war of 1870, an affair that many did not believe in. They say that it's the same with the cut woman of Saint-Ouen who died a natural death in the hospital and who is now posing as the object of an alleged crime.[125]

These neighborhood police reports indicate the extent to which the public had shown an interest in this affair and the sense that the government was heavily invested in spectacle—in this case as entertaining diversion from other possibly more important and pressing issues. The reports also make clear that the crowd, in fact, went to the morgue for distraction and entertainment.

Aside from its important place in the press, this *fait divers* was probably sung in *cafés-concerts* since song sheets, available at a music store on the rue du Croissant in the middle of the newspaper district, sold "La complainte de la femme coupée en deux morceaux." The song revolves around the display at the morgue, turning it into a court of popular justice. Its moral, however, was directed neither against violent crime nor at the sad state of Parisian life. Rather, it advised the murderer to be sharper:

> If you cut up a woman,
> Don't throw her in the water;
> It's light, this pretty creature,
> A woman floats.
> It would be better to burn it
> In order not to be worried.[126]

The moral of the story is to burn the corpse or it will enter into the realm of public spectacle and become tomorrow's entertainment for the masses. Rumors, press coverage, the extended public exposition, police photographs and such popular songs all contributed to the spectacularization of the morgue display.

By November 24, *Le Voleur* estimated that between three and four hundred thousand people had filed through the morgue without making a positive identification. Even when there were no developments in the story, dailies mentioned the morgue in their *faits divers* columns, if only to report that there was no news about the case. *Le Journal illustré* featured "La femme coupée en morceaux" (fig. 10) in the pages of its

125. Ibid., November 30, 1876.
126. The song was probably written when the body was on display at the morgue; it did not mention Billoir and stressed the search for the murderer.

10. "La femme coupée en morceaux," from *Le Journal illustré,* November 26, 1876.

November 26 issue. As in an illustrated serial novel, the page turned the investigation into narrative. Its five images, moving from the discovery of the body in the Seine, to the police photograph of the victim's upper body, to the police showing the photo around the neighborhood where the corpse had been fished from the Seine, to the bottom of the page, which depicted the "lines and conversations" outside the morgue, centered on the scene inside the morgue. Here, the image makes clear the large number of visitors, the crowd's diversity, and shows the victim (or actually the wax head on a mannequin) laid out in the center of the window, facing the visitors. As with the "enfants de Suresnes," the mise-en-scène represented in the newspaper illustrates how the body had been pulled out of the context of the other corpses in the display window, creating a further dramatization of what had already been "framed" by its placement in the window.

The case was finally solved when, at the beginning of December, a group of men who had seen the woman's picture (either in the paper, or in the photograph circulated by the police) came to the morgue to identify the corpse as that of Marie Le Manach, Joseph Billoir's mistress. For another two weeks, the wax figure continued to be displayed in the exhibit room and attracted crowds of between three thousand to ten thousand daily until it was finally removed on December 15 when the administration was convinced that the corpse had actually been properly identified. At this point, the story shifted from that of "la femme coupée en morceaux" to "l'affaire Billoir"—a narrative that continued to fascinate the public until Billoir's execution as Alan Mitchell has shown. Interestingly, although perhaps as many as a half a million people had filed past Billoir's victim, only between three hundred to six hundred people attended his execution.[127]

Ten years later, the cover of *Le Journal illustré* featured another doyenne of the morgue, this time the "enfant de la rue du Vert-Bois" a four-year-old girl found in a stairwell at 47, rue du Vert-Bois, near the Conservatoire des Arts et Métiers (fig. 11). The corpse, which was transferred to the morgue, showed no apparent signs of injury except a slight bruise on the right hand. The newspapers reported that the display attracted "a considerable crowd," which by August 3 was estimated at

127. See APP, BA 81. While visits to the morgue grew more popular during the last third of the nineteenth century, the attendance at public executions waned. To prevent crowds from gathering, the police increasingly confined them within the prison courtyard at La Roquette, and the government announced the time of executions only at the last minute. The last public execution was in 1938. See APP, BA 887.

Le Journal illustré

VINGT-TROISIÈME ANNÉE — N° 33   DIMANCHE, 15 AOÛT 1886.   PRIX DU NUMÉRO : 15 CENTIMES

LES ANNONCES SONT REÇUES AU BUREAU DU JOURNAL, 61, RUE LAFAYETTE ET 16, RUE GRANGE-BATELIÈRE

LE MYSTÈRE DE LA RUE DU VERT-BOIS

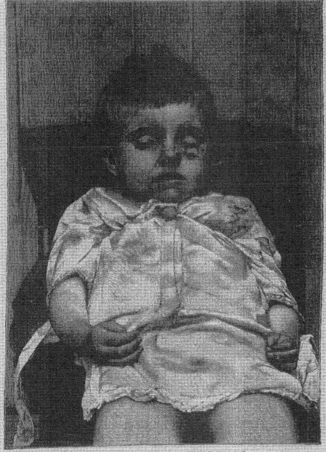

PORTRAIT DE LA PETITE FILLE

11. "Le mystère de la rue du Vert-Bois," from *Le Journal illustré*, August 15, 1886.

about fifty thousand.[128] The body, clothed in a dress, was mounted in the exhibit room, "on a chair covered in a red cloth that brought out the paleness of the little dead one even more" (fig. 12).[129] *Le Matin* reported that despite the extra policing that had been set up, the size of the crowd forced the traffic in front to a halt and vendors hawked coconut, gingerbread, and toys, turning the quai de l'Archevêché into "a genuine fairgrounds."[130]

By August 5, *Le Matin* estimated that one hundred fifty thousand people had filed past the body (in groups of no more than fifty at a time, in rows of five, who were forbidden to stand in front of the glass). Each night the corpse was put in a refrigerated case to preserve it. In order to avoid altering it in any way, morgue attendants simply strapped the corpse to the red velvet chair and deposited the complete display in the refrigerator.

Still, the body began to decompose so the morgue doctors decided to perform an autopsy on August 6.[131] *Le Petit Journal* reported the sentiments of the crowds that had gathered that day, only to "have been disappointed not to have caught sight of the child displayed on its little chair."[132] After the autopsy, doctors concluded that the child died of natural, if accidental, death: she suffocated by choking on an earthworm.

Images of both the child and the crowd at the morgue appeared in the popular press throughout the period of display. *Le Journal illustré* featured an illustrated narration (fig. 13). The scene opens with the building on the rue du Vert-Bois. Next, two people discover the corpse in the building's stairwell. The crowd outside the morgue occupies the center of the page, and the scene in the exhibit room covers the bottom. When these illustrations appeared on August 15, the cause of the child's death was already known. Buried on August 17 and despite the photograph that remained on display at the morgue's entrance for months, her identity and her abandonment remained a mystery.[133]

Corpses were not the only objects displayed in order to connect the morgue to sensational real-life dramas. For example, a trunk that had contained the body of Toussaint-Auguste Gouffé, a bailiff, murdered in 1889 by Michel Eyraud with the aid of Gouffé's former mistress, was

128. *Le Petit Journal,* August 3, 1886.
129. *Le Matin,* August 2, 1886.
130. Ibid., August 4, 1886.
131. APP, morgue register, 1886.
132. *Le Petit Journal,* August 6, 1886.
133. APP, morgue registers.

PARIS.   LE MYSTÈRE DE LA RUE DU VERT-BOIS : EXPOSITION DU PETIT CADAVRE A LA MORGUE. (Dessin d'après nature de M. Paul Destez.

12. Morgue interior, with inset of the child, from *Le Monde illustré,* August 15, 1886.

displayed in the morgue window. On the street outside, street peddlers sold toy trunks with secret openings that had "L'Affaire Gouffé" written across the front.[134] Ruelle wrote in his poem:

> And since this *Fait Divers*
> Through the hundred trumpets of the press,

134. The real trunk and a toy trunk can still be seen in Paris at the police museum. The APP contain numerous files on the "affaire Gouffé" (BA 85). Pierre Darmon has recently written a book titled *La malle à Gouffé* and the case is described in Alain Monestier, *Les grandes affaires criminelles* (Paris: Bordas, 1988), 209–11. See also Ruth Harris, *Murders and Madness.*

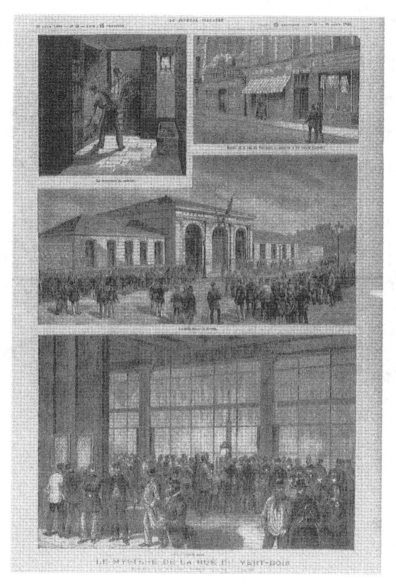

13. Narration of the story of the "enfant de la rue du Vert-Bois,"
from *Le Journal illustré*, August 15, 1886.

Has made the tour of the universe,
All of Paris crowds to see it.

In another instance, the "assassinat du passage Saulnier" in which a registered prostitute, Marie Fellerath, was murdered in February 1879, the incriminating evidence—a Japanese knife, its sheath, and a button, presumably from one of the murderer's sleeves—were exhibited at the morgue.[135]

The morgue was plunged further into *faits divers* narratives as a site that might draw a criminal to his victim. It was commonly believed that the murderer would come to the morgue to see his victim, as does Laurent in *Thérèse Raquin*. Tardieu explains that "sometimes we have seen the murderer himself slide by," recognized by the guards.[136] Perhaps visitors flocked to the morgue hoping to catch part of a drama in action, thinking that an arrest of a notorious criminal might take place in their presence.

Murderers did make appearances at the morgue, much to the crowd's delight. Often, the police would bring a suspected murderer to "confront" his victim's corpse in the back room of the morgue in the hope that the criminal's reaction, which might even elicit a confession, would verify his guilt. The newspapers routinely announced the "confrontation," unleashing what Clovis Pierre described for *Le Figaro,*

The day of a confrontation, the area around the morgue is always invaded by the crowd that detects, one only knows how, a sensational show. When the crowd is more evil or excited than usual, sometimes there are cries when the car arrives from the Mazas [prison]. The crowd screams: 'To the water' [where the back entrance to the morgue was located], and despite the police's efforts, the accused takes the chance of receiving a few punches or hits with an umbrella.[137]

In such an instance, Parisians might get to participate in the *fait divers* itself. They knew to go to the morgue to witness the criminal on the day of the "confrontation," because they anticipated its enactment as part of the newspaper crime narrative with which they were quite familiar.

135. APP, BA 1612, with a March 22 handbill touting the serial novel *L'affaire Lerouge* as "almost identical" to the case of the passage Saulnier, with sketches of objects from this case displayed at the morgue. The handbill ended by claiming that *Le Nouveau Journal républicain* "could no longer delay the publication of the work that responds so well to the preoccupations of the public."

136. Tardieu, "La morgue."

137. *Le Figaro,* September 9, 1893. Note the umbrellas of bourgeois participants.

In reporting on the display at the morgue, newspapers promoted public interest and did what they did best: transform the banal and the everyday into sensationalized urban spectacle. The corpses at the morgue became enveloped in the frame of current events and constant change that characterized newspaper culture. Guillot pointed to the newspaper as the source that stimulated public interest for what "the papers call the daily special."[138] He complained that in newspapers readers could learn about the details of an autopsy, the testimony of criminals, or read descriptions of a confrontation. He concluded that if the morgue could be referred to as the "theater of crime," then certainly more than one newspaper "serves as its program."[139] These links between the newspapers and the morgue suggest that the former stimulated interest in the latter.

Other commentators suggested that the morgue was some *version* of the newspaper. *L'Eclair* described it as "this living illustration of a serial novel mystery," and Gaud echoed this comparison when he remarked that women workers, whose spirits had been haunted by serial novels, came to look at the corpses.[140] The interest in visits to the morgue was attributed to the influence of "realism" as well as the fascination with reality. An English newspaper did not stop at blaming newspapers, rather it identified "the passion developed more and more by a diseased realism in the world of fiction" as promoting an interest in the horrible.[141] But both the press and the morgue administration mediated this reality whose compelling nature resided in its sensational narratives.

"It's in real life that can be found the sensational incidents that excite the crowds and increase newspaper circulation,"[142] one newspaper quipped about the morgue, explaining the public's interest in real life. "What if rather than your stories, your most frightening paintings, they prefer reality, and what a reality," wrote Firmin Maillard.[143] An article in *Le Paris* boasted that "these are not imitations, not trompe l'oeil."[144] What made the morgue's display exciting was that the bodies shown were real flesh and blood, which might reveal that reality was more fer-

138. Guillot, *Paris qui souffre*, 182.

139. Ibid., 258.

140. *La Presse*, March 22, 1907.

141. *The Morning Advertiser*, January 14, 1893. See Walter Kendrick, *The Thrill of Fear* (New York: Grove Weidenfeld, 1991), for an account of the interest in "scary entertainment."

142. *Le Voleur*, August 19, 1886.

143. Maillard, *Recherches sur la morgue*, 94–95.

144. *Le Paris*, August 31, 1892.

tile than the novelist's imagination. Maillard claimed that the morgue's "actual drama is a thousand times more striking than all your inventions." He might have added, "who needs fiction when life is so dramatic?" Macé echoed these sentiments by saying that "the reality of the facts will be sufficient in writing the morgue's history."[145] Yet the exhibit room, its curtain, the lines outside the morgue, wax masks, corpses dressed and seated on chairs, and newspaper illustrations all guaranteed that the morgue's reality was re-presented and mediated, orchestrated and spectacularized.

The Closing of the Morgue

In March 1907 Louis Lépine, the prefect of police, ordered the morgue to be closed to the general public. The decree dated March 15 explained "that it is agreed, except in exceptional cases, to give access to the exhibit room . . . only to those people who might be able to provide useful information about the identity of a displayed corpse and thus to set aside all those people who come out of curiosity."[146] From then on, the morgue was open only to those who had reason to search for the corpse of a loved one. Given the language of the order, we might conclude that, at the time of its closing, the morgue still drew large crowds of curious visitors and its closing therefore did not result from a lack of public interest.

The year 1907 marks the end of an intermittent campaign to close the morgue to the public. An impassioned critique of the practice of the exhibition had already begun by 1887, when Adolphe Guillot wrote *Paris qui souffre,* a study written to advocate the end of public executions. Guillot's line of attack had nothing to do with the effectiveness of the public display for identification purposes. Rather he argued, "Even admitting that once in a while the display leads to an identification, we would prefer, from a social standpoint, that a few more pathetic souls remain unidentified and that we stop this spectacle that demoralizes and pushes people toward crime."[147] His attitude echoed the many bourgeois voices raised against bloody sights in Paris, although his con-

---

145. Gustave Macé, *Mon premier crime* (Paris: Charpentier, 1885).
146. Arrêté concernant l'accès à la morgue, March 15, 1907, APP, DB 210.
147. Guillot, *Paris qui souffre,* 248.

cerns had nothing to do with hygiene but rather focused on the moral quality of the spectacle. He believed that familiarity with what he called "bloody spectacles" (and this despite the very sanitized corpses in the window) made people less respectful of human life and perverted the soul. But what troubled him most was that this sight was open to the masses (and perhaps here Guillot reflects the influence of the burgeoning field of crowd psychology):

Bloody spectacles, always dangerous, are certainly dangerous in periods when savage and sensual passions invade the masses. . . . The publicity of the executions of assassins and the display of the corpses of victims are two things that I don't hesitate to think of as having contributed, in large measure, to developing the taste for blood among youths.[148]

Guillot went on to draw a direct correlation between the rise in crime committed by youths and visits to the morgue because of the corrupting nature of the sight. The book thus hoped to end to this "public danger" by stopping public visits to the morgue. In 1887, it seemed to have had no immediate consequences.

Five years later, in 1892, the popular press exploded in a debate about the exhibition of bodies—a debate that seemed to be stimulated by the Conseil général de la Seine's interest in moving the morgue. On August 29, L'Eclair demonstrated that the random visit rarely provided a positive identification. Of the 750 adults admitted the year before, 680 had been identified. 405 had been made through the special investigation by the morgue. 165 had been "recognized on admission" (forensic autopsy, etc.), "55 by their clothing after the corpse's burial, 10 through photographs, 5 by l'anthropométrie and 40 through display. Of these 40, the paper argued that it was likely that they were all "intentional viewer identifications and not the product of chance."[149]

Almost every major daily had something to say about this article and most agreed with it. Le Voltaire echoed L'Eclair: "The display at the morgue is practically useless and inexcusable. We've got to stop it!"[150] La Justice noted that "what has to be stopped is this useless mise-en-scène, it's a pretext for gawking."[151] Interestingly, Le Petit Journal, one of the most popular Parisian dailies, argued against the closing of public expositions: "No matter how small a number there are of corpses

148. Ibid., 258–59.
149. L'Eclair, August 29, 1892.
150. Le Voltaire, September 22, 1892.
151. La Justice, August 30, 1892.

identified by random passersby, we cannot deny them the help that the public display gives."[152] Another popular newspaper, *La Petite Presse*, claimed that closing the morgue would not work because people would lie in order to "momentarily gaze on their favorite show."[153]

The entire debate seems to have been lost on the municipal and general councils of the Seine, on the police and the morgue administration. In fact, all the materials and reports from the 1880s through the early twentieth century show a preoccupation with the inadequacy of the actual building space, ignoring the efficacy or morality of the public display of dead bodies. Overflowing with corpses, the facility simply no longer sufficed. Paul Brouardel, director of the forensic instruction that began regularly at the morgue in 1877, also wanted to expand the functions and facilities of medical research, for which he needed more space. Alpy, on behalf of the seventh commission of the Conseil général, suggested building a separate but adjacent Institut médico-légal.[154] When concerns arose about the morgue's location (the Seine was eating away at the floor), Arthur Rozier suggested that it be relocated, along with the dog pound, to the quai St-Bernard.[155] In *all* the published records of both councils, there is not one mention of stopping the practice of public exhibition. In fact, in a meeting on December 26, 1906, only four months before the morgue was closed, plans for a new morgue, slated to be moved to the place de Mazas, included an exhibit room.[156]

Nevertheless, the morgue was decreed closed to the public at large by the police in March 1907, and the press generally concurred except for the complaints on behalf of free theater. There is no indication of popular protest, but the press, which at this point favored the measure, might have hesitated to report it, and the police records are simply too incomplete.

152. *Le Petit Journal,* August 30, 1892.

153. *La Petite Presse,* September 8, 1892.

154. June 1891 report to Conseil général on creating an Institut médico-légal. Bibliothèque administrative.

155. Dausset and Lemarchand, *Reconstruction de la morgue,* 179. See the report of the first department's service of architecture, June 6, 1906, at the Archives de Paris, D2N1 304 (1906), which rejected the move: "quiet and calm were to reign" in the morgue, and at the dog pound "stray dogs were known to bark all the time."

156. All the municipal and general council published debates and reports are housed in the Bibliothèque administrative de la ville de Paris—but no materials discuss closing the morgue to the public—and the morgue records at the Archives de Paris have nothing on the subject. Within the unclassified papers of the Conseil municipal and the Conseil général for 1906 and 1907 I found no trace of a discussion on closing the morgue.

That the decision seemed abrupt can be gauged in the surprised tone of the objection lodged by Pierre Jolibois, representative from the quartier Notre-Dame, first to the municipal council on June 10, 1907, and then to the general council on June 19. The petition he presented on behalf of the merchants located in the morgue district indicated that the morgue had been a popular attraction and attempted to reopen the question of the closing of the morgue. Jolibois had many complaints. First, he said that "it was only through the declaration of its closing that I was even aware of the issue." Further, he protested that the second commission of the general council of the Seine, which decided in favor of the closing, had done so in collaboration with the police and without notifying the district councilman. Third, although he admitted that unseemly types such as prostitutes and pimps had frequented the morgue, he suggested that added surveillance staff might eliminate any immorality among the crowd at the morgue: "All you have to do is get them moving through, and watch them, and since most of them are not eager to be better known to the police, a simple warning would suffice to empty out the room."[157] In his report to the general council the next week, he elaborated on this question:

It's the task of the administration, which seems to have forgotten that guardians of the peace are intended for public services and not for private ones. Today, many agents are sent to theater box offices and to music halls in a moralizing role to forestall all discussion between the public and the cashiers of these private establishments: it's not their place. By the same token, they can be found in banks, where they don't belong. Other times, they guard the equestrian arenas of the Seine-et-Oise . . . another task that the law has not charged them with. The tax-paying Parisian doesn't pay them for this task. It's time to restore agents to their proper function and make monuments [public buildings] their destinations.[158]

Jolibois's complaint that the police were spending too much time controlling the interaction between the crowds and the box offices at private establishments (and not controlling the crowd) suggests that he envisioned the morgue as another site of popular entertainment, but one that the police actually had the obligation to patrol because its *patrons* used tax monies.

<hr>

157. *Bulletin municipal officiel* no. 38, June 11, 1907.
158. Pierre Jolibois, June 19, 1907, cited in Dausset and Lemarchand, *Reconstruction de la morgue*, appendix 31, 212.

Armand Grébauval, president of the second commission, reiterated that it was necessary to avoid the "scandalous spectacle" of prostitutes, pimps and tourist groups who came for entertainment. To this, Jolibois responded, "It's not acceptable that we close the morgue because immoral people go there. Do we prevent traffic on the boulevards because there are dishonest people there?" Jolibois likened the morgue to the boulevards—both seemed a natural part of Parisian life, a life in which the dishonest might be integrated into "respectable" urban activities such as strolling on the boulevards and going to the morgue, or so he advocated.

And like boulevard culture, the morgue transformed the banality of everyday life by spectacularizing it. To us, looking at dead bodies seems at best an exercise in morbid curiosity. And some of the late nineteenth-century Parisian press did consider the attraction rather morbid. Yet, as cultural critic Jay Ruby has argued, assuming morbidity as the impulse to represent death merely reflects "our culturally encouraged need to deny death."[159] In fact, although the morgue clearly displayed dead bodies, the discussion of the popularity of public visits to the Paris Morgue generally placed it outside the death-related and morbid topics of its day: cemeteries, slaughterhouses and executions. Instead, the morgue was characterized as "part of the cataloged curiosities of things to see, under the same heading as the Eiffel Tower, Yvette Guilbert, and the catacombs."[160]

The morgue transformed anonymous corpses into Parisian sensation, and a large public gathered to consume this spectacularized reality; one whose reality-effect was bolstered by the spectacle's re-presentation of other sights with which the morgue's crowd was no doubt familiar—from mass-circulated newspapers, police memoirs written for a popular audience, and even wax museums.

The fame of the Paris Morgue and its association with popular entertainment resided in its connection to a peculiarly sensational Parisian reality. In fact, the Paris Morgue represented the so-called realities of urban life well beyond the city limits. A catalog of the Copenhagen wax museum, the Panoptikon, published in the early twentieth century, described its display of "La Morgue:" " 'La morgue' in Paris is regarded as a first-rate attraction, not just by tourists and strangers, but also by

159. Ruby, *Secure the Shadow*, 52.
160. *Le Voltaire*, July 22, 1892.

the populace itself. . . . 'La morgue' is a paragraph of an exciting novel, an entire series of effect-filled closing chapters."[161] It is no surprise that the morgue should appear in this wax museum or at the one in Paris, the Musée Grévin—which it did from its opening day. If the boulevards, the mass press and the morgue all displayed a reality spectacularized, such entertainments as wax museums, and panoramas and cinema re-presented this sensationalized reality in the form of realist spectacle. It is to the spectacular realities of novelty entertainments that we now turn.

161. Panoptikin catalog (1902). I thank Mark Sandberg for this reference and its translation.

CHAPTER 3

The Musée Grévin

Museum and Newspaper in One

In 1887 the theater critic and Parisian man-about-town Jules Lemaître described a detour that took him from his evening stroll on the boulevards into the Musée Grévin, "in order to review our glories, to recollect the year's remarkable accomplishments."[1] He was quick to add that the world reproduced inside the Musée Grévin was authentic because in this museum, as in his own world, "all is wax and all will melt, sooner or later. A clear expression of the futility of objects."[2] We hardly imagine most museums as ephemeral years-in-review or as institutions that inspire visitors to remark on the futility of objects. But of course the Musée Grévin was no ordinary museum.

Opened on June 5, 1882, in the heart of "modern" Paris on the boulevard Montmartre, next to the passage Jouffroy and across the street from the Théâtre des Variétés and the passage des Panoramas (see fig. 1), this lavish wax museum took Paris by storm. The *Petit Journal* heralded, "The Musée Grévin's success is guaranteed."[3] Another newspaper noted that "the crowd presses morning and night" to see the display.[4] An immediate success, the Musée Grévin received roughly half a million visitors yearly.[5] Still in business today, it remains the oldest Pa-

---

1. Jules Lemaître, *Impressions de théâtre*, 8th ed. (1887; Paris: Société française de l'Imprimerie, 1897), 324. I thank Marcus Verhagen for the reference to Lemaître.
2. Ibid., 330.
3. *Le Petit Journal*, June 6, 1882.
4. *Le Voltaire*, June 11, 1882.
5. Report of the administrative council to the general assembly of the Musée Grévin, March 30, 1883, Musée Grévin archives, hereafter MGCA for Musée Grévin's administra-

risian institution of commercial entertainment opened during the end
of the last century. Why did this wax museum capture the public imagination in late nineteenth-century Paris?

A cartoonist depicting the opening of the wax museum gives us a
clue. In it (fig. 14), two working-class men gape at a wax figure laid out
on a slab. One says, "Gawd, you'd think it was a real stiff." His friend
replies, "This is almost as much fun as the real morgue."[6] In short, the
wax museum's strikingly realistic representation of the morgue's spectacular reality became the basis for the pleasure it elicited. In an ingenious formula that combined an already appealing content with the
novelty of the museum's particular form, the museum both mirrored
and further contributed to the spectacularization of reality in late nineteenth-century Paris. Upon its opening, the wax museum made explicit
that it would create an institution where "the public would find those
people who occupied their attention reproduced with a scrupulous respect for nature."[7] And, we might add, it would capitalize on the spectacular reality that was already exploited by the Parisian mass press and
appeal to a broad and diverse public.

The wax museum's engagement in transforming life into spectacle
did not reside entirely in its reproductive aesthetics through which wax
sculpture uncannily doubled reality. After all, the museum's aesthetic,
like any other, operated in a particular historical context that produced
the cultural standards of what acceptably passed as realistic representation. At the Musée Grévin, the familiar "real-life" narratives depicted
in the tableaux and the accumulation of objects and details that formed
the cornerstone of the diorama displays were as important as the likenesses of the wax casts in affecting the "real."

Since most visitors would not really know the subtle differences of
the physiognomy of a well-known person or certainly whether the wax
figure's setting in, for example, the president of the republic's study,
was faithfully reproduced, why did the museum go to so much trouble
to make everything look real?[8] The museum's devotion to reproducing

---

tive council reports, MGAG for its general assembly reports and MGA for Musée Grévin
archives.

6. Cartoon found in the MGA.

7. *Catalogue-almanach du musée Grévin,* 2d ed. (Paris, 1882), 4.

8. The museum's late nineteenth-century visitors most likely had little visual basis
upon which to assess the likeness of the various personalities represented other than than
cartes de visite (calling cards with photographs) or press engravings.

— Non de d'là, regarde donc si on ne dirait pas un vrai machabée!
— Cré nom! c'est presque aussi rigolo qu'à la vraie Morgue!

14. Cartoon spoofing the opening of the Musée Grévin, June 1882. Probably from *Le Monde illustré,* Musée Grévin archives.

"the real thing" embodies a desire to naturalize as "real" and "Parisian" what was actually an interested representation. This insistence on authenticity also gave its self-proclaimed status as a museum legitimacy. With this legitimacy, the museum could not only insist on its institutional respectability but could also gain the freedom to challenge the museum-form that enhanced its popularity and its financial gain alike. By exploiting the power of the wax verisimilitude to represent contemporary Paris in a lifelike three dimensions, the museum combined the legitimacy of the museum-form with the popularity of the press and thus found and sustained its public through its spectacular depiction of reality.

Early Wax Displays

Wax sculpture as entertainment was hardly a novelty of the late nineteenth century. A favorite medium of anatomists since the sixteenth century, during the eighteenth century wax displays moved beyond anatomical and religious iconography (its other typical use) and into the burgeoning commercial sphere.[9] One of the earliest examples in France of a wax *diorama*—that is, the grouping of several figures in an appropriate setting—was Antoine Benoist's *cercle royal*. Benoist, a successful portrait artist, received a *lettre patente* of September 23, 1668, which allowed him to display his collection publicly. He grouped the circle of the French court "in the manner in which they appear at the Louvre . . . all the major people who make up the court are represented in wax and are dressed with pomp and glamour," noted the *Gazette* of 1669.[10] In 1688 he was given a thirty-year monopoly to display his royal circle as well as "the figures of the ambassadors of Siam, Morocco, Moscow, Algeria, the doge of Genoa and other extraordinary figures in wax in Paris and the provinces."[11] At his *cabinet* on the rue des Sts-Pères his *cercle* received visitors as noble as Madame de Sévigné, La Bruyère and even the king and twenty courtiers.[12]

Benoist's diversion for aristocrats preceded the entrepreneurial exploits of Philippe Curtius, an anatomist by training and the man most directly linked to the foundation of wax museum-like displays. Born in Germany as Kreutz, Philippe Curtius came to Paris in 1766 at the insistence of the prince de Conti and opened a shop on the boulevard St-Martin in 1770. He then moved to the Palais-Royal in 1776; in 1782 he opened a second showroom at 52, boulevard du Temple.[13] There, his

9. For this, and an extensive history of wax sculpture, see Lemire, *Artistes et mortels*.
10. Ibid., 70.
11. Ibid.
12. Ibid.; and Jean Adhémar, "Les musées de cire en France, Curtius, 'Le Banquet Royal,' Les Têtes Coupées," *La Gazette des Beaux-Arts* (n.d.), from the Tussaud archive. I thank the staff of Madame Tussaud's for giving me generous access to their archival collection.
13. Lemire, *Artistes et mortels*, 88.

exhibit was part of what Robert Isherwood has described as "the greatest show in prerevolutionary Paris, the center of a renaissance of marketplace culture."[14] The boulevard hosted "the inferior shows" (including that of Curtius).[15] Curtius took care to establish himself very close to the celebrated popular theaters of Nicolet and Audinot.[16]

Curtius's collection included mostly wax busts. As one observer described, "One sees his heads at his showroom on the boulevard du Temple and at fairs . . . they attract a large crowd of the curious of all kinds by the ease of getting this pleasure for only two sous."[17] His collection can best be described as eclectic, including such contemporary luminaries as Voltaire, Rousseau, Benjamin Franklin, Necker, the duc d'Orléans; more notorious personages such as Mesmer and the actress Louise Contat and more anatomically oriented and almost salacious displays such as a tableau of Pyramus and Thisby, whose body could be opened to show her vital organs.[18]

His major attraction, however, was a tableau, not unlike Benoist's "Grand couvert à Versailles," which featured the royal family seated around a large dining table (fig. 15). Yet verisimilitude seemed not to extend to a figure's entire body. As a contemporary almanac noted, "Most often, the bottom half of the body was nothing but a shapeless mannequin" while the bust and face were so well done as to "produce an illusion."[19] By 1784, Curtius expanded his collection to include a cavern of great thieves, which featured the infamous criminals of the day and attracted a broader audience. Louis-Sébastien Mercier even included Curtius's wax showroom in his *Tableau de Paris,* describing the

14. Isherwood, *Farce and Fantasy,* 161.

15. L. V. Thiery, *L'almanach du voyageur à Paris* (Paris, 1786) from Tussaud archive, London.

16. On the history of these theaters see Isherwood, *Farce and Fantasy;* and Root-Bernstein, *Boulevard Theater and Revolution.*

17. Mayeur de Saint-Paul, *Le chroniqueur désoeuvré, ou l'espion du boulevard du Temple* (1781), cited in *Le Temps,* March 27, 1925.

18. Lemire, *Artistes et mortels,* 88. For more on the popular wax anatomy museums, see Giuliana Bruno, *Streetwalking on a Ruined Map* (Princeton: Princeton University Press, 1993); Christiane Py and Cécile Ferenczi, *La fête foraine d'autrefois: les années 1900* (Lyons: La Manufacture, 1987); and Ludmilla Jordanova, *Sexual Visions* (Madison: University of Wisconsin, 1989); and Jann Matlock, "Censoring the Realist Gaze," in *Spectacles of Realism,* ed. Margaret Cohen and Christopher Prendergast (Minneapolis: University of Minnesota Press, 1995). I omit wax anatomy museums because they dealt more in popularizations of science than spectacular realities, and also because full-scale wax museums deliberately excluded anatomical displays—to show their own highbrow character.

19. Lemire, *Artistes et mortels,* 89.

Le Sallon de Curtius

15. "Le grand couvert" of Philippe Curtius's salon, ca. 1780. Bibliothèque nationale, cabinet des estampes.

barker outside: "Enter, enter sirs . . . come see the *grand couvert,* it's all like at Versailles."[20]

By late 1789, however, it was hardly wise to display the king and his family at Versailles. In fact, Curtius managed to shed his early association with the court and became an avid revolutionary. On July 12, 1789, when revolutionary leaders rushed to Curtius's showroom to demand the busts of Necker, who had just been fired, and that of the duc d'Orléans, well-known enemy of the queen, Curtius happily volunteered the busts that were then paraded through the streets of Paris, draped in black crepe.

Two days later, Curtius joined the crowd that stormed the Bastille. Ever the businessman, he brought with him his student Marie Grosholtz, later to become Madame Tussaud. There, she made masks of de Bernard-René Jourdan, the marquis de Launay and Jacques de Flesselles.[21] From that point forward, his display featured a rapidly changing group representing the victors of the moment. Curtius joined the Jacobin Club and the National Guard. Sent to the Rhine, he was among those besieged at Mainz in 1793.

In many ways, the Revolution created the terms that became the essential poles of the leisure industry a century later. Its promotion of social and cultural change and its own highly volatile political climate were critical in establishing the centrality of novelty and creating what became known as current events. In addition, the treatment of the public, from noting its whims to giving it proper instruction, became of great political concern.

While revolutionaries were reclaiming the great works of art for "the nation," especially in the founding of the Louvre, popular exhibits like that of Curtius drew fire as charlatanism that preyed on the credulity of the common citizen.[22] At a meeting of the Société républicaine des arts, Athanase Détournelle proclaimed his disgust and warned of the possible dangers of popular entertainments:

Those citizens who are not artists must get out of the habit of seeing mediocre, even monstrous productions. . . . Nicolet's theater, Curtius's salon

---

20. Louis-Sébastien Mercier, *Le tableau de Paris,* cited in ibid.

21. Grosholtz, whose mother worked for Curtius in Berne, was born in Strasbourg in 1761 and moved to France at the age of six. She served as art tutor for Madame Elisabeth, sister of the king but was called back to Paris by Curtius not long before the Revolution began.

22. For a history of the Louvre, see Andrew McLellan, *Inventing the Louvre: Art, Politics, and the Origins of the Modern Museum in Eighteenth-Century Paris* (Cambridge: Cambridge University Press, 1994).

must be empty. . . . . The peaceful countryman takes a portion of his salary out of his pocket, goes into these foyers full of admiration for the waxes that are far from representing nature. . . . . It is time to open people's eyes to charlatanism; that Curtius wins money from a credulous amateur who wants himself reproduced, I am far from preventing; but that he [must] not publicly display these ridiculous busts whose false illusion easily fools those without acquired knowledge. . . . . I will cite more than one example of the danger of displaying these cold copies; I have seen volunteers, preferring Le Peletier and Marat in these stories to beautiful paintings of the Convention.[23]

The republicans—who encouraged the popularization of state-sponsored "high art"—could not tolerate the profit-oriented "cold copies" of the wax display that were beginning to find favor among a truly popular audience.

Détournelle, however, did not have his way. Under the direction of Mlle Grosholtz, the collection became more of a portrait gallery as she abandoned the format of the *grand couvert* display.[24] Instead, she featured various portraits of the celebrities of the moment and even claimed to have molded the death masks of the king, the queen and Philippe-Egalité during this period.[25] After the fall of the Jacobins, Curtius switched allegiances to the victors of Thermidor but did not live long into that period. He died in August 1794, leaving his estate and collection to Grosholtz, who, the following year, married an engineer, François Tussaud.

While the collection continued to be shown on the boulevard du Temple, in 1802, Philipstal, a magic lantern entertainer, invited Madame Tussaud to tour England with him.[26] She and her collection of wax figures traveled around England for over thirty years until she opened a permanent collection in London on Baker Street in 1835, at the age of seventy-four. In Paris, her husband ran the collection, but its vogue had passed. According to the Parisian chronicler Gourdon de Genouillac, "the characters that one saw were nothing but crude dummies,

---

23. Athanase Détournelle, *Aux armes et aux arts! Journal de la société républicaine des arts* (Paris: Détournelle, 1794), 18. I thank Robert Simon for this reference.

24. Lemire, *Artistes et mortels*, 98.

25. According to Lemire, the claim has never been verified, and a death mask of the king's mutilated head is highly unlikely (ibid.).

26. Lemire dates her departure to 1802 (ibid.); but Pauline Chapman, in her *Madame Tussaud's Chamber of Horrors* (London: Constable, 1984), dates her departure as 1801. Lady Chapman was the archivist of Madame Tussaud's until her recent retirement and meticulously gathered materials about Curtius and Madame Tussaud.

more likely to attract the curiosity of peasants and children."[27] Tussaud eventually sold the collection. Its site was demolished in 1847 to make way for the construction of the place de la République (then the place du Château d'Eau).[28]

In London, Madame Tussaud's gallery-like collection flourished. There, in an almost random manner, such figures as Tom Thumb appeared next to Victor Hugo, Shakespeare side by side with the Irish patriot Daniel O'Connell.[29] Yet in Paris, the city of Madame Tussaud's beginnings, no collection of wax celebrities thrived. Scientific collections used for teaching by anatomists were fairly common; the best known among them was the Musée Dupuytren, a museum of *anatomie pathologique*, and the Musée Orfila, a museum of comparative anatomy, both at the Paris Medical School. In 1856 Pierre Spitzner exploited the popular interest in science and the prurience of anatomical displays by opening his Grand Musée anatomique et ethnologique in the Pavillon de la Ruche at the place du Château d'Eau; it later became an itinerant exhibit.[30] In 1866 Jules Talrich, an anatomist who modeled in wax, opened a museum on the boulevard des Capucines. Its display was arranged "like groups of *tableaux vivants*," according to an article written by Théophile Gautier.[31]

These collections must have been neither popular nor well known, because the *Grand Dictionnaire universel* of 1867 remarked that "today, the collections of wax figures are only displayed, we repeat, at fairs. . . . At the moment, Paris is bereft of wax exhibits."[32] The entry mentions a Musée Hartkoff opened by the Swedish phrenologist Professor Schwartz in the passage de l'Opéra in 1865. The museum was open only to men and "has less in common with old wax exhibits than with modern scientific collections." While it featured the masks of certain Swedish monarchs, as well as Voltaire, Schiller, Robespierre and Auerbach, it

27. Gourdon de Genouillac, *Paris, à travers les siècles*, 4:28.

28. Lemire, *Artistes et mortels*, 100.

29. G. A. Sala, *Catalogue of Madame Tussaud's Exhibition* (London, 1892).

30. In *Artistes et mortels*, 341–45, Lemire claims that Spitzner's museum lasted there until 1885, when the pavillion burned down but offers no details. I found no mention of its existence in Paris by 1882.

31. Gautier gives no source for his article (in Bibliothèque de l'arsenal, collection Rondel, Ro. 13.740), and I found no other mention of the museum on boulevard des Capucines. Jules Talrich's father, Jacques Talrich, made a mask of Jeremy Bentham in London; his son made the mask of "la femme coupée en morceaux" (see chapter 2) and opened another museum in 1876 on the rue Rougement.

32. "Cabinets de cire," *Le Grand Dictionnaire universel* (Paris, 1867), 3:17.

also offered a private showroom, which included the head after which Victor Hugo had modeled Quasimodo along with other unnamed items that made the display "more like the Musée Dupuytren and the Musée Orfila than Curtius's show."[33] The museum does not appear to have been open for long.

Wax collections similar to Curtius's did not flourish in Paris during the first three quarters of the nineteenth century. In fact, while fairs, often featuring traveling waxworks, especially of the anatomical variety, continued outside Paris and in the provinces, they were forbidden inside the city limits until the second half of Napoleon III's rule. Thus, waxworks became associated with mediocre standards and an unsophisticated audience.

When in 1881 Arthur Meyer, director of *Le Paris-Journal* and *Le Gaulois*, sought investors for the Musée Grévin, an exhibition of wax figures to be opened on the former site of a popular boulevard café, he promised that it would be a "unique artistic institution . . . a new and national enterprise."[34] He would justify his daring selection of the term *musée*. While Meyer's enterprise was in no way France's first waxworks, it can claim the title of being its first "wax museum."

Paris Gets a Wax Museum

The idea for a new Parisian waxworks did not originate with Meyer. In fact, a Belgian company that had recently opened a *galerie historique* in Brussels was the first to propose opening one in Paris. Their Eden-Galerie had been modeled after Madame Tussaud's in London. After a great success in Brussels, they determined that "Paris was a natural for the start of its extension."[35] They contracted Alfred Grévin to be the institution's artistic director. Grévin was a very well known caricaturist, whom the Eden-Galerie's stock prospectus described as "the most original spirit . . . the creator of a number of exquisite types, and father to a generation of charming women . . . [created] in three strokes of the pencil."[36] They next found "a vast site" at

33. Ibid.
34. Stock prospectus for Musée Grévin, BHVP, actualités anciennes (AA) series 102.
35. Stock prospectus for Eden-Galerie de Paris, 1880, BHVP, AA 102.
36. Ibid.

27, boulevard des Italiens and were ready to issue stocks and open in April 1881.

Then they met Arthur Meyer. The director of *Le Paris-Journal,* he became interested in the project and proposed to arrange for its publicity.[37] When Meyer learned, however, that the stock was being sold in Paris for twice the price per share as in Brussels, he refused to work with the Belgians.[38] Outraged by their audacity, Meyer bought out the Belgian company, confident that the project was a guaranteed success because of Grévin's association with it. As the stock prospectus for Meyer's Musée Grévin explained,

Rather than raise the capital of a Belgian company, it seemed preferable, in terms of capital as well as from the perspective of national artistic genius, that the business have an exclusively French and eminently Parisian character.

We wanted to associate no longer with a deal that was offering the public overpriced stock. Above all, we specified that the stock had to be tendered equally, in order to guarantee that none profit unfairly from the benefits already assured them.[39]

Meyer called his new French-directed project the Musée Grévin. He selected a site for the museum near his own newspaper offices and domicile—at the former Café Mulhouse, 10, boulevard Montmartre—in the heart of the most lively part of the city. He also hired a young architect, M. Esnault-Pelterie, to design and decorate the vast space that he promised potential investors would be "lavish." Started with capital of a million francs, the public company was divided into 2,000 shares worth 500 francs each.[40]

That the Musée Grévin is Meyer's most permanent legacy is fitting, although he might not have thought so. He made no mention of the museum in his three volumes of memoirs, perhaps because he left the direction of the project in 1883 after many battles with Grévin. Yet the museum reflected his *esprit boulevardier* and his amazing eclecticism. Born to Jewish parents in Le Havre in 1844 (he later converted to Catholicism when he married a minor aristocrat), Meyer attended the Ly-

37. Meyer went back to *Le Gaulois* in 1882.

38. Report presented to the Musée Grévin's general assembly of stockholders, March 7, 1881. MGA.

39. Stock prospectus for Musée Grévin, MGA.

40. The original list of investors included the writer Octave Mirbeau and Albert Millaud, a publicist and son of the founder of *Le Petit Journal,* as well as the bankers Nissim and Isaac de Camondo.

cée Bonaparte, where he befriended Albert Millaud, son of the important Jewish entrepreneur, Moïse "Polydore" Millaud, founder of *Le Petit Journal*. The two young men traveled the provinces selling the newspaper. On his return to Paris, Meyer founded the short-lived *Nouvelle Revue de Paris* in 1864 employing Henry de Pène, Jules Claretie, Aurélien Scholl, Victorien Sardou and Georges Feydeau; an important cast of Parisian boulevard literati. After the journal's failure, Meyer headed into provincial administration but decided he was not destined for a bureaucrat's life and missed Paris too much.

He returned to the capital and, with Edmond Tarbé, founded *Le Gaulois* in 1865 as a voice of the prince impérial, Eugène Louis Napoléon. As he put it, "I thus acquired *Le Gaulois* to defend the fourth dynasty in the person of the prince impérial. I was a dynastic Bonapartist."[41] He felt betrayed by Napoleon III's "acting like a republican" in posing his "candidacy in front of the deputies," and when the prince was killed, not long after the founding of *Le Gaulois*, Meyer believed this was a great loss to antirepublican hopes.[42]

Meyer also actively supported the campaign of the popular General Boulanger in the hopes of eventually restoring the monarchy. Of monarchy, he said, "it would have the power to resist the fluctuations of public opinion!"[43] Like many monarchists, Meyer was also an anti-Dreyfusard. He blamed the republic for fomenting anti-Semitism through what he identified as its virulent anti-Catholicism: "The republic governed for the Jews against the Catholics, and anti-Semitism was born and bred as a pious protest."[44]

Like many behind Boulangism, he despised the thought of being *vieux jeu* and advocated that royalism appeal to contemporaries by being brought up-to-date. For royalism to triumph, he argued, "it can't be old hat, but on the contrary, very modern."[45] His conservative politics were coupled with a profound comprehension and exploitation of the modern forms and methods of communication. Emile Faguet, who wrote the preface to the memoirs' first volume, astutely described

41. Meyer, *Ce que mes yeux ont vu,* 55.

42. The right-wing *Le Gaulois* never had a very large circulation before its brief shift to republican views. Meyer also ran *Le Paris-Journal* when he left *Le Gaulois;* he returned just before the Musée Grévin opened and eventually merged *Le Paris-Journal* and *Le Clairon* with *Le Gaulois*.

43. Meyer, *Ce que mes yeux ont vu,* 260.

44. Ibid., 188.

45. Arthur Meyer, *Soyons pratiques* (Paris: Lucotte, 1888), 14–15.

Meyer: "One senses . . . a man who is impassioned, for all his life, by conservative ideas . . . and who at the same time, and this is his mark of originality, was infinitely curious about all novelty and had an eye and ear for all spectacles and for all the noises of this world."[46] Meyer believed in the mass-circulated press, respected men such as Emile de Girardin and Polydore Millaud, yet complained and seemed almost remorseful that freedom of the press had led the press to seem like a carnival, complete with the "the noisy *parade* [sideshow] in front of the barracks."[47] He endorsed such cutting-edge technology as photography in journalism as an important asset, arguing that "if reproduction no longer has exactly the character of art that artistic interpretation gives it, it gained a precious documentary value for newspapers."[48] In short, Meyer embraced new technologies of communication although he seemed conflicted about what he perceived as the crassness of the new mass culture these technologies encouraged.

Maurice Talmeyr, a fin-de-siècle commentator, referred to him as "one of the stars of elegance" and Jules Bertaut, in his book *Le boulevard,* described Meyer's important social position in Paris: "He will have occupied an important place in Parisian life. . . . He loved being represented in the year-end reviews . . . to be sung about at the Chat noir or caricatured in *Le Rire* or *La Vie parisienne* because he knew at heart it was publicity for him and his newspaper."[49] In sum, he was, as the *Larousse du XXe siècle* put it, "*boulevardier* and journalist at heart."[50]

It would not be difficult to see in Alfred Grévin the artistic equivalent of Arthur Meyer. Also born in the provinces, in Epineuil in 1827, Grévin drew caricatures for the flourishing Parisian press. He began his career in 1859 at *Le Journal amusant,* then went on to do the front pages of the weeklies *Le Petit Journal pour Rire* and *Le Charivari.* Grévin portrayed what was known as *la vie parisienne* in his caricatures and was best-known for his *parisiennes,* described as "silhouettes of women, natty and sprightly, slender-bodied, with a quick eye . . . the frivolous creatures as light in moral sensibility as birds in the field."[51] His representations of women were considered "plus parisienne que la parisienne" and were so well known that in 1876 the Théâtre des Variétés

46. Faguet, preface to Meyer, *Ce que mes yeux ont vu,* xxiii–xxiv.
47. Meyer, *Ce que mes yeux ont vu,* 406.
48. Ibid., 395.
49. Jules Bertaut, *Le boulevard* (1924; Paris: Tallendier, 1957), 99.
50. *Larousse du XXe siècle* (Paris, 1931).
51. *La Nouvelle Revue* 76 (May–June 1882): 610–11.

featured a review, "Les jolies femmes de Grévin."[52] Grévin was considered an important artist in this "modern medium" of the illustrated press. Pierre Véron, editor of *La Revue de Paris,* remarked, "He is not Gavarni II, but Grévin the first."[53] He also designed costumes and sets for popular theater.

Like Meyer, he was associated with boulevard culture of the Second Empire. As one critic put it, "If his work does not bear a profound witness to his era, it is the image nevertheless of a certain tendency of spirit; formed under the Second Empire, Grévin kept the same vision his whole life."[54] Few men were as well connected to bourgeois Parisian life and one of its great achievements—the popular press—as Arthur Meyer and Alfred Grévin.

As a result of their decided association with what at the time was known as *parisianisme,* both men insisted that the Musée Grévin would be no French version of Madame Tussaud's, as the Belgians had proposed of the Eden-Galerie. In fact, Grévin and the architect Esnault-Pelterie visited the popular London attraction in March 1881. In a letter describing his visit, Grévin assured Meyer that the two institutions would differ: "Grévin must be to Tussaud what Paris is to London, what our boulevards are to Regent-Street, what the Parisian woman is to the London woman, that-is-to-say, charm, taste, spirit (and if I dare say so) to vastness and bad taste."[55] In keeping with its self-proclaimed "artistic" values, the collection on the boulevard Montmartre was to elevate the status of the wax showroom, exhibition and even gallery. This exhibit would be a museum.

The logic of this museum, however, seemed to announce itself as an anti-museum. As one review noted, in pointed distinction to the Louvre, "The Musée Grévin does not live off the success of archeological bibelots. It is very Parisian and very modern."[56] The wax museum, after all, fabricated the objects that it then represented as a collection, as opposed to the art museum, which gathered what it considered valuable objects for display. In addition, unlike most nineteenth-century museums that were constructed as definitive and permanent collections decided on by state officials, the Musée Grévin's display changed fre-

52. Henri Beraldi, *Les graveurs du XIXe siècle* (Paris: Conquet, 1885), 7:253.
53. Ibid., 242.
54. Philippe Roberts-Jones, cited in Marcus Osterwelder, *Dictionnaire des illustrateurs, 1800–1914* (Paris: Hubschmidt et Barret, 1983), 459.
55. Letter from Alfred Grévin to Arthur Meyer, March 27, 1881, MGA.
56. *Le Temps,* June 9, 1882.

quently, and its success was ultimately in the eye of the beholder. Rather than a definitive collection decided on from above, the Musée Grévin held a rapidly changing collection whose content was contingent on the public's interest and visual recognition.

The museum's insistence on its artistic qualities belies a different and even "modern" notion of what might count as art, for the major artists directly associated with the museum, Alfred Grévin and, later, Jules Chéret, epitomized the explosion of commercial art. When Grévin fell ill in 1891, Jules Chéret, the "master of the poster," and designer of most of the museum's publicity posters, replaced him as the museum's president and artistic director. The fin-de-siècle art critic Roger Marx celebrated Chéret's work for its documentary quality: "Browse through the lithographic work of Chéret, it will seem to you to be an illustrated chronicle of the era, the prepared documentation for historians curious about the details of our way of life."[57] Marx's remark suggests a new and modern aesthetic: rather than a timeless and eternal artistic standard, Chéret's work could be valued for documenting its own era.

While the "artists" involved with the Musée Grévin attest to the fin-de-siècle mixing of art, industry and commerce, the museum also managed to embrace and capitalize on more traditional notions of art in order to bolster its legitimacy and separate it from Tussaud's or from lowbrow, almost pornographic, itinerant wax anatomy collections, which traveled the fair circuit. For example, the museum's lavish décor, with its colonnaded and gilded main room, reflected the relation between opulence and "the most delicate and pure art," one reviewer noted.[58] In its *salle de la coupole,* complete with skylight, the museum drew even more explicit ties to classical styles. Arches of dazzling blue mosaic from Venice inlaid with gold, busts of Michelangelo, Benvenuto Cellini, Germain Pilon and Jean Goujon decorated the corners of the room, and four large allegorical statues of the seasons stood below them. In the eight doubled arches decorated with garlands and railings, one could see the symbols of sculpture, painting, architecture, music, comedy, tragedy, war and commerce, representing the themes contained within the museum. A reviewer for *Le Voltaire* described "a marvelous setting, worthy of *1,001 Nights,* guilloche colonnades, deco-

57. *La Plume,* November 15, 1893, 495. For more on the aesthetic and political status of the poster see Marcus Verhagen, "The Poster in Fin-de-Siècle France, That Mobile and Degenerate Art," in *Cinema and the Invention of Modern Life,* ed. Leo Charney and Vanessa R. Schwartz (Berkeley: University of California Press, 1995).

58. *Le Gaulois,* June 2, 1882.

16. "Les coulisses d'un panorama." Musée Grévin archives.

rated, gilded, flowers and many hangings, enchanting lighting."[59] This pastiche of allegory and classical stylization announced the museum's insistent embrace of legitimate "art" while conforming to an architectural aesthetic that was fairly typical of large palaces of consumption such as department stores and later movie theaters.[60]

When the museum actually represented artists among its wax figures, they favored academic painters. In the tableau "Les coulisses d'un panorama," the distinguished military painter Edouard Détaille puts the finishing touches on his panorama of the battle of Rezonville (fig. 16). Gathered in his studio are such contemporary luminaries as Gérôme, Bouguereau, Carolus Duran, Jean-Paul Laurens, Cabanel and Vibert. By showing these assuredly respectable artists supporting commercial

59. *Le Voltaire,* June 7, 1882.

60. Gustave Rives, who later designed the expansion of the Musée Grévin, was the architect of the Magasins-Dufayel. For more on department store achitecture, see Rosalind Williams, *Dream Worlds.* On early movie theaters, the definitive study is Jean-Jacques Meusy, *Paris-Palaces, ou le temps des cinémas (1894–1918)* (Paris: Centre national de la recherche scientifique, 1995).

artistic production, the museum reinforced its own artistic status and that of another visual entertainment: panoramas. The museum catalog also pointed out the "artistic value" of their tableau, which included an exact reproduction of Détaille's panorama, whose production at the wax museum he had supervised.[61]

If the museum seemed to exploit the legitimacy of art as part of its commercial scheme, its opening epitomized the institution's self-construction as a respectable institution. The museum first opened its doors on June 5, 1882, with a fundraising event for two charities, the Amis de l'enfance and the Société de bienfaisance italienne, under the patronage of the comte de Béthune and the comte de Camondo respectively.

Under the halo of charity, the crowd that gathered for the opening was an elegant group that included the comtesse Aimery de la Rochefoucauld, the marquise de Gallifet and the comtesse de Brigode.[62] The newspaper reviewers insisted on the event's distinguished tenor as well as its success: "From noon to midnight, the entrance to the room was jammed; never has the faubourg Montmartre seen so elegant a crowd."[63] Another simply proclaimed: "All of Paris was at the Musée Grévin."[64] The event raised 40,000 francs for charity; at 10 francs a ticket, the figure represents at least four thousand guests in attendance on June 5.[65]

Both the museum's founders and the journalists who reported the opening described the Musée Grévin as "Parisian." "Only after the Louvre, which is a universal museum, was there room for a Parisian museum. . . . I must say a boulevard museum," one newspaper noted.[66] Le Journal amusant reported it as an "event of the most immediate Parisianness."[67]

The museum's site and interior design reinforced the bourgeois definitions of parisianisme that were critical in constructing this wax collection as a "legitimate" museum. As one newspaper noted, "Located in the heart of the boulevards, in this corner that the refined people consider the only true Paris, that is to say between the faubourg Mont-

61. The wax museum serves as a useful corrective to a history of art that lionizes the avant garde and leaves these academic painters, obscure in the historiography.

62. Le Moniteur universel, June 6, 1882.

63. Le Clairon, June 6, 1882.

64. Le Gil Blas, June 7, 1882.

65. If 40,000 francs are not gross but net receipts, even more people attended. MGA.

66. L'Evènement, June 6, 1882.

67. Le Journal amusant, June 10, 1882.

17. Exterior of the Musée Grévin, ca. 1892. Musée Grévin archives.

martre and the chaussée-d'Antin, at the corner of the passage Jouffroy, across from the Variétés, it occupies a unique position in the world" (fig. 17).[68]

Yet, as one preopening review duly noted, "It is not from the Institut [de France] that Grévin will solicit the vote, but from the public."[69] This comment lays bare the fact that, of necessity, the Musée Grévin created a bourgeois tone but actually cultivated an audience much broader than the Parisian bourgeoisie. While museums were public institutions, they were not required to function as popular institutions.

The Musée Grévin was, in fact, a smash hit with the *grand public. Le Voltaire* noted, "The crowd presses morning and night."[70] Meyer's publicity barrage no doubt helped attract visitors. The regular edition

68. *Le Contemporain*, June 3, 1882.
69. *Le Monde illustré*, May 22, 1882. The patronage of the Institut de France would bring a museum the most prestigious and selective artistic and academic audience it might have.
70. *Le Voltaire*, June 11, 1882.

of *Le Paris-Journal* available on newsstands the day the museum opened was nothing but three pages of publicity for the museum. The front page featured an illustration of the interior of the museum crowded with visitors, drawings of Meyer, Grévin, Esnault-Pelterie and the presidents of the benefit committees.[71] The newspaper's columns were filled with descriptions of some of the tableaux, with autographs and "endorsements" of those celebrities featured within the museum.

The issue sold out its ten thousand copies the first day and a second printing was ordered for the next day. On June 13, the paper continued its publicity by publishing an article, "Le Musée Grévin devant la presse," which reprinted portions of rave reviews from other newspapers. The museum's directors also paid for articles in *Le Figaro, Le Gil Blas, L'Evènement, Le Clairon, Le Voltaire,* but the event was reported by Parisian dailies and weeklies that ranged from the more highbrow variety such as *Le Moniteur universel* to very popular papers like *Le Petit Journal.*[72]

While its opening day established this spectacle as appropriate entertainment for the bourgeoisie, the papers also explained that because the display was respectable and affordable, it would draw a diverse range of visitors. The admission of two francs during the week and one on Sundays, noted *Le Parlement,* "was affordable to all."[73] Other reviewers stressed the good value visitors would receive for their admission fee: "The visit lasts about an hour and a half. Note that in panoramas, where the price is the same, visits barely last ten minutes."[74]

Whichever of these qualities drew the public, many people visited the new attraction on the boulevard Montmartre during the summer of 1882. Daily receipts amounted to between 6,000 and 7,000 francs, and much greater figures on Sundays in June 1882.[75] One newspaper reported that the museum's receipts for August 18, 1882, were 4,020 francs and that during the last three days the museum had earned 11,000 francs.[76] During its first year of operation, the museum grossed

71. The room as illustrated appeared far larger than it was.

72. MGCA, March 28, 1882. The museum paid 200 francs to *L'Evènement*, 250 to *Le Gil Blas* and *Le Voltaire*, 300 to *Le Clairon* and had a special deal with *Le Figaro* for an article and advertisements paid in two sums of 3,000 francs.

73. *Le Parlement,* June 6, 1882.

74. *L'Evènement,* June 6, 1882.

75. Financial report on museum, June 1882, MGA.

76. *Plaisirs et bureaux de Paris,* August 19, 1882. It is impossible to determine whether the newspaper cites income from admissions alone. Receipts in the museum archive denote

about 40,000 francs a month and netted about 20,000 francs.[77] The museum could not have gotten off to a better start.

The Museum as Three-Dimensional Newspaper

The journalists who in overwhelming numbers positively reviewed it, glorified the Musée Grévin because it represented the Paris that they and their newspapers had so heavily invested in creating.[78] *Le Petit Journal* raved that "the Musée Grévin's success is guaranteed; it's an ensemble of varied and amusing, interesting and artistic things and people."[79] Another paper called it "a true spectacle," and still another noted that "the public . . . has not been disappointed in its wait."[80] If the Musée Grévin's definition of Parisian was decidedly bourgeois, it should come as no surprise that the mass press, controlled by bourgeois interests, should so laud the museum's representation of Paris since it so explicitly reflected a press-version of contemporary life. Such was both the association of the press with a certain Parisianness and the presence of the press in the museum that one reviewer snidely remarked, "We would be wrong to say, however, that the Parisian element does not figure in this exotic creation. It's there, alas, it's represented by the press, the organizers of this show think they have done it all when they introduced the press."[81] The author went on to mock the imagined surprise of a visitor from a foreign country or from the provinces, who arrives in Paris to be greeted by the wax figure of journalist Albert Wolff, yet another *boulevardier,* who wrote for *Le Figaro* and authored the preface to the museum's first catalog.

But it was not only because the Musée Grévin reflected the press construction of Paris that it won the praises of the press reviewers. The museum also claimed it would be a *journal plastique*—a newspaper molded and formed in three dimensions like other forms of the "plas-

---

"admissions, catalog sales, . . . advertising by poster at the museum entrance and inserts in the catalog."

77. MGCA, March 30, 1883.

78. Of the sixty-two articles about the museum's opening I read, only three or four were negative.

79. *Le Petit Journal,* June 6, 1882.

80. *La Vérité,* June 8, 1882; and *Le Télégraphe,* June 7, 1882.

81. *Revue littéraire et politique* 2, no. 24 (June 1882): 762.

tic" arts. The museum's promotional material touted that it would "represent the principal current events with scrupulous fidelity and striking precision. . . . To bring together, in short, before the eyes of the Parisian public, all the elements of curiosity, instruction and information. . . . To create what we call a 'living newspaper.' "[82]

Meyer imagined the museum as the latest improvement in modern communications, picking up from where the new illustrated press had left off. The wax museum's edge on the written word inhered in its visual realism. According to Albert Wolff, writing in the preface to the museum's first catalog, "Given the public taste for current events, written reporting has not entirely satisfied Parisians."[83] The Musée Grévin would do so by illustrating current events.

Reviews in the dailies and weeklies characteristically echoed the museum's message: "To do with wax figures what illustrated newspapers do with their drawings . . . to reproduce the characters and scenes that interest the public, that is the goal of the organizers of the newest Parisian novelty. It will be a type of three-dimensional newspaper, full of celebrities of all varieties, with the usual eclecticism of the press."[84] The Musée Grévin mimicked the eclecticism of newspapers in the range of figures and tableaux displayed: celebrities of the moment (such as dancers, actresses and boulevardiers) stood alongside more traditionally historically significant figures: presidents, kings and explorers.

Modeling itself on the newspaper reinforced, rather than opposed, the Musée Grévin's status as a museum. In the same way that the universal survey museum such as the Louvre functioned as a summary of all knowledge, the press claimed to represent all of contemporary life.[85] The museum's insistent classificatory schemes matched the newspaper's rubrics: the feuilleton, the échos and the fait divers. In addition, both the component parts of the museum and the newspaper did not consist of a developmental narrative in which one section followed the next in any particular logic; rather their parts combined instead to create a summary whole.[86]

82. Stock prospectus for Musée Grévin, BHVP, AA.

83. Albert Wolff, preface to Catalogue-almanach du musée Grévin, 2d ed. (Paris, 1882), 3.

84. Le Temps, June 7, 1882.

85. Carol Duncan and Alan Wallach, "The Universal Survey Museum," Art History 3 (1980): 448–69.

86. For more on the narrative structures of the mass press, see Terdiman, Discourse/Counter-Discourse.

The wax museum also mimicked the newspaper in its commitment to rapid reporting and constant change. Referred to as a "chronicle in action" by *Le Paris,* the wax museum would replace its displays to keep current.[87] *Le Petit Journal* informed its readers that even in its first week, the museum began work on two new displays: a figure of Garibaldi, whose death had generated a great deal of press coverage, and a tableau featuring the Arabi-Pacha, the leader of the revolt against the Khédiv Tewfick, who had recently been imprisoned by the English.[88] That same week, the "crime de Pecq," the story of the murder of a pharmacist by his former mistress and her husband on the outskirts of Paris, filled the pages of every newspaper. The museum immediately announced that it would do a series of tableaux reproducing the story. In this way the wax museum would also serve as another outlet for sensationalism.

In fact, the museum often literally rendered newspaper illustrations in wax, as in its reproduction of the "crime du Kremlin-Bicêtre." In December 1897 the story of the brutal murder of an innocent receipts clerk by the Italian-born mushroomer Carrara filled newspaper columns with the events in Le Kremlin-Bicêtre. The mushroomer, terribly in debt, robbed and murdered the young man who regularly carried large sums of cash as part of his job. Carrara then boiled his victim's corpse in a mushroom cleaner. The illustrated supplement of *Le Petit Journal* published three engravings of the incident on December 26, 1897. When the Musée Grévin decided to do a two-tableau series featuring the crime a few weeks later, one of their tableaux reproduced almost exactly one of *Le Petit Journal's* engravings (figs. 18–19). Thus, while the museum claimed to represent the stories one might find in the newspaper, it also copied the images right out of the newspaper.

Jules Claretie, journalist for *Le Temps* and eventual director of the Comédie-Française, celebrated both the museum's commitment to rapid change and its embrace of ephemerality: "O glorious transitory wax figures! Celebrities of the day! Pantheon of the moment!"[89] Claretie's phrase, "pantheon of the moment" encapsulates the seeming contradiction of the enshrinement of fleeting celebrity so associated with mass cultural forms. People, like news items, were served as the *plat du jour;* a modern, mass-cultural pantheon would tout the transitory over the eternal.

87. *Le Paris,* June 6, 1882.
88. *Le Petit Journal,* June 11, 1882.
89. Jules Claretie, *La vie à Paris* (Paris: Victor Havard, 1883), 275.

The museum's focus on the present seemed to oppose it to other museums that venerated the artistic production of the past as a means of representing current glory. One English visitor indicated the extent to which the museum seemed to monumentalize contemporary Parisian life: "Your journalists are of no interest to me and I would rather see the great men of the battlefields than the heroes and heroines of the boulevard. . . . Where are your historical memories? Where are the characters from your history?"[90] The Musée Grévin memorialized the present, lionizing "modern life" seemingly at the expense of the great moments and accomplishments of the past.

By calling the museum a pantheon, Claretie, either wittingly or unwittingly, connected the museum to one of the celebrated moments in the midcentury mass press: the creation by Nadar, who became France's first great photographer, of his pantheon (fig. 20). Although an eventual commercial failure, Nadar's pantheon set out to illustrate, in caricature, the thousand most celebrated figures of the day.[91] The Musée Grévin's pantheon also featured celebrities in "typical poses" as did caricature, but its wax figures approximated photographic representation rather than the early press mode of caricature.

Like other examples of Parisian spectacle, the museum attempted to present a microcosmic and encyclopedic whole, the sum of whose parts was *le tout Paris*. As Paul Bourget noted in his review of the museum, "In three or four rooms is it not the abridged version of the modern city?"[92] Like the mass press, the arcades and boulevards, department stores and expositions, the Musée Grévin offered the "universe in a garden."[93]

As a pantheon, the museum insisted on its selectivity. And yet its criterion appeared to be, as the catalog put it, "the interest of the public." Unlike other museums whose organizers claimed the authority of selection, the Musée Grévin claimed to be ruled by the "public." By promoting itself as a slave to public opinion, the Musée Grévin reinforced its reputation as a "popular" institution.

Aside from responding to its patrons' interest in actually seeing the latest story they had read about, the museum also changed its display

90. *La Gazette de France,* June 8, 1882. This paper was the oldest and most old-fashioned in Paris.

91. Nadar only completed one of the four projected lithographs because at 20 francs, he sold only 136 copies. See *Nadar—La Connaissance des Arts,* special issue, no. 56 (1994), 16.

92. *Le Parlement,* June 8, 1882.

93. Maurice Talmeyr, cited in Rosalind Williams, *Dream Worlds,* 61.

CRIME DU KREMLIN-BICETRE
Le cadavre brûlé Scène reconstituée d'après les aveux de l'assassin

18. Engraving from *Le Petit Journal*, December 26, 1897.

19. "Le crime du Kremlin-Bicêtre." Musée Grévin archives.

20. Panthéon Nadar, 1854. Maison Victor Hugo. © Photothèque des musées de la Ville de Paris.

in response to complaints from the crowd. For example, many newspapers reported that the figure of Madame Judic, the well-known actress, did not resemble the actual person. In fact, people in the crowd on opening day yelled, "That's not Madame Judic . . . get another Madame Judic."[94] That evening, the directors decided that she would be remodeled.[95]

The museum's association with "popular" tastes can also be seen in the disdain some critics held for it. One reviewer in the *Revue littéraire et politique* ranted about the presence of Francisque Sarcey in this "vulgar pantheon." He complained that the museum catered to the coarse tastes of the public: "Sarcey has an unmatched respect for the immunities of the crowd. He thinks that his being, like his writings, belongs to the crowd and he gives himself up without hesitation."[96] He singled

94. *Revue littéraire et politique*, 763. The reviewer also noted this as a particularly egregious flaw since people had seen her face on wine labels.

95. *Le Figaro*, June 6, 1882.

96. *Revue littéraire et politique*, 763.

Sarcey out as shamelessly catering to the public and his use of the term "crowd" (*la foule,* an undifferentiated mob) suggests just how "popular" he perceived the museum's patrons to be.

The potential for financial profit in establishing the museum as a journalistically inspired pantheon of the present should not be overlooked. Just as the new mass press exploited and created current events to warrant the daily purchase of the newspaper, the museum constantly changed its displays to encourage people to visit and then revisit the museum. While state-run museums, memorials and monuments might captivate public attention and draw a large audience, their very existence did not, by definition, depend on the number of visits made to them and they did not assume they would possibly need repeat visitors to survive. As always, novelty drove commercial culture because the promise of something new solicited a perhaps yet untapped audience at the same time that it kept previous visitors returning for more.

Novelty at the Musée Grévin went beyond changing the tableaux. Over the years and under the leadership of Meyer's cousin by marriage, Gabriel Thomas, one of the fin-de-siècle city's most important entrepreneurs of commercial culture, the museum promoted novelty and sought out opportunities for publicity at every turn.[97] In May 1883 the museum introduced the *théâtrophone*—which linked the museum to the Eldorado, one of the largest music halls in Paris—by allowing museum visitors to listen to live performances and thus "transporting" them to another site of modern diversion. In 1884 the museum introduced electricity, making it one of the first Parisian entertainment institutions to do so.[98] Electricity offered an improved, steady lighting for the museum's displays and mitigated both the heat and the discol-

97. Born in Passy in 1854, Gabriel Thomas was one in a long line of financiers. By 1882, when he joined the Musée Grévin as its accountant, he had already made a fortune in the stock exchange. In addition to becoming the museum's chief administrator in 1883, its artistic director in 1887 and president in 1914, he was chief administrator and president of the Eiffel Tower Company, invented the Bateaux-Mouches and served as chief administrator of the moving sidewalk company for the 1900 exposition. In the high-cultural domain, he assembled the well known artistic team of Antoine Bourdelle and Maurice Denis to design the interior of the Théâtre des Champs-Elysées.

98. See advertisement for the Société Edison in *Catalogue-almanach du musée Grévin,* 32d ed. (Paris, n.d.). The museum lagged behind only the Bank of France, the Gagne-Petit Department Stores and city hall in the amount of electricity it bought from the Edison Company. Like most other customers, the museum hooked up to the Edison's current only in an emergency. Its own generators in the basement often broke down, judging from the archival material. See both MGCA and a report of the Commission technique d'électricité de la préfecture de police from May 22, 1897, APP.

oration of the tableaux that resulted from the use of gas lighting. Beyond that, however, the museum capitalized on electricity's novelty and even opened its "Machine Room" to the public.

In the years before the First World War, visitors to the Musée Grévin might watch a panoply of entertainments: a magician in the Cabinet fantastique, gypsy orchestras, automats, Chinese shadow theater, lifesize marionettes, X-rays, the Palais des Mirages—a light and mirror show—and might even hear a phonograph operate. Most of these attractions played with creating illusions in one way or another and thus, aside from their sheer novelty, seemed to fit with the project of the wax tableaux in that they created a reality effect.[99] But, perhaps most significantly, long before the Lumière brothers patented their *cinématographe,* Gabriel Thomas approached several people to find a way to present projected moving images in the service of an even more "realistic" representation of the world, which we examine in chapter five.

Beyond its use of novel attractions as a means of generating publicity, the museum employed innovative advertising techniques and attempted to appeal to as broad an audience as possible, reinforcing its status as a modern institution designed for mass consumption. The museum used the rather popular *publicité rédactionelle* (paid newspaper copy), which could be found alongside unpaid articles in every newspaper in Paris.[100] It also relied heavily on poster advertising, which exploded in the 1880s because of advances in color lithography and the liberal press laws of 1881.

The vast majority of the museum's posters were illustrated by Jules Chéret, whose four-color lithography made his name synonymous with the poster.[101] Chéret designed more than twenty-five posters for the Musée Grévin in addition to a painted curtain for the museum's theater, which opened in 1900.[102] In fact, Chéret's posters for the Musée

99. See Barthes, "The Reality Effect." Also see Tom Gunning, "An Aesthetic of Astonishment: Early Film and the (In)-Credulous Spectator," *Art and Text* 34 (spring 1989); and also Neil Harris, *Humbug: The Art of P. T. Barnum* (Boston: Little Brown, 1973).

100. By using the museum's records of paid editorial copy, I separated ads from actual reviews.

101. For more on Jules Chéret, see Verhagen, "The Poster in Fin-de-Siècle France"; and Marcus Verhagen, "Refigurations of Carnival: The Comic Performer in Fin-de-Siècle Parisian Art" (Ph.D. diss., University of California, Berkeley, 1994). See also Robert Herbert, "Seurat and Jules Chéret," *Art Bulletin* (March 1958): 156–58.

102. The theater, with its bas-relief by Antoine Bourdelle, was named a cultural monument by André Malraux in 1964. Very few posters remain at the Musée Grévin, but the Bibliothèque nationale has a significant collection of Chéret's Musée Grévin posters.

Grévin were so popular that the museum printed inexpensive copies to sell to the museum's visitors.[103] Chéret and his posters situated the museum with other lavish and large-scale institutions of the burgeoning leisure industry such as cafés-concerts, music halls, circuses and hippodromes, but Chéret's presidency of its board of directors seems to signal the importance of the Musée Grévin as a leader among these new institutions.[104]

The museum plastered posters on the prime and expensive space of the Morris columns, the oriental-style advertising spaces found all along the boulevards, on *voitures-affiches* that went through the major areas of the city, on rotating advertising columns at the six major hotels and, of course, on the well known café-concert curtains, like that at the Café des Ambassadeurs, among other places.[105]

Aside from the permeation of spaces for poster art, the museum constantly cultivated different sources for, and sites of, publicity. In an effort to attract bourgeois tourists, the museum worked with the British Thomas Cook tours, placed large albums containing photographs of the dioramas in major hotel lobbies in Paris such as the Grand Hôtel and the Continental, and in hotels at the thermal stations and seaside resorts.[106] During the universal expositions of 1889, the museum gave the panorama of "Tout-Paris" a few wax figures in exchange for publicity; in 1900 it placed forty posters on lighted billboards at the moving sidewalk attraction.[107] The museum also featured dioramas at the Exposition of Industrial Arts in 1886 and at the Exposition of Decorative Arts in 1892.[108]

In order to appeal to people who lived in the provinces, the museum put posters in railway stations, gave a priest from Aveyron a wax saint in exchange for advertising the museum in his parish, and participated in the "pleasure trains" with the Railway Companies of the North and the West. The companies paid the Musée Grévin forty centimes per ticket, instead of the usual two francs during the week and one on weekends, and visitors who came to Paris from the provinces on the trains

103. MGCA, April 8, 1891.

104. See Verhagen, "The Poster in Fin-de-Siècle France," 107.

105. Information scattered through MGCA records.

106. The museum archive contains two such albums and the records of the weekly meetings refer to placing such albums in tourist resorts.

107. Heading the museum and the moving sidewalk company was one individual: Gabriel Thomas.

108. The former was a failed "ascension des Alpes," the latter a copy of Moreau's "Délices de la maternité."

were admitted to the museum free of charge. In 1891, for example, 10,760 people visited as part of the package. The museum administration considered its success:

We think this deal is lucrative for our company and is worth pursuing. The bargain is for an underprivileged clientele that no doubt evades us; in addition, we have only allowed entrance on these tickets during certain hours in order not to obstruct our galleries when those paying full tariff arrive in large numbers. We should also add that the advertisement of the deal by the railroad companies offer our business publicity that should not be scorned. . . . The benefit is even greater since we have not recently had the chance to solicit public interest by the announcement of a work of attention-getting current events that attracts the crowd.[109]

Here it is clear that the museum's directors wanted to reach this poorer provincial crowd. The museum also made clear that their exhibit was not merely for city slickers by placing the wax figure of a *paysan endimanché* (dressed-up peasant), looking at a poster for the museum at its entrance in the final months of 1883.[110] Finally, the museum also engaged in publicity stunts and gimmicks. For example, it sent a carriage full of wax figures to the Grand Prix and sent another representing a wedding party to drive around the city, both accompanied by posters and banners bearing the museum's name.

The museum thus also mimicked the newspaper in its aggressive commercialization. The wax museum and other major institutions of entertainment learned from the tricks of the mass press that saturating public space with advertising functioned as a critical means through which to became associated with modernity and thus solicit visits from natives and tourists eager to participate in the spectacle of modern life by consuming it.

Reality at the Wax Museum

The museum brilliantly constructed itself as bourgeois entertainment through its association with museum culture yet survived because it worked like, and re-presented the realism of, the mass

109. MGAG, March 30, 1892, summary of 1891.
110. The figure replaced the more Parisian *sandwich-afficher*. I do not know how long the peasant figure lasted there. MGCA September 29, 1883.

press, including reaching its audience of newly and/or barely literate readers. By depicting the world as represented in newspapers, the wax museum's realism was both topical and aesthetic. The verisimilitude of wax sculpture was not the sole element in the museum's realist aesthetic. Rather, the museum used dioramas and in them compiled detail on detail to affect verisimilitude. So if at once the museum touted its artistic element, it also aestheticized reproduction in even the smallest details. Accessories, ornaments, the framing effect of the diorama, and even the dioramas' narratives created the illusion of reality at the same time that they turned reality into an aesthetic.[111]

Unlike most waxworks that preceded it, the Musée Grévin employed the full-scale diorama. The tableaux offered recognizable, taxonomic and appropriate settings for the figures, creating "peepholes" into Parisian life.[112] As the *Moniteur universel* reported, "at the Musée Grévin resemblance is perfect, striking, extraordinary. You begin to ask yourself whether you are in the presence of the real person."[113] But an English guidebook to Paris reveals that the key element in the museum's aesthetic went beyond the wax figures: "The particular boast of the Grévin is its groups."[114] The museum catalog also touted "the composition of groups, in showing individuals in their 'milieu'—famous writers in the halls of the Comédie-Française next to famous actors, painters in a studio, watching the work of a colleague."[115] An appropriate setting and taxonomic grouping helped define the realistic element of the diorama. If less than one hundred years earlier revolutionary aesthetics found no place for Curtius and his wax collection, the Musée Grévin could successfully bank on "reproduction loyal to nature and respect for the truth in the smallest details" as the aesthetic guide on which the museum was founded.

The museum reproduced the details of the diorama settings as closely as possible. The library of Jules Grévy, the president of the re-

---

111. See Naomi Schor, *Reading in Detail* (New York: Methuen, 1987), 139, on detailism and the uncanny. Bringing the accessory (detail) to the center, she notes, is critical in establishing an uncanny effect.

112. See Donna Haraway, "Teddy Bear Patriarchy: Taxidermy in the Garden of Eden, New York City, 1908–1936," *Social Text* (winter 1985): 20–63. Haraway argues that dioramas at the American Museum of Natural History—"peepholes into the jungle"—socialized the natural order, and I suggest that the Musée Grévin's dioramas naturalized the social order.

113. *Le Moniteur universel,* June 6 1882.

114. Lucas, *A Wanderer in Paris,* 246.

115. *Catalogue-almanach du musée Grévin,* 2d ed. (Paris, 1882).

21. Arrest of Russian nihilists. Musée Grévin archives.

public, "was copied exactly from [his library] at the Elysée." And the success of the dramatic arrest of Russian nihilists (fig. 21) lay in its details, according to one review: "Not a detail is missing, the icons, papers, cartons, thick newspapers."[116] The tableau included paper imported from Russia on which real Russian characters were written, and a samovar and tea glasses that came from Moscow. While in the president's library the museum featured facsimiles or "doubles," in the Russian tableau it displayed "authentic" Russian items.

But concern for authenticity did not stop at conventions of representation. A few years after its opening, the museum introduced its first historical diorama because it had the opportunity to acquire the actual tub in which Marat had been murdered (fig. 22). The scene, which opened in the fall of 1886, also included a real map of France from 1791, copies of Marat's newspaper *L'Ami du peuple,* and a knife and a pike dating from the period. In an annual report to stockholders, the museum directors reported that "this scene, whose reconstitution is perfectly loyal to the official reports of the era . . . was well worth the ex-

116. *L'Indépendance belge,* June 12, 1882.

22. Death of Marat. Musée Grévin archives.

traordinary price of 5,000 francs paid for the tub. The authenticity of
the tub has increased the attraction of the tableau tenfold" and contributed, they argued, to a significant rise in receipts in the two months
following the tableau's opening.[117] From this point forward, the museum began to mix current events with scenes from the past, hoping
to boost the tableaux's authenticity by eliciting the aura of "real" objects from the past, breathing life into wax reproductions of historical
figures.

The museum's aesthetic can in part be understood in the context of
Naturalism, a contemporaneous literary movement, often distinguished
from realism in its celebration of details for their own sake and in its
dedication to the exact reproduction of real life.[118] *L'Illustration* noted,
"Wax figures are the triumph of Naturalism."[119] In a letter to Emile

117. MGA, board of directors' report to the general assembly of stockholders, March
28, 1887.
118. For more on naturalism, see Colette Becker, *Lire le réalisme et le naturalisme*
(Paris: Dunod, 1992), Philippe Hamon, *Texte et idéologie* (Paris: Presses universitaires de
France, 1984); and Henri Mitterand, *Le regard et le signe: poétique du roman réaliste et
naturaliste* (Paris: Presses universitaires de France, 1987).
119. *L'Illustration,* December 10, 1881.

Zola requesting a suit for his wax effigy, Grévin linked the museum to the author's aesthetic, promising that "The Musée Grévin will be naturalist or will not be."[120] Here he echoed Zola's own well known phrase, "the republic will be naturalist or will not be," which itself echoed Adolphe Thiers, the President of the Republic, who announced that the republic would be conservative or would not be.

But if the Musée Grévin was to be guided by Naturalism, it would also alter the rules of representation as needed. In January 1886 the museum opened a scene from Zola's novel *Germinal,* which originally appeared in serial form in the newspaper *Le Cri du Peuple* in 1885. The tableau claimed to depict the scene from the theatrical adaptation of the novel that had recently been forbidden by the censors. The museum chose the moment at the novel's end when the mine floods: Etienne kills Chaval, and he and Catherine—caught in the mine—make love with the corpse nearby. The tableau illustrated the moment following the sexual encounter and depicted the lovers clutching each other as they confronted the corpse (fig. 23). The museum catalog boasted of the "scrupulous exactitude" of the representation and reported, "All the accessories, hats, lamps, tools, are authentic. The mine is the exact copy of the gallery at Anzin, from where the museum got some of the wood and blocks of schist in order to give the public a complete illusion."[121] While the museum claimed to represent a scene from a play, it did not make copies of the play props. Rather, because the play was "naturalist" theater based on a "naturalist" novel, the wax museum went to what was believed to be Zola's source: the mine at Anzin. Yet the museum would never have built a tableau of the mine at Anzin had it not figured as part of Zola's fiction. In this case, the familiarity of both the novel and the play bolstered the reality-effect of the representation of the mine.

The tableau's evocation of, and the crowd's familiarity with, Zola's *Germinal* were critical to the "realism" of the spectacle although reviewers commented solely on the diorama's verisimilitude—as though its mere illusionism constituted its success. *L'Illustration,* for example, wrote, "Here is a real mine shaft, black and deep with pieces of real coal and its timbers that were taken from the depths of the shafts at Anzin. Everything is of the most exact nature. . . . As we already said,

120. Bibliothèque nationale, mss n.a.f. 24519, 410, letter from Grévin to Zola, July 6, 1881.

121. *Catalogue du musée Grévin,* 39th ed. (Paris, n.d.), probably 1886.

23. Scene from *Germinal*. Musée Grévin archives.

all is real . . . the timbers, the lamps, the tools, right down to the clothing that is worn by *real* miners."[122] What was "real" in this tableau? Its
recreation of the theatrical adaptation, of Zola's novel, or of a mine?
What was the claim to reality of this novelistic/theatrical scene when
juxtaposed with other scenes at the Musée Grévin, such as a tableau of
the Chamber of Deputies? Perhaps for the visitors who might never see
the president of the republic or a coal mine, the diorama's simulations
were satisfyingly real.

If the museum and the critics alike noted the verisimilitude in the
figures, the clothes, the settings, and the accessories, the diorama's construction of a sustained narrative contributed to enhancing the effect
of the real. This may explain why the "Histoire d'un crime" emerged
as the museum's first big hit. The crowd's behavior led one reviewer to
remark, "These tableaux of a striking realism, are those that interested
the crowd most; it was difficult to get close; the crowd was so big."[123]
In them the museum represented a crime from start to finish in seven
tableaux, as a serial novel (figs. 24–30). While this conceptualization

122. *L'Illustration,* January 2, 1886.
123. *Le Temps,* June 7, 1882.

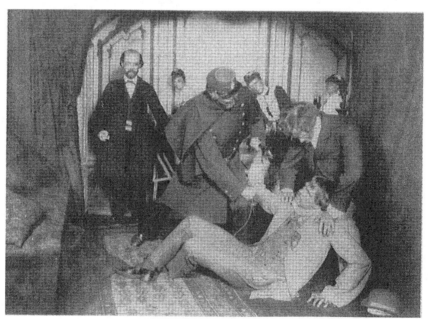

24–25. The crime (*above*); the arrest (*below*). "L'histore d'un crime,"
Musée Grévin archives.

26–27. Confrontation at the morgue (*above*); the trial *(below)*. "L'histoire d'un crime," Musée Grévin archives.

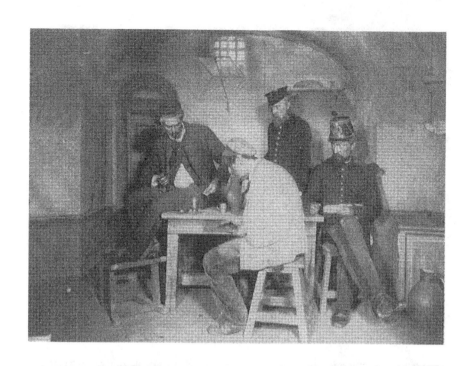

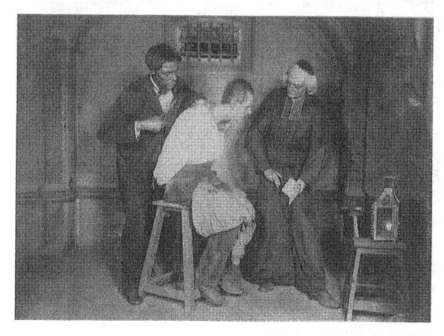

28–30. Waiting in the cell (*above left*); preparing for the execution (*below left*); being led to the execution (*above*). "L'histoire d'un crime," Musée Grévin archives.

thus already compared the display to a form of representation—the serialized novel—the catalog also pointed out that the dramatization was divided "comme au théâtre" into seven distinct tableaux. It described each tableau in terms of plot advancement, and the seven-tableaux structure mimicked that serial installation of illustrated reports of a crime investigation (see figs. 6, 9).

Despite these explanations that clearly rooted the display in other forms of representation, reviews insisted on its striking realism, calling it "a *fait divers* in seven tableaux, of an extraordinarily realistic execution that creates an intensity of effect that is stunning."[124] Another review described it as "a living *fait divers*."[125] Just as the morgue's "realism" was embedded in newspaper narratives, the familiar narrativity of "l'histoire d'un crime" effected the "real." Essentially, the tableaux series seemed "real" because they evoked familiar stories. They offered three-dimensional representations of newspaper *faits divers* that represented real-life Paris.

"L'histoire d'un crime" depicted narrative development through the serial juxtaposition of seven tableaux. Other *fait divers* displays relied on the viewer's ability to make intertextual links as a means of building narrativity into the exhibit. The litany of contemporary criminals displayed over the years at the museum offered a vivid depiction of the voyeuristic thrills that abounded in the mass press. The newspaper coverage of a crime, however, functioned as more than the pretext for its representation as part of the museum's display. Sometimes rendered simply and almost always accompanied by little catalogue copy, these tableaux, if taken at face value, might seem to epitomize what many scholars have labeled the non-narrative quality of late nineteenth-century "spectacle." These "snapshot" *faits divers,* however, presumed the visitor would have prior knowledge of the crime narrative from the newspaper and thus relied on the viewer's ability to relate the display to an already known investigation. Narrative and realism, among these exhibits, relied on the viewer's "reading" intertextually; moving not only across media (from newspapers to wax tableaux) but also through shifting modes of perception (from the written word to the three-dimensional wax sculpture).

The tableaux, with their backdrops, objects and wax figures, may have built a lifelike scene, but they also served as clear demarcations through settings that made the spectator aware of their artificiality. De-

124. *L'Express,* June 7, 1882.
125. *Le Parlement,* June 6, 1882.

31. The papal cortège. Musée Grévin archives.

spite the absorptive qualities of such a display, the museum attempted to further naturalize its exhibit by removing the imaginary fourth wall from time to time. For example, the museum strategically placed a wax figure of a resting gentleman on a bench intended for use by its live visitors. Visitors were thus invited to do a double take—to be momentarily tricked by the casually displayed figure, whose location outside a tableau seemed to announce him as "one of us." Strategically located outside the obvious "display" spaces, such a figure enhanced the deceptive illusion of the wax sculpture and also allowed museum visitors to insert themselves into the show and mingle with luminaries.[126]

In addition, the museum sometimes presented entire "scenes" outside a framed setting. The papal cortège (fig. 31) occupied the center of the museum's ornate main room, the *salle des colonnes,* and was set up as though in procession. This grouping offered a scene already in motion for the spectator, who could thus find herself in the midst of a papal procession. The spectator's ability to see it from any angle gave

126. To this day, the wax reproduction of an actual museum guard (known as Bibi) stands ready to guide visitors who enter the basement.

her a viewing position that in reality would not actually be accessible but functioned, nevertheless, to bolster the display's realism.

Rather than simply represent reality, the Musée Grévin was a representation of a representation of reality: it had the reality of a newspaper, which most people enjoyed as reality, despite the fact that it was packaged and sensationalized for everyday consumption. Yet the Musée Grévin's aesthetic lays bare the fact that reproduction was inscribed in layers of representation, and that dioramas could mix the "actual thing" (like Marat's tub, or a miner's "real" clothes) with replicas, like that of the president's library. Looking at the opening of the Musée Grévin in 1882 and the discourse of both the museum's administration and the Parisian press, we discover that the display on the boulevard Montmartre used the bourgeois respectability of the museum to sell a three dimensional representation of the sensationalism of the mass press. Its modernity resided in its celebration of the present, in its commitment to rapid change, in the wide-range of its pantheon, and in its emphasis on the importance of responding to public interest. The museum's popular appeal resided in no small measure in its insistent evocation of a reality effect.

If dioramas were "windows onto knowledge," then the Musée Grévin could be considered a "peephole into Paris." We turn now to the museum tableaux and their construction of spectatorship, for it was in large measure through the tableaux themes and visual organization that the museum empowered and thus attracted its visitors.

Panoramas and Peepholes

In a summary to its stockholders after its first year of operation, the directors happily reported that "the public . . . proves by its volume, that we have satisfied its curiosity."[127] What relation did the museum create between its displays and its visitors that satisfied the public as its directors happily proclaimed? What did the tableaux offer their viewers? What was the museum's appeal to its large and diverse public?[128] For if the wax museum, like the boulevard, the press, and the

127. MGAG, March 30, 1883.

128. To "read" the dioramas at the wax museum, I begin with Fredric Jameson's notion of mass culture's "utopian or transcendent potential," rather than the Frankfurt school critics' concentration on cultural production that ignores the mass appeal of a particular cultural form except as people are manipulated into enjoying it. See Fredric

morgue, represented and spectacularized reality, its particularity as a spectacle resided in both its content and the viewing positions enacted through the tableaux and the museum spaces more generally.

The Musée Grévin's organization was decidedly modern in its deliberate ambiguity and in its peripatetic qualities. If its reproductive aesthetic seemed at great distance from the blur of impressionist painting, its visual indeterminacy loudly echoed that of Impressionism and thus can be seen as reinforcing what T. J. Clark has called the "myth of modernity."[129] In particular, the multiple subject-positions and visual perspectives the museum offered spectators promoted a certain ambiguity and fluidity in this otherwise seemingly didactic exhibition. For Clark, of course, the modernist myth found no way to picture class adequately and thus advanced, rather than contradicted, bourgeois ideology, especially on the subject of urban life. The wax museum, in fact, repeated the visual experiences of the city, especially in the way that it transformed the museum visitors into *flâneurs* of sorts. And yet the transformation of everyday life into spectacle built social bonds among strangers, who now belonged to a community because they had visual evidence that such a community existed. By taking the popularity of the wax museum seriously—as more than successful bourgeois ideology—we begin to understand ways that the consumption of life as spectacle was not necessarily alienating, that *flânerie* had possibly liberating and even democratizing effects.

For the *flâneur* is not really a person of any particular class or gender but is rather a historically specific positionality of power—one that the Musée Grévin invited its visitors to assume. Through *flânerie*, spectators commanded the spectacle: they participated in it at the same time that they believed it was constructed for them. They also occupied a variety of viewing positions: both ocular and socially determined. Visitors inhabited multiple perspectives—panoramic views—at the same time that the displays often offered privileged access: peepholes into Paris. While the museum reinforced the system of celebrity, it offered visitors seeming proximity to those well-known people. Further, visitors occupied a wide variety of identificatory viewing positions that transgressed boundaries of class, gender, geography and even temporality.

Jameson, "Reification and Utopia in Mass Culture" (1979), in *Signatures of the Visible* (New York: Routledge, 1990), 29–30.

129. The modernist reworking of the myth of modernity is Clark's central thesis in *The Painting of Modern Life*.

The attraction also relied on the actual mobility of the human being who moved across, through and even into the display, allowing the spectator to command the spectacle: to set its story in motion, to freeze its narrative and to literally dissolve the boundaries between self and spectacle—to blur reality and representation. The ambiguity of the wax figures and the eclecticism of the tableaux and their viewing positions, turned the Musée Grévin into a crowd pleaser by existing in and through the visitor's interaction with the display.

The wax museum consciously materialized a democratized social order. The museum, with what seemed like "intrepid whimsy," filled its "Parisian pantheon" with celebrities.[130] That the café-concert singer Yvette Guilbert and the president of the republic might stand side by side suggested that the wax museum also echoed the basis of political legitimacy in Third Republic France in which politicians—like performers and artists—rose and fell in connection to a broad constituency of voters.

The museum also reinforced a culture of celebrity and then offered its visitors a special privilege through proximity to these celebrities in the wax tableaux. One newspaper review explained, "The likenesses of our great men, of our famous artists or society people pleases us . . . and it is to see them up close that the public crowds to the Musée Grévin."[131] In a letter to her friend in the provinces, reprinted in *Le Charivari*, one Parisienne explained that "there is, in effect, a mix of celebrities of all kinds . . . one sees there in review all those who count in the *tout Paris* from Victor Hugo to Judic."[132] Another newspaper concluded that "it is to see them [celebrities] that the public goes in masses to the Musée Grévin."[133]

Visitors experienced the centrality of "celebrity" in the museum in its first room whose center was occupied by a tableau titled "Le tout-Paris chez Grévin," which changed to the "Salon de célébrités parisiens" after five years. In the former, Grévin sketched a young woman, while the "celebrities of arts and letters" milled around his studio: journalists such as Albert Wolff, J. J. Weiss and Francisque Sarcey; the painters Détaille and Vibert, the composers Massenet and Gounod. Unlike a recreation of the Chamber of Deputies or a scene from a play, the

130. Lemaître, *Impressions de théâtre*, 325.
131. *L'Indépendance belge*, June 12, 1882.
132. *Le Charivari*, June 11, 1882.
133. *L'Indépendance belge*, June 12, 1882.

fame of the characters (aside from the verisimilitude of the wax sculpture) served as the tableau's measure of reality. The scene depicted a possible as opposed to an actual moment whose plausibility resided in the fact that the people represented might or should know each other but all somehow "belonged" together because they were "celebrities." Over the years, Grévin's studio dropped from the tableau, but the essential theme of the diorama remained unchanged as celebrities came and went, in or out of vogue. The seeming ease with which one figure traded places with another was not lost on some visitors such as Lemaître, who reasoned this way:

Not being able to take them all, they took any old one. This is not at all unfair. As there is no measure by which to judge them exactly, it was better to leave it all to chance. This is also very philosophical. Talent, after all, is but a lottery. Celebrity, too, is but a lottery. From these first winners, a second has been drawn, that's all. . . . And this drawing signifies, in the end, that apart from the five or six geniuses of each century, one man of letters is worth another, or just about.[134]

Here was a display whose duration suggested the importance of celebrity in the wax museum and whose structure made it eminently suitable to the museum's constraints. In fact, it matched the structure of modern life as constructed by its various representations: the category of fame could be filled by an endlessly changing parade of wax figures.

The tableaux afforded museum-goers something special: intimate settings and views of dignitaries who might otherwise only be seen at official functions, if seen at all. Visitors saw the famous explorer Savorgnan de Brazza relaxing in his tent (fig. 32), and Bismarck meeting with Marshal von Moltke in a "private visit" at Varzin, where he "often rested from the fatigues of politics."[135]

The museum not only put visitors in the same room as celebrities, but it also allowed them to get close enough to touch them.[136] For example, visitors might come on François Coppée and Juliette Adam (fig. 33) in midconversation or admire the model of a monument to Admiral Courbet while standing alongside its artists, the well known academic sculptors Falguière and Mercié with Charles Alphand, minister of

134. Lemaître, *Impressions de théâtre*, 328.

135. *Catalogue-almanach du musée Grévin*, 32d ed.

136. In contemporary wax museums too, visitors armed with instamatic cameras can be photographed with a waxen celebrity. The video camera destroys this effect, capturing human motion and waxen immobility.

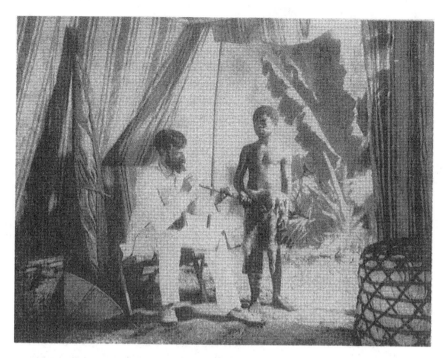

32. Savorgnan de Brazza. Musée Grévin archives.

33. François Coppée and Juliette Adam. Musée Grévin archives.

Public Works. Celebrities were mingled throughout spaces that seemed to belong to the museum's visitors.

Over the years, one of the standard themes of Musée Grévin tableaux was the *coulisses* (the theater wings): representations of a perspective *not* usually accessible to most spectators and the domain most often reserved for the allegedly privileged gaze of the *flâneur*. In these tableaux, *their* voyeurism was extended to every visitor who could pay the museum's small admission price. Thematically, the *coulisses* tableau offered a peephole into an exclusive Parisian site. The catalog underscored the privilege of the diorama's perspective: "Everything works to give the spectator the illusion of a visit to so curious a corner of the grand Parisian stage, a visit only permitted an elect few."[137] If visitors found this potential for the extension of certain elite voyeurism appealing (an appeal that also found a venue for display in impressionist paintings), the museum spectator's particular privilege resided in the tableau's offer of more than one view at a time—that of both a spectator of the show and a spectator of other spectators.[138] In 1885 the museum represented a dancer's loge at intermission. The scene (fig. 34) showed a dancer being visited by an elegant man. In 1890 this tableau was replaced by "Les coulisses de l'Opéra: le foyer de la danse" (fig. 35).[139] Here, the visitor saw both onstage and off, at the same time. The display's three-dimensionality and verisimilitude were touted as effecting the illusion of presence or reality in a way that paintings simply could not.

If sites of exclusivity offered voyeuristic peeks into Parisian high life, the city's more "popular" characters were also depicted in this social zoo. Thus, visitors might encounter such Parisian types as a *chiffonier* (rag-picker), the *homme-sandwich*, a diorama of a troupe of circus performers or that year's queen of the laundresses.

The museum offered its spectators the ability to travel not simply to Parisian locations, high and low, but also to colonial settings—compressing space in keeping with other modern technologies such as the railway and the telegraph.[140] For example, in November 1895, the mu-

137. *Catalogue du musée Grévin,* 82d ed.

138. As Robert Herbert has noted, this theme occurs in many impressionist paintings and in other more popular images as well. Herbert, *Impressionism* (New Haven: Yale University Press, 1987), 104.

139. Both tableaux are evocative of Degas's series of sketches *La famille Cardinal* and his painting *The Curtain.*

140. For more on the compression of time and space, see Wolfgang Schivelbusch,

34. A dancer's loge. Musée Grévin archives.

35. "Les coulisses de l'Opéra." Musée Grévin archives.

36. Human sacrifices in Dahomey. Musée Grévin archives.

seum opened a panoramic diorama of Tananarivo in Madagascar, which had just become a French protectorate. Another tableau depicted the exotic other of human sacrifices in Dahomey (now Benin), in which King Béhanzin, surrounded by "his women," orders the sacrifice of several of his slaves (fig. 36). But the museum reminded Europeans that the empire had already been brought to Paris in other "ethnographic" spectacles, such as the Javanese dancers and a Cairo street from the universal exposition of 1889 (fig. 37).

The museum also played with notions of time. Its evocation of "the present" in many respects allowed its visitors "to be there" as witnesses and even as participants in "current events." By emphasizing current events and celebrity, the wax museum offered a sort of "instant and living history" that not only emphasized the ephemeral but also seemed to extend the duration of the present. Its displays coupled ephemerality with an eternal present in much the same way that photographs would

The Railway Journey (Berkeley: University of California Press, 1977); Stephen Kern, *The Culture of Time and Space* (Cambridge, Mass.: Harvard University Press, 1983); and David Harvey, *The Condition of Postmodernity* (Cambridge: Basil Blackwell, 1989).

37. A Cairo street, universal exposition of 1889. Musée Grévin archives.

eventually do in the press. As Siegfried Kracauer explained about the uses of photography in newspapers: "the world is turned into a photographable present and the photographed present is completely eternalized."[141] However quickly the museum installed a new display, its exposure there far outlasted its coverage in the newspaper. Yet both the newspaper and the wax museum attest to the fact that *l'actualité* (current events) described a state of the present that exceeded an actual moment yet whose significance was derived from the sense that the event or person would be "of a moment."[142] The museum, in fact, pre-

141. Kracauer cited in Martin Jay, *Downcast Eyes* (Berkeley: University of California Press, 1993), 135.

142. For two interesting discussions of ephemerality and the moment, see Jeannene Przyblyski, "Moving Pictures: Photography, Narrative, and the Paris Commune of 1871," and Leo Charney, "In a Moment: Film and the Philosophy of Modernity," both in *Cinema and the Invention of Modern Life*, ed. Leo Charney and Vanessa R. Schwartz (Berkeley: University of California Press, 1995).

38. The coronation of the czar. Musée Grévin archives.

served the present. Intense newspaper coverage tended to last at least as long as the fabrication of a tableau. In a sense then, the museum served to prolong the present by keeping alive a story that might have already dropped from the newspapers.

The museum tableaux represented an eternal present in two other ways. First, they froze an action that the visitor seemed to catch in medias res. Visitors, for example, could witness the arrest of Russian nihilists (see fig. 21) or the anarchist Duval, the czar's coronation (fig. 38), and the bombing of the forts in Amman, Cochin China, by Admiral Courbet. Spectators encountered these tableaux whose narratives were already in the process of unfolding. The tableaux insisted on their presentness through their relation to the narratives they depicted—narratives with which people were already familiar or with which the museum catalog familiarized them. Thus, the pleasure of these spectacles was moored in narrative—an element that served a key role in the museum's visual spectacle. The tableau's visual mimesis thus relied on nonocular knowledge contained either in the viewer's head by virtue of newspaper-reading or through the written catalog narratives.

39. Rivière dead in Tonkin. Musée Grévin archives.

In addition, the museum's many displays of the almost dead and the recently deceased—suspended, it seemed, somewhere on the threshold between life and death—played with temporal as well as corporeal presence.[143] Whether a display of Colonel Rivière at the moment of his death in an ambush in Tonkin (fig. 39), or Victor Hugo on his deathbed, mourned by an allegorical representation of France, these tableaux enhanced the effect of wax sculpture in their suspension of animation. They also gave great credence to the notion that the wax museum could arrest the ephemeral and eternalize the present. The verisimilitude of the wax sculpture and its setting in a tableau, and therefore in some form of narrative time, breathed life back into an effigy that represented a corpse. The tableaux might even beat back death by halting a narrative before or at the moment of death.

If the museum's investment in the present came in part from its aspiration to be a plastic newspaper, its presentness also contributed to its realism. Yet the museum could never match the speed with which

143. See Mark Sandberg, "Missing Persons," for a parallel discussion of life and death in wax tableaux.

events and people fell in and out of the public eye. Although they installed their own studio in 1883 and produced, designed and costumed the dioramas in the museum, production was merely too slow to match the rapid pace of newspapers. Initially, the museum changed its dioramas fairly rapidly. For example, Bou-Amena, which belonged to the museum's first collection, was replaced only three months later by General Wolseley in Egypt. Nine months later, that tableau was replaced by the crowning of the czar. The tableau of the Chambre des Députés, which lasted five years, worked somewhat like the celebrities diorama featuring different speakers at the Tribune: in 1882, Gambetta; in 1883, Clemenceau; in 1884 and 1885, Jules Ferry. The tableau of the scene from the opera *Francesca da Rimini* lasted for less than a year, and Prince Jérôme for only eight months. The museum's early production was marked by the creation of new tableaux, all of which were used as occasions for publicity.

This task could neither be sustained by the studio nor by the museum's finances. Over time, the museum's collection changed less frequently. The 1883 tableau of the earthquake at Ischia lasted only a year, the fire at the Opéra-Comique of 1887 and l'affaire Gouffé of 1890 lasted three years, but the anarchist Ravachol occupied a place in the basement for six years, starting in 1892. The dancer Rosita Mauri, although in different costumes, greeted visitors as the first figure in the museum for twelve years and the "Foyer de la danse" was open for well over eleven years, topped only by the "Histoire d'un crime," which lasted for eighteen years.

But the museum's inability to keep up with current events and perhaps the public's familiarization with reproduction in wax as a novel technique of realist representation led to the eventual increase in the number of historical tableaux displayed. If it proved difficult to freeze the present, the museum would instead breathe life into the past by animating it.

In an article describing the Musée Grévin's new tableau, "Une soirée à Malmaison" which opened in April 1900, historian Frédéric Masson explained, "It is understood that here is a new attempt at a democratic and popular history, inspired by the national passion, served by illustrious artists, and toward whose completion no amount of money, work or research was spared."[144] Masson continued, "In effect, these are no longer wax figures, it's part of history, it's *History*. . . . The best teach-

144. *Le théâtre,* numéro spécial: le musée Grévin, 1900.

ing, according to the modern patois, is that which we learn with the eye—the lesson of things."[145] The museum's popular and democratic visual history seemed contingent on the dissolution of distance from the past and on the possibility of giving visitors a privileged viewing position.[146]

The museum's "histories for the masses" personalized history and politics by giving dramatic public events a personal face. They offered visitors an intimate view of historical luminaries and ecumenical interpretations of the past, establishing the "something for everybody" quality necessitated by the institution's attempt to appeal to a large and diverse audience. For example, a tableau of Napoleon seeking shelter from the snow on his retreat from Russia represented the emperor huddling in the cold. The catalog asked visitors to note, "Napoleon's look is poignantly filled with anxiety: you can already see foreshadowed there the empire's destiny."[147] French and foreign viewers found the country's fate in its leader's emotional physiognomy as opposed to its battlefields.

The Malmaison tableau amplified this model on a large scale. Two years in the making, the diorama represented a party at Napoleon's château at Malmaison in July 1800 following the decisive victory over the Austrians. Rather than illustrate the battlefield victory, the museum chose to represent the moment, as Masson put it, when "for the first time, he considered himself ruler."[148] The museum spent a fortune scouring antique stores for "authentic" period furniture, paintings and clothing and appealed to the descendants of those who had been in the emperor's entourage for any objects that might have belonged to Napoleon. The scene depicted Josephine seated on a small couch, looking admiringly at the scene, while Napoleon stood in the center of the drawing room where guests played cards, chatted, enjoyed the refreshments served them by black servants and perhaps flirted (fig. 40). This tableau, not unlike the "Tout-Paris chez Grévin" tableau, consisted of a gathering of celebrities and, perhaps inadvertently, presented a past that seemed much like contemporary Parisian society. Rather than stressing the difference between eras, the tableau materialized the social order of fabricated nobility, parvenus and "talent and merit" that pro-

145. Frédéric Masson, in Le théâtre, 9.
146. For contemporary notions of history see Kern, Culture of Time and Space; and Stephen Bann, The Clothing of Clio (New York: Cambridge University Press, 1984).
147. Catalogue du musée Grévin, 54th ed.
148. Masson, in Le théâtre.

40. "Une soirée à Malmaison." Musée Grévin archives.

duced the Paris captivated by "celebrities" of the fin de siècle on which
the museum thrived.

As noted earlier, the museum first turned to representing the past
when the opportunity arose to buy Marat's tub in 1885, three years after
the museum opened. With the approach of 1889, the museum decided
to join in the festivities to commemorate the centennial of the French
Revolution and opened a gallery of the French Revolution.[149] This series represented a succession of personal moments and individual tribu-
lations for members of multiple political factions: Louis XVI and the
royal family at the Temple on September 3 1792, on hearing the news
of the murder of the princesse de Lamballe; the fallen king imprisoned
in the tower of the Temple; Marie Antoinette under constant surveil-

149. Pascal Ory's article, "Le centenaire de la révolution française. la preuve de 89,"
in *Les lieux de mémoire*, ed. Pierre Nora (Paris: Gallimard, 1984): 1:523–60, makes no
mention of the Musée Grévin or much else that was not state-sponsored, as though the
only commemorations of 1789 were "official ones."

41. Dignitaries visit the Eiffel Tower. Musée Grévin archives.

lance at the Conciergerie; the young Louis XVII alone and imprisoned in a rat-infested cell. The museum catalog described the *tragédie royale,* and these representations of familial and solitary settings no doubt attempted to evoke empathy as opposed to analytic distance among museum-goers.

If the visitor in 1889 could not feel any pity for the royal family, radical revolutionary sympathizers might be moved by the reconstitution of Marat's death. Mirabeau, Bailly and Lafayette were grouped together in conversation as were Danton and Desmoulins with Robespierre. Jacobins did not represent all of the revolutionary forces: Girondists found their martyr in a tableau of Madame Roland's trial.

The museum's display did not offer a chronological unfolding of the French Revolution. It combined "great revolutionary figures" (celebrities from the past, we might say) with sensationalized events depicted as personal tragedies: imprisonment, condemnation to death, starvation and murder. As in most official commemorations of the centennial

42. Workers on the Eiffel Tower. Musée Grévin archives.

of 1789, the collective actions of the crowd remained unrepresented.[150] The museum did not attempt to construct a crowd with which its own crowd might identify, leaving the moment of revolutionary crowds behind.

But the wax tableaux's narratives were not the only means of constructing the relation between the viewer and the subjects represented. The three-dimensional tableaux created a particular visual relation between the spectator and the display which functioned as one of the museum's lasting attractions. In the 1889 tableau of the Eiffel Tower, the museum showed the tower under construction during a visit by Eiffel and exposition and Parisian officials Lockroy, Alphand and Berger (fig. 41). The scene included workers whose labors had been interrupted represented as though watching the visiting dignitaries (fig. 42). The museum visitor, therefore, saw what few people had seen: the view from

150. See ibid. Ory perceptively links this lack to officials' fears of *Boulangisme* in 1889.

the tower still under construction. At the same time, the scene depicted a panoramic view of the capital, a privileged view of a privileged view of Paris. Not one but three sights confronted the museum visitor: the panoramic view of Paris, the view of the visitors Eiffel and company, and the view of the workers watching the visit.

The museum's tableaux not only unmoored spectators' vision by taking them to a variety of places and offering multiple perspectives on one scene, they also addressed and relied on ambulatory spectators. For example, an 1887 diorama of a rehearsal at the Comédie-Française represented the director's loge during a dress rehearsal (fig. 43). Here the museum's visitors observed Juliette Adam, editor of *La Nouvelle Revue*, Ambroise Thomas, director of the Opéra, Jules Claretie, director of the Comédie, and Edouard Pailleron, author of *La Souris*, watching a scene from that play. The tableau's structure played on its own three-dimensionality and the visitor's mobility. It was assumed that the spectator would approach the tableau from the left, where the figures in the box appeared to be watching something. As the spectator walked to the right, he or she could then see the inset of the dress rehearsal as it would appear through the eyes of those seated in the box and, because of its angle, as the museum visitor could glimpse only when she aligned herself with the visual perspective of the wax figures. Through her own motion, the spectator thus enabled the unfolding of the scene's narrative.

"L'histoire d'un crime" also relied on a spectator's mobility to generate its narrative quality. While the realism of this seven-tableaux series seemed embedded in its similarities to newspaper *faits divers*, its effectiveness as a serial narrative that presented a sequence of freeze-frames required the onlooker to walk through the display. The act infused it with at least one of its seemingly lifelike qualities: serial motion. In this way, "L'histoire d'un crime" was already a series of moving pictures. It is therefore no surprise that Ferdinand Zecca, an early filmmaker for Pathé, established his fame with a 1901 film of the same name, based on the Musée Grévin's display.[151]

These tableaux offered its spectators the power to introduce motion

151. The museum displayed the tableau series from its opening in 1882 until a fire in the basement in 1899 forced it to drop the tableau of the courtroom. Most historians interpret Zecca's omission of the trial as an attempt to save money. See Georges Sadoul, *Histoire générale du cinéma* (Paris: Denoël, 1948), 2:187; Alan Williams, *Republic of Images* (Cambridge, Mass.: Harvard University Press, 1992), 46; and Richard Abel, *The Ciné Goes to Town* (Berkeley: University of California Press, 1994), 97–98. Abel misidentifies the installation date as 1899.

43. A rehearsal at the Comédie-Française. Musée Grévin archives.

into the museum display—an effect that the museum actively pursued in another way. In 1892 the Musée Grévin became the first institution to offer projected moving images in the form of Emile Reynaud's *pantomimes lumineuses.*[152]

152. See my article, coauthored with Jean-Jacques Meusy, "Le musée Grévin et le cinématographe: l'histoire d'une rencontre," *1895,* no. 11 (December 1991): 19–48.

The content of the dioramas and the way they situated spectators helped turn museum visitors into *flâneurs* of sorts. Spectators also were at times asked to identify with the figures in the tableaux through mechanisms of positioning, through the presentness effected by the figures and their narratives, and through their placement inside the wax museum's narrative space. These viewing positions promised everyone access and was thus conceived and enjoyed as "modern" by virtue of its seemingly democratic nature. In sum, when Jules Claretie remarked that "those who write the history of the Musée Grévin recount a chapter even of today's history," he was commenting on more than the museum's content.[153]

153. Jules Claretie, *La vie à Paris*, 278.

CHAPTER 4

Representing Reality
and the O-rama Craze

"One panorama arrives and another goes. That's the picture of life," summarized a newspaper article reporting the opening of a new panorama at the Carré Marigny on the edge of the Champs-Elysées in 1883.[1] The slightly ambivalent tone of this observation sharpens its social commentary. Whether we take it to refer to rapid change, to the popularity of panoramas and other such entertainments or even, inadvertently, to the verisimilitude attempted by the genre, to speak of panoramas was to speak of contemporary Parisian culture.

Panoramas and dioramas, both early nineteenth-century attractions, have drawn the interest of scholars as technological innovations of the early nineteenth century that led to film. In particular, scholars have noted how they marshaled vision to transport spectators in time and place through the illusion of realistic representation.[2] But we need to look at panoramas and dioramas as more than steps in the technological telos that culminated in film. Although these attractions became available at the start of the nineteenth century, their popularity ebbed and flowed until the 1880s when this revival well surpassed that of their earlier favor. Cassell's 1884 *Guide to Paris* remarked that "with the last few years there has been a perfect eruption of panoramas in every quar-

---

1. *Ville de Paris*, May 19, 1883.
2. Friedberg, *Window Shopping*, 20–22. Jonathan Crary noted that the panorama compels spectators to turn their heads and look around, while the diorama actually turns them, changing them to components of the machine. Crary, *Techniques of the Observer*, 113.

ter of Paris."[3] Indeed, in 1880 Parisians and visitors could see only one panorama, the defense of Paris during the siege, which had been open on the Champs-Elysées since 1872. By 1882 Paris boasted eleven panoramas and by 1889 seventeen, including those featured as part of the exposition.[4] What was behind fin-de-siècle *panoramania?*

The popularity of panoramas in the late nineteenth century depended on their status as another outlet for spectators in Paris to experience reality as spectacle. But representing the real was no straightforward matter, as the Musée Grévin makes clear. In fact, the panoramas' reality effects changed over the course of the century in terms of both content and form. Whereas they initially favored representations of landscapes, which were more effectively suited to creating the "panorama-effect"—its illusion of reality—by the end of the century they joined wax museums in constructing reality as some version of the newspaper. In addition, their technology pushed toward simulating experience.

In that way the panorama engaged its spectators differently than the wax museum, which seemed to offer spectators multiple views and a certain degree of power over the spectacle. Instead, the panorama took charge of its spectators—removed their points of reference, jostled and shook them and offered them an experience that engaged all five senses—going beyond the visual illusion of spectacle, or perhaps redefining it as more than an image.

Early Panoramas and Dioramas

Legend has it that the effect of light falling vertically on the prison cell wall of Robert Barker, a Scottish painter imprisoned by his creditors in the 1790s, inspired the first panorama. A composite of two Greek words—*pan,* which means all, and *horama,* which means view—panorama signifies a total view.[5] Panoramas were enormous circular paintings, lighted with natural light through slits in the ceiling

3. *Illustrated Guide to Paris,* 117.

4. François Robichon, "Les panoramas en France au 19e siècle" (thèse de IIIe cycle, Université de Paris, Nanterre, 1982), appendix.

5. Richard Altick, *The Shows of London* (Cambridge, Mass.: Harvard University Press, 1978).

that were meant to give the illusion of nature. Spectators entered a darkened passageway that led to a platform on which they stood in the center of the room, where they were enveloped by the tableau whose borders were invisible. The panorama thus prescribed the spectator's viewing position. The removal of all other visual points of reference outside the panorama made it difficult for spectators to judge size and distance. The circularity of the tableau created the illusion of depth. These elements comprise the "panorama-effect." The panorama's visual trick, which relied on its erasure of the spectator's point of reference, also facilitated the sense that the panorama, a representation that effaced its status as representation, became a substitute reality.[6]

Turning the illusion of depth on a flat surface into a commercial venture, the "English Fleet at Portsmouth" opened in London's Leicester Square in 1794.[7] The American Robert Fulton, better known as the inventor of the steamboat, owned a patent for the panorama technique. He went to Paris, whereupon he and James Thayer, who owned a large townhouse and much land on the boulevard Montmartre, built two rotundas, both seventeen meters wide and seven meters high to house two panoramas: "A View of Paris and its environs, as seen from the top of the Tuileries Palace" and "The Evacuation of Toulon by the British in 1793," which opened in 1799. A year later, the passage des Panoramas, the first of the capital's many *passages,* opened with these panoramas as its endpoint. From the start, this realist entertainment mingled geographically with what would soon become the sites of *flânerie.*

Panorama spectators were given bird's eye views; they were placed as though standing on a hill, overlooking the scene. The object of panoramas was "to offer views of entire towns and their surroundings."[8] An early form of "armchair" tourism, panoramas might substitute for travel and, additionally, offer more convenience at less expense. As a British observer remarked, "Panoramas are among the happiest contrivances for saving time and expense. . . . What cost a couple of hundred pounds a year a half century ago, now costs a shilling and a quarter of an hour."[9]

6. Bernard Comment, *Le XIXe siècle des panoramas* (Paris: Adam Biro, 1993), 51.

7. Altick, *Shows of London,* 129.

8. "Notice sur les panoramas et les dioramas," *Annales mensuelles de l'industrie manufacturière . . . et des beaux-arts* (1827): 206–16. APP, DA 129.

9. *Blackwood Magazine* (1824), cited in Altick, *Shows of London* 181.

Panoramas during the first half of the century were frequented by people no lower than the *moyenne bourgeoisie* owing, at least in part, to their cost.[10] Admission prices ranged from 1.50 francs to 3.00 francs and some even had varying prices depending on where you stood, suggesting an expectation of some sort of hierarchy of viewers, based on social rank and ability to pay. Nevertheless, the cost remained more than a worker's daily wage. In 1833 one reviewer complained, "The panorama owners would have served themselves and their public well to lower the admission price."[11] It was not until the last third of the century that workers could afford panoramas, or most large-scale commercial entertainment for that matter. Yet increasing accessibility of commercial culture was not simply a function of a rise in wages. As the mass press, department stores and the like burgeoned, their commercial logic bred a notion that people across classes should share these cultural activities and entertainments since these institutions relied on large numbers of participants. As with the price of newspapers, admission prices fell over the course of the century, and the panoramas found a truly "popular" audience.[12]

Panoramas were initially taken quite seriously for their potential scientific quality, which might advance knowledge and instruction. Such was the "legitimate" interest in panoramas that in the year VIII (1800), the Institut de France charged the architect and painter Dufourny to study the origins, effects and development of the panorama.[13] He marveled that "the more one studies a panorama, the less one is convinced that one is seeing a mere illusion."[14] Dufourny's praise of panoramas expressed the bourgeois values of instruction and utility that served to legitimate most sanctioned public entertainment throughout the nineteenth century:

Were this ingenious application, of still more ingenious principles but a stimulus to curiosity; were it good for nothing other than to present the exact and literal view of cities and the most interesting sites of the globe, it would still be a contribution to the general interest and under these cir-

10. Robichon, "Les panoramas en France," 183.

11. *L'artiste* (1833), cited in Robichon, "Le panorama, spectacle de l'histoire," *Le Mouvement social* (April–June 1985): 73.

12. See ibid., 76–77.

13. See Dufourny's report to Institut de France on panorama, BHVP, AA 103. See also Brigitte d'Helft and Michel Verliefden, *Monuments historiques* 4, no. 3 (1978): 54–60.

14. d'Helft and Verliefden, op. cit., 56.

cumstances alone would merit the greatest encouragement as an object of both instruction and utility.[15]

The panorama served an educational purpose by replicating views and sites. Dufourny showed no discomfort with the imitative nature of the panoramas, nor with the audience's willingness to be deceived. Panoramas, after all, offered the art of deception and never willfully deceived without the spectator's participation. Yet the illusion lay not so much in the actual quality of the panorama's realistic representation of a particular place (for few in the audience would have stood before the actual site and therefore could not judge the quality of the copy) as in its technological illusionism. The panorama's first spectators marveled at the panorama-effect and appreciated its substitute reality. The subjects represented played a secondary role.

The success of the first two panoramas led Thayer to build yet another rotunda in 1807, in a more densely residential street between the rue Neuve St-Augustin and the boulevard des Capucines. Larger than the first, it featured paintings by one of David's students, Pierre Prévost, and continued to thematize cityscapes and recent battle scenes. There over the years, Parisians saw Antwerp, London, Jerusalem and Athens, "the meeting at Tilsit" and the battle of Wagram. A most-likely apocryphal tale has it that on visiting this panorama in 1810, the emperor Napoleon decided to undertake the enormous project of popularizing his victories by building eight rotundas in the Champs-Elysées that showed his battle victories and the important cities he had captured. The events of 1812 halted the project.[16] True or not, the story indicates the extent to which the panoramas were perceived as having a potentially didactic quality.

Because the panorama's early success was based on the seeming realism of its point of view, it should come as no surprise that the technique was modified over time in order to achieve greater realism. What seemed "more real," however, was not self-evident. The original point of view offered visitors was clearly inspired by the tradition of landscape painting; spectators were placed as though in a privileged position, most often above the scene represented. Breaking with this positioning of the spectator, one trajectory of panoramas brought the spectator even

15. Dufourny's report, 9. BHVP, AA 103.
16. d'Helft and Verliefden, op. cit., 56. They report the project as factual, but it has been cited elsewhere as apocryphal.

closer to the action in an attempt to enhance the spectacle's "realism." For example, in 1831, the military painter Charles Langlois opened a panorama of the battle of Navarino (in which the combined English, French and Russian fleets defeated the Turkish navy in support of Greek independence in October 1827) that departed from the original formula.

Spectators entered the panorama through a dark passageway and found themselves on an actual French battleship that Langlois had transported to the panorama's site on the rue des Marais-du-Temple. Described as "an enormous step toward perfection, by adding to all the other illusions that of the actual site that could hold the spectators,"[17] passengers entered the ship through the officers' cabin at a moment sometime after the battle had begun. Visitors then climbed a small staircase to the captain's quarters, which featured actual chairs, tables and nautical equipment. From there, visitors climbed up to the poop deck, from which point they observed the battle, as though it were going on. The leaflet describing the attraction exclaimed, "All around there were flames, smoke, noise" although the room was neither actually engulfed in flames and smoke nor filled with the sounds of battle.[18] In effect, the leaflets, which appear to have been distributed at the entrance to a panorama, used narrative to boost the display's visual realism.

Spectators boarded a ship that was meant to be actually in the midst of the combat. Langlois's attraction, described as a "tour de force of art . . . and of an ingenious skill to arrive at the maximum illusion," proved a highly successful formula.[19] He followed it with several other panoramas in a new building on the Champs-Elysées opened in 1838 with battles such as Sebastopol and Solferino, the capture of Algiers or Moscow on fire.

If Langlois improved the panorama-effect—by placing spectators within the action and incorporating "real" sets and objects—two of Prévost's students, Bouton and Daguerre (better-known for his contributions to the development of photography), began to address another element that would aid the project of verisimilitude: the incorporation of motion into the spectacle. In a building on the rue Sanson, right off the place du Château-d'Eau (now the place de la République), crowds in July 1822 attended the diorama. It was of the diorama that David

17. Hittorf, "Description de la rotonde des panoramas," in *Revue générale de l'architecture* 2 (1841): 502.
18. Description of panorama of Navarino, BHVP, AA 103.
19. Hittorf, "Description de la rotonde," 502.

was alleged to have said to his students, "Truly, gentlemen, you should come here to study nature."[20] Seated as though in a theater, spectators watched as an enormous painted canvas whose borders they could not see (it was 20 meters wide and 13 meters high) represented scenes that appeared to move. The canvas stood thirty to thirty-five feet from the spectators and the scene often contained life-sized props in the foreground such as stuffed and mounted goats or a chalet for a scene depicting the Alps. Daguerre, a well known set designer for the Opéra, among other theaters, used theatrical lighting against this painted backdrop to create the effect of motion. Lauding the improvements of the diorama over the panorama, one observer explained its qualities:

Its goal is to resolve the problem that has been recognized for a long time and has remained unsolved; to find and gather the means by which, through imitation, to render nature as it is seen, that is to say to incorporate the changes over time produced by wind, light, mist. . . . Their project was never to produce general views, but only interesting perspectives.[21]

At each "showing" spectators watched two programs, one an interior and the other a landscape. For example, when the diorama opened in 1822, visitors saw the interior of Trinity Chapel at Canterbury Cathedral and also Sarnen Valley in Switzerland.[22] The change in scenes, which were separated by partitions that were not apparent to the audience, took place through the rotation of the entire seating area, which was suspended on rollers. Thus, while the actual tableau seemed to move through lighting, the building moved and also featured change by showing two different scenes.

Daguerre, in 1831, introduced the *diorama à double effet*, which incorporated the illusion of significant temporal change into each scene, injecting a narrative progression into what might have been thought of as a freeze frame. Using one canvas painted on both sides, which he lit first from the front and then from the back, Daguerre represented one site changing over time. The first of these featured midnight mass at St-Etienne du Mont. The scene opened with a view of the empty

20. Scott Wilcox, "The Panorama and Related Exhibitions in London" (Master's thesis, University of Edinburgh, 1976). I thank Ralph Hyde of the Guildhall Library, London, for access to this thesis. See also Ralph Hyde, *Panoramania: The Art and Entertainment of the 'All-Embracing View'* (London: Trefoil Publications, 1988).

21. "Notice sur les panoramas et dioramas," 211.

22. Other subjects included the port of Brest, Chartres cathedral, Holyrood in England, the port Santa María in Spain, Roslyn Abbey in Scotland, Rouen in fog and snow, the environs of Paris near Meudon. Ibid., 215.

church interior during daylight. Eventually night falls, the sanctuary is illuminated with candles and the pews fill with people.

The diorama's success prompted Bouton to go to London to open a diorama in Leicester Square which featured such scenes as Napoleon's tomb at St. Helena, St. Peter's in Rome and Goldau Valley in Switzerland.[23] The diorama on the rue Sanson burned down in 1839, and Bouton reopened it in 1843 on the boulevard Bonne Nouvelle (Daguerre was at this time preoccupied with photography). The attraction continued to entice large crowds; as the *Moniteur universel* reported in 1845, "An enormous crowd visited the diorama" for the opening of a tableau representing St. Mark's in Venice.[24]

Because their novelty formed a basic part of their appeal, when it waned, so did public interest in panoramas and dioramas. Although there seems to have been no diorama after the 1850s, Langlois's panorama continued to be featured in the Champs-Elysées until the siege of Paris in 1871. Another limit on the proliferation of such spectacles in the first half of the century was the relationship between wages and admission prices which limited the attractions' potential clientele.

In the 1870s Philippoteaux's painting of the defense of Paris, which had been commissioned during the armistice and opened in January 1873, was the sole panorama that could be seen in Paris. Continuing battle thematics that had become standard panorama fare, the tableau featured a heroic but devastated city. A great success, it remained open for ten years, most likely because it was the only attraction of its kind and because of the patriotic and commemorative purposes it seemed to serve.

Visitors were guided through and told they were inside the fort of Issy. Conceding that the panorama was not a "pure art object" but rather a "work of sensations" the reviewer for *La République française,* described how "the earth, the stones, the destroyed trees, cry eternal hatred louder and longer than human lungs could. Nature, herself, never becomes hoarse from moaning of her sadness and mourning."[25] The painting, copied from photographs, attempted to capture nature, in which could be found the real signs of the devastation of the siege.

Yet the reviewer explained how the panorama brought back his own memories of starvation, of salads made from grass, of doing the wash-

23. Altick, *Shows of London,* 172. It remained open until 1853.
24. *Le Moniteur universel,* June 10, 1845.
25. *La République Française,* February 24, 1873.

ing in the St-Sulpice fountain in the freezing night air surrounded by bombardment, of watching a countess wait among the common people to receive a grain of rice from the city coffers. "I remember . . . that spontaneous fusion of classes, those unexpected friendships cemented by the blood of the country bled dry." Rather than a simply personal memory, he also remembers the way the siege broke down barriers among Parisians. Panoramas, I suggest, did the same thing.

Fin-de-siècle *Panoramania*

Panoramas can be contextualized as part of the general growth of commercial entertainment during the period, benefiting from the larger audience of tourists who traveled to Paris, and from the increased accessibility of their exhibits that followed the drop in admission prices and the increase in worker salaries since the 1850s. But the panoramas of the 1880s and 1890s differed from their predecessors in ways that connect them more directly to the other cultural forms and representations of reality as spectacle already discussed in this book. First, they represented real-life events and people. Gone was the sublime quality of the diorama's representations. Second, they did so with an increasing attention to their technology. The "realism" of their varied technologies of representation described below increasingly hinged on the notion that to capture "life," a display had to reproduce it, not simply represent it. The display had to fit motion and the entire bodily experience of its viewers into the spectacle.

"We are entering *panoramania*," declared an article in *Le Voltaire* in 1881 in response to the opening of the third panorama in a year's time.[26] Although all discussions of the resurgent interest in panoramas indicate that critics were fully aware that panoramas were not really novel entertainment, they were exploited nonetheless as "novelties" and reviewed in terms that matched the era's particular construction of reality—a reality that went far beyond the optical effect produced by a "panoramic" canvas.

Many panoramas continued to thematize important battles. While battle paintings always served nationalistic zeal, French victories at Wagram, Navarino and Sebastopol dominated early panorama depictions,

---

26. *Le Voltaire*, January 3, 1881 cited in Robichon, "Les panoramas en France," 216.

at a time, it should be noted, when panorama audiences were composed of the aristocracy and wealthy bourgeoisie. During the panorama revival, most military panoramas represented French defeat. The predominant theme, needless to say, was French martyrdom at the hands of the Germans during the Franco-Prussian War. As already noted, the first panorama during the Third Republic represented the siege of Paris. Others followed. In 1881 "La bataille de Reichshoffen" (fig. 44) opened, depicting the battle known in France as the battle of Froeschwiller, in which 35,000 French troops fought 140,000 Germans in August 1870. The catalog that accompanied the display (and sold for 75 centimes) explained that "this battle lost, it was the invasion, France mortally wounded."[27]

Battle panoramas used defeat to spark nationalism. For example, the battles of Buzenval and Champigny, both fought on the outskirts of Paris during the Franco-Prussian War, also opened in the early 1880s. One newspaper reviewer explained that he told Edouard Détaille, the well known military painter responsible along with Neuville for the "Bataille de Champigny," that "I admire [this panorama], but you are instilling rage in people's hearts." Détaille responded by saying, "That's exactly what we wanted to do."[28] An English guidebook, clearly not quite understanding why the French would represent a defeat, described the panorama of the battle of Champigny as one in which "the French army gained a decided success over the besieging Germans."[29] The French newspaper, on the other hand, spoke of the value of remembering the hard times and chastised those people who objected to the depiction of such a subject as valuing the easy life and not wanting it disrupted by any unpleasantness.

Even those panoramas that depicted other military exploits referred back to the Franco-Prussian War. The painter Poilpot insisted that he decided to represent the great French victory at Iéna in 1806 under Napoleon when he visited the Berlin panorama that portrayed the Prussian victory at Sedan. He said, "And all of a sudden I thought of Iéna, almost the same battle but with the roles reversed."[30] Iéna would somehow

27. "La bataille de Reichshoffen," exhibit catalog (Paris: Société des Grands Panoramas, 1881), in BHVP, AA 103.
28. Newspaper article, no source, 1882. Ibid.
29. *Guide to Paris* (London: Cook, 1885), 81–82.
30. *Le Petit Journal*, April 15, 1899.

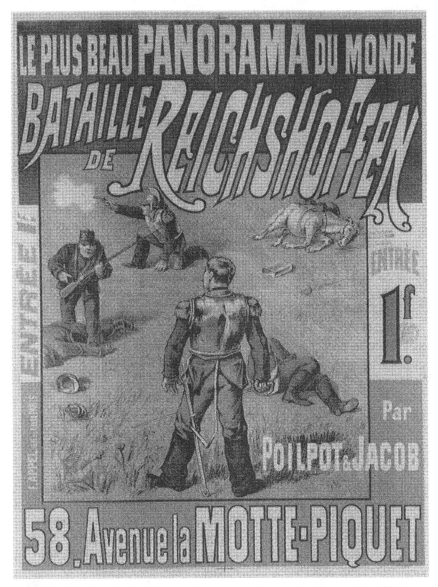

44. "La bataille de Reischoffen." Musée Carnavalet. © Photothèque des musées de la Ville de Paris.

compensate for Sedan. These attractions cultivated patriotism through collective victimization. Yet they could only achieve their patriotic ends by quite literally "moving" their visitors to such sentiments through the power of verisimilitude. The power to inspire visitors and cultivate patriotism and feelings of *revanchisme* came through the success of the attraction's technology of realistic illusion.[31]

Artists worked to enhance the verisimilitude of their panoramas throughout the century. The invention of photography helped in two ways. Some panorama painters painted from photographs and also projected enlarged slides onto the canvas and then traced the projected images. They also mixed three-dimensional objects with the painted canvas to improve the display's realism. Langlois had incorporated a "real" set in the 1830s that soon thereafter became standard in all such attractions. The 1880s and 1890s witnessed a proliferation of added objects as "realistic" details in the panoramas. For example, Poilpot used tinsel on his canvas for weapons and for the buttons on military costumes. Wax figures were scattered around the part of the exhibit between the canvas and the spectators' platform, strewn among the "realistic" sets. The catalog of the "Bataille de Reichshoffen" acknowledged the sculptor Jules Talrich for providing the wax figures that "represent the bodies strewn-out on the natural setting in such an astonishing and true manner."[32]

The caricaturist Robida mocked the increasing verisimilitude of panoramas in a cartoon featuring the "Panorama de la bataille de Champigny," adding several features that the panorama had not yet incorporated (fig. 45).[33] One of the captions explains that to give the sense of life during the siege people had to stay three days and have only one smoked herring each to eat. Another caption notes that the attraction was freezing cold and visitors could be drenched by a simulated rainstorm. With shells exploding and military music in the background, Robida concluded that "one deserved a military medal on exiting." He warned that shells actually exploded on the visitors' platform once in a while and that the simple word "exit" excited visitors to make a military charge for the door and to stay in formation outside on the

31. *Revanchisme* denotes the burning desire for vengeance against Germany after the Franco-Prussian War, including efforts to regain the lost provinces of Alsace and Lorraine.

32. "La bataille de Reichshoffen," BHVP, AA 103. Jules Talrich also sculpted the wax bust of the woman cut up into pieces (see chapter 2).

33. A. Robida, *La Caricature*, May 1882.

45. A. Robida, "Panorama de la bataille de Champigny." *La Caricature*, May 1882.

Champs-Elysées. Although clearly no panorama at the time went as far as Robida's parody, his point was clear: people delighted in the realistic recreation of this event.

The new panoramas delivered their "realism" by enveloping spectators. By manipulating the spectators' bodies, the scene intended to move the spirit as well. The collective body of the nation was to be built through the literal sensations of individual bodies. For at least some visitors to these attractions, the sensations mixed with memories they already had from childhood or even from firsthand experience with the moment represented. The spectacle thus embellished a narrative visitors already knew through visual representation and sensation.

But recent military defeats did not monopolize the explicitly didactic and patriotic attractions.[34] The exposition years of 1889 and 1900 served as moments for historical representation and commemoration in official and commercial culture. The centennial of the storming of the Bastille occasioned a panorama representing the event on the place de Mazas near the former site of the prison. In addition, it featured a reconstruction of the Bastille itself inside the exposition, a reconstruction of the Châtelet, an eighteenth-century Breton village, the opening of a Historical and Patriotic Museum that featured a panorama of the life of Joan of Arc located at the Pont de l'Alma just outside the exposition, and the celebrated "Histoire du siècle," a panoramic retrospective history of the century in France, representing the "celebrities" of each era.[35]

"L'histoire du siècle" is perhaps the most interesting of the historical panoramas because it departed from the traditional panorama formula of illustrating either a single moment or a timeless landscape. The canvas represented an entire century by portraying approximately six hundred fifty "noted figures from 1789–1889.[36] Grouped together by political regime, the clusters of "celebrities" were painted in the Tuileries gardens (where the actual panorama was located). The people represented were increasingly not celebrated for their roles in political life

---

34. The proliferation of military and historical panoramas also suggests that "historical" painting did not die to be replaced simply by genre painting after the midcentury, as Patricia Mainardi suggests. While she may be correct that it left the salon and "high art," some form survived in commercial culture. See Patricia Mainardi, *Art and Politics of the Second Empire* (New Haven: Yale University Press, 1989).

35. P. Bluysen, *Paris en 1889* (Paris: P. Arnould, 1890), 39–40.

36. According to *L'Art industriel,* November 5, 1888, not fewer than two thousand people were represented.

46. Stevens and Gervex, "L'histoire du siècle" 1889. Bibliothèque historique de la ville de Paris.

but rather for their cultural and social status; the Third Republic constituency dominated by sheer number. The panorama's classification scheme was thus explicitly narrative in that it unfolded chronologically. The figure separating the start and finish of the tableau, posed next to two allegorical sculptures of France, one representing work and the other the defense of the fatherland, was none other than "the hinge of the entire century around which everyone else pivoted": Victor Hugo (fig. 46). The painters responsible for the tableau, Stevens and Gervex, explained that they chose Hugo because his birth in 1802 linked both centuries, but no doubt also because he was an appropriately republican symbol.

An article discussing the future attraction explained that the panorama would be "the exact representation of all the people who figured in the annals of the last one hundred years. Is it a panorama? Better, it's a museum of contemporary history."[37] Proud of the tableau's celebration of the contemporary regime, Gervex boasted of its educational value: "The schoolchildren of France themselves can know the principal groups, a publishing house even had the idea to reproduce it

37. *L'Evènement*, October 4, 1888.

on the covers of school notebooks."[38] Calling the display a museum and reprinting portions for schoolchildren indicates the extent of the panorama's didactic purposes; this panorama would edify as well as entertain.

The panorama's educational qualities seemed to compensate for the fact that the attraction did not provide the optical illusion that was most effectively rendered through painting bird's eye views and landscapes. Its "realism" resided in its thematic representation of "important" and genuine historical figures. "We cannot do enough . . . for the practical education of the people," explained one newspaper.[39] An American journalist summarized the display's value: "A visit means a pleasant hour and a better, because a more vivid and speaking knowledge of French history, than could be learnt in a twelve-month from the cyclopaedias."[40] Visually identifying each regime's celebrities somehow gave visitors a history lesson, as though seeing famous people conferred meaning in and of itself.

Although these military and historical tableaux of the 1880s and 1890s built on early nineteenth-century panorama themes, they rescripted them to fit neatly with the Third Republic agendas of *revanchiste* patriotism for the masses and universal education through popular history lessons. For the first time, however, panoramas attempted to capture contemporary life. The views of Paris that visitors had seen in the first panorama on the boulevard Montmartre may have been of the contemporary view from atop the Tuileries Palace, but the artist only consciously represented that particular view for the sake of creating verisimilitude. Visitors were meant to be fascinated by the illusion; the subject illustrated proved less engaging. Over time, the realism of the panorama seemed to rely less on its form and increasingly on its content, especially its depiction of social and human life as opposed to the spectacle of nature.[41]

By the 1880s panoramas began to serve as visual corollaries of the popular press. They represented particular moments of the daily events reported in newspapers: the czar's coronation or the visit by the president to the Russian fleet. A definition of panoramas and dioramas from

38. *Revue de Paris,* November 15, 1923, cited in Robichon, "Les panoramas en France," 497.

39. *L'Art industriel,* November 5, 1888.

40. *The New York Herald,* June 23, 1889, AA 103.

41. See Nicholas Green, *The Spectacle of Nature* (Manchester: Manchester University Press, 1990), on panoramas and nature earlier in the century.

47. Charles Castellani, "Le Tout-Paris," 1889. Bibliothèque historique de la ville de Paris.

the 1890s described their realism as entirely generated by the subjects they represented: "Scenes of current events have the knack of attracting the crowd that is still struck with emotion about a recent event, a catastrophe, an execution or a famous assassination. They reexamine the accident or the crime in a tableau which creates the illusion of reality."[42] Despite the fact that the illusion created by panorama painting was not as effective when portraying individuals and moments as opposed to landscapes, the influence of the press in delivering reality can be seen in many of the new panoramas.

The panorama craze of the 1880s and 1890s benefited from the same fascination with representing current events, modern life and celebrity that led to the great success of the wax museum. For example, Charles Castellani's "Tout Paris" offered a painted "pantheon of the moment." The tableau grouped Parisian celebrities at and around one of the symbols of the new Paris: the Opéra (fig. 47). The spectator was positioned facing the Opéra; the tableau's backdrop represented the Opéra, the adjacent boulevard des Capucines, the Grand Hôtel, the rue du Quatre

42. *Encyclopédie enfantine recommandée pour les écoles,* n.d., BHVP, AA 103.

septembre, the Café de la Paix and the Louvre at the end of the long avenue de l'Opéra. A review celebrated the choice of the place de l'Opéra: "no better place could have been chosen in this shining and noisy Paris to represent Parisian life in all its ardor, vigor and feverishness."[43] Unlike the more self-consciously uplifting panoramas, "Le Tout-Paris" was intended to satisfy public interest and curiosity—one that was clearly tied to boulevard and press culture. One review explained that the panorama would attract many people who "always wanted to know and see the poets, writers, painters, sculptors, actors and politicians whose names they read in the newspaper every day."[44] This gallery served as a visual corollary to print culture and allowed the spectator both access to and objectification of celebrities.

Unlike "L'histoire du siècle," popularity, familiarity and "Parisianness" seemed to guide Castellani in his choice of subjects. Characters were grouped in a sort of flexible taxonomy: the painters Gérôme and Poilpot were pictured with the architect Charles Garnier; Jules Chéret stood with Alfred Grévin.[45] Jules Claretie, the writer and director of the Comédie-Française, stood near the Opéra star Rosita Mauri. Louise Michel stood alone. The press was well represented: Mariani, then-owner of *Le Petit Journal,* Albert Wolff of *Le Figaro,* Henri Rochefort of *L'Intransigeant,* Arthur Meyer of *Le Gaulois,* and Aurélien Scholl, critic-at-large, among others. Despite the intended order and logic behind the groupings, Castellani explained in his memoirs that almost all the people represented complained about their placement in the panorama; most asked to be put alone and in the foreground.

Although politicians found their rightful place among the celebrities represented, the panorama's greatest controversy surrounded the presence of General Boulanger, whose political popularity had recently challenged the stability of the Third Republic. When the project began, *Le Figaro* reported that the painting would represent no particular political agenda: "The painter of this important work is bothered neither by coteries nor factions."[46] After the April 1889 elections and Boulanger's departure to Belgium, the government asked Castellani to delete Boulanger from the panorama. As one newspaper reported the official

43. *Le Figaro,* February 23, 1889.

44. *Le Petit Moniteur,* May 16, 1889.

45. Aside from their links to popular image-making, the placement of Chéret with Grévin seems a clear allusion to the Musée Grévin.

46. *Le Figaro,* February 23, 1889, cited in Robichon, "Les panoramas en France," 501.

objections, "M. Castellani gave General Boulanger a relatively important role, placing him in uniform in the foreground, while the President
of the Republic, M. Carnot, is represented half-hidden in a carriage, at
the back of the canvas."[47] Upon Castellani's refusal to change his panorama, the government simply prohibited the exhibition's opening.[48]
Facing financial ruin, the panorama's backers insisted that Castellani
back down. Eventually, Boulanger was replaced by a figure of the shah
of Persia. Another controversy then ensued because the Persians did
not want the shah placed next to M. Turquet, a Boulangist minister. In
the end, the shah was also erased, but only after being immortalized in
the panorama's catalog.[49]

The panorama faced other potential financial liabilities that resulted
in its foregoing many of the techniques that visitors had become accustomed to relying on as evidence of a panorama's verisimilitude. For example, it contained none of the foreground objects because its backers
wanted to keep costs to a minimum, fearing poor attendance because
of what they feared was a poor location. (Despite the fact that the panorama was located on the Esplanade des Invalides, within the actual exposition site, its site was nevertheless considered undesirable).[50] Castellani complained about the attraction: "We had neither accessories, nor
false terrains, nor any of the things that are absolutely indispensable for
producing what the public likes: trompe l'oeil and illusion."[51] The reviews of the panorama suggested, however, that the illusion of life
might be generated in other ways.

Popular despite the poor location that had worried its financial backers, the panorama remained open for the entire exposition, during
which time over three hundred thousand people visited it.[52] Aside from
celebrating the range and sheer number of celebrities represented, reviews noted the "the astonishing expression of activity and life that
animates the entire composition."[53] A simple circular painting, without
props and sets, we might imagine that it could not compete with other

47. Le Figaro, May 5, 1889, cited in Robichon, ibid., 502.

48. See The Graphic of May 1889, cited in Wilcox, "The Panorama and Related Exhibitions," 218.

49. Robichon, "Les panoramas en France," 502.

50. See Charles Castellani, Confidences d'un panoramiste (Paris: Maurice Dreyfous,
n.d.), 281.

51. Ibid., 281.

52. Rearick, Pleasures of the Belle Epoque, 173.

53. Le Rappel, March 12, 1889.

panoramas in terms of its verisimilitude. It was as though its subject matter somehow animated the composition itself. Another review described the panorama as though it were a freeze-frame—an instant captured:

seized while passing by in a carriage, on horseback, in groups, with even more truth than an instant photograph can give the idea of. What's more, isn't there the charm of color, the representation of gestures and looks, the entire Parisian spirit spread among the brilliant, animated crowd who is so lively that we have the perfect illusion of its movement and its reality?[54]

Why did Castellani's panorama receive so much praise when it broke with the conventions of panorama painting by foregrounding people as opposed to landscapes? Although the painting did not portray an actual moment, it depicted an idealized and ostensibly real moment in Parisian life that most Parisians and the readers of the daily press, above all, could imagine because of their familiarity with the location and the people populating it. The painting seemed "real" because it echoed a familiar narrative of the "real"—that of the Parisian press. Further, it reinforced the lionized image of a spectacular city: a glitzy and celebrity-filled whirl of sensation.

The lifelike qualities that were used as evidence of the display's realism—its trompe l'oeil effect, aided by its effacement of the panorama's status as representation, its use of scenery, including the placement of spectators on real boats, the use of props such as stuffed goats and wax figures, and its reliance on familiar narratives of contemporary life—in many ways matched the wax museum's standard of verisimilitude. The later panoramas, however, also sought literally to "animate" their displays by incorporating motion into them and in this way outpaced the wax museum. Several new panoramas took the idea of motion quite literally and attempted to simulate it to achieve greater verisimilitude.[55]

The first moving panorama involved the fleet of the Compagnie générale transatlantique; visitors boarded a recreation of the company's newest steamer, *La Touraine*.[56] Opened in May 1889 on the quai d'Orsay within the exposition grounds, the attraction received more than 1.3

54. *Le Courrier des Expositions,* March 1889.

55. The diorama incorporated motion even earlier but did so by representing it through special effects created through lighting.

56. Many of these attractions had sponsors, companies that marketed such trips on their modes of transport. This fact should serve as a corrective for those who associate corporate "entertainment" with twentieth-century America and the Disney theme parks, in particular.

million visitors.[57] Poilpot served as the artistic director of the display, which incorporated a view of the entire port of Le Havre in which visitors could see the company's eighty other ships harbored. The attraction also featured eleven other canvases and a coastal landscape that moved as the ship apparently went by. Passengers climbed aboard this life-sized reproduction of the ship through an elegant vestibule, walked up a set of stairs and out onto the captain's deck in the supposed open-air. Wax figures of crew members in lookout positions and of the captain describing the port to a female passenger mingled with live sailors and officers dressed in the uniforms of the Transatlantic Company.[58] Reviewers noted that "he [Poilpot] has succeeded in reconstituting scenes from life on board in its most minor details with surprising fidelity. . . . The artist has completely achieved his goal; he has mixed reality and fiction in such a way that we are practically fooled."[59] In his book about the 1889 exposition, Paul Bluysen described the trip once aboard:

La Touraine, thus loaded, left the port of Le Havre, and the décor through which she moved was not less beautiful than the steamer itself: the sea stretched out all around her, one saw different kinds of warships gathered, graceful fishing boats moving at a quick pace, even with the water level.

Further, the entire French coast circles by, from the elegant beach where one can pick out the Hotel Frascati to the pointe de la Hève jutting out in to the sea. One passes a charming hour on the deck of La Touraine, where one is reminded of wonderful summer outings, safe from abhorred lurching and pitching.[60]

What the review makes clear is that the coastline moved across the viewer's field of vision although it was constructed to work as though the spectators themselves were positioned on a moving boat. In addition, the reviewer celebrated the fact that the ride was even more pleasant than an actual boat trip because these simulated seas could be controlled and therefore remained calm.

With as many visitors as the attraction had, all paying the small sum of one franc, it should come as no surprise that reviewers remarked on the diversity of the crowd, which included peasants, workers (who had never seen the sea, the reviewer noted), bourgeois men and women, shopkeepers and diplomats.[61] Visitors of different classes must have had

57. Robichon, "Les panoramas en France," 504.
58. It is not clear whether they worked for the company or were hired actors.
59. Bluysen, Paris en 1889, 19.
60. Ibid., 20.
61. La Nature, June 15, 1889, cited in Robichon, "Les panoramas en France," 507.

divergent experiences on *La Touraine*. As Bluysen's review suggests, the trip might be evocative of "real" sea voyages already taken. Those visitors could judge the quality of the simulation. For others, it might be the first time that they had set foot on a "ship," and one imagines that the Compagnie générale transatlantique hoped that this would not be the last. Even if the panorama competed with the company's business by providing an easier, more comfortable and more affordable option, the company nonetheless made money from people who perhaps did not have the means, the time or even the interest to go on a real cruise.

Between 1892 and the next exposition in 1900, many attractions successfully simulated motion. Parisians could see projected moving images for the first time in the form of the *pantomimes lumineuses* at the Musée Grévin starting in October 1892. In 1894 they could see moving photographs in Edison's Kinetoscope and as of December 1895, the Lumière brothers' films could be seen at the Grand Café.[62] Entrepreneurs sought to incorporate moving pictures into already existing amusements because, as the following examples suggest, the entertaining qualities of moving pictures in their own right were not self-evident.

Rather than imagine that moving pictures threatened panoramas, entrepreneurs initially incorporated films into their displays with great enthusiasm. In 1898 Louis Régnault opened "Maerorama" on the boulevards across from the porte St-Martin. A simulated boat ride, it incorporated the moving platform idea that Poilpot had used in *Le Vengeur* and added compressed air to make wind and waves. The exhibitor, dressed in a captain's uniform, explained, "We announced that those susceptible to falling seasick should abstain."[63] The lights then dimmed, and instead of a painted canvas rolling by, visitors watched "movies" of coastal views photographed from boats: the Corsican coast, Africa, the Italian lakes and finally a view of Marseilles—where, after two toots of the ship's horn, passengers were asked to descend and allow other tourists, "eager to experience the wonders of 'Maerorama,'" to be given their chance.[64] Régnault presented a similar attraction at the 1900 exposition; there, passengers were seated in a funicular instead of on a boat.

Whether cinematic or mechanical, many of the attractions at the

---

62. See chapter 5 for the history of early cinema in Paris.

63. R. M. Arlaud, *Cinéma-bouffe* (Paris: Jacques Melot, n.d.), 66. I thank Jean-Jacques Meusy for this reference.

64. Ibid., 67.

1900 exposition emphasized simulating motion through voyage. Raoul Grimoin-Sanson's Cinéorama put passengers in a hot-air balloon and attempted to show them a "panoramic" view photographed by movie cameras.[65] But the advent of film did not replace mechanical panoramas. For example, at the exposition visitors could attend Hugo d'Alési's "Maréorama," a "living panorama,"[66] the "Tour du monde," an animated panorama-diorama sponsored by the Compagnie des Messageries maritimes, and the "Transsibérien," sponsored by the Compagnie internationale des Wagons-Lits, to name but a few.

The realism of these attractions derived from both the subject they represented and the technology that put passengers in the middle of things and simulated motion. "Maréorama" (figs. 48–49), which lasted half an hour and held as many as seven hundred spectators at once, offered a plausible itinerary to various ports. The boat departed from Villefranche and cruised the Mediterranean to the small port of Sousse on the Casbah, then traveled on to Naples, Venice, and finally arrived at Istanbul. Although the panorama compressed a long journey into less than an hour's time, the tableaux that passed across the passengers' fields of vision incorporated elements of temporality: Sousse was painted with the noon sun shining, Venice at sunset and Istanbul at sunrise. Between Venice and Istanbul passengers experienced a full-blown simulated storm complete with turbulence, water, the smell of the sea and thunder. Here, the tableaux literally moved, as did the spectacle through its incorporation of narrative. Suffice it to say that the enormous boat also rocked back and forth, with either calm or turbulence depending on the moment being represented. In fact, the prospectus suggested that the landscapes formed a secondary attraction, instead, "the great attraction, for the majority of the public, resides in the illusion of a boat ride . . . in the movement of the ship, in the foghorn's blast, in the smoking chimney, in the piercing wind."[67] The attraction, in order to "make an impact on all of the senses at once and to obtain the most complete realistic effect," featured a symphony played by an orchestra that could not be seen.[68] "Maréorama" multiplied the panorama's sensory address, becoming an experience for all

65. Many people describe the Cinéorama of 1900 but, as Jean-Jacques Meusy notes, it never worked. See Meusy, "L'énigme du cinéorama de l'exposition universelle de 1900," *Archives*, no. 3 (January 1991).

66. "Maréorama" prospectus, BHVP, AA 122.

67. Ibid., 4.

68. BHVP, AA 103, "Maréorama" program.

48. "Maréorama," 1900. Bibliothèque historique de la ville de Paris.

49. "Maréorama," 1900. Bibliothèque historique de la ville de Paris.

the senses. The measure of the attraction's reality resided in its push beyond visual simulation. If the attraction promised to transport spectators elsewhere, they would now experience the ride.

Other attractions suggest that multiple-sense realism and motion dominated the technologies of the panoramas at the exposition. The "Transsibérien"—a cross between the "Transatlantique" from 1889, because its train was a replica of one belonging to the Compagnie des Wagons-Lits, and "Maréorama," because the train and the panorama moved—shortened a two-week trip from Moscow to Peking to forty-five minutes (fig. 50). This attraction employed the same techniques as "Maréorama" but also simulated the landscape as it would appear from the window of a train—with foregrounded objects that moved by at a more rapid pace than objects at a distance. The panorama used four separate backdrops operating at different speeds to approximate a single vista.

The novelty of the "Tour du monde—panorama-diorama animé" resided in its combination of almost every available attraction (fig. 51). Sponsored by the Compagnie des Messageries maritimes, it formed a "multiplex" *avant la lettre*. The enormous building stood in a central exposition location—next to the Eiffel Tower between the Esplanade des Invalides and the Champ de Mars, with its front door facing onto

50. "Le Transsibérien," 1900. Bibliothèque historique de la ville de Paris.

the main exposition square. The interior of this pagodalike building contained a restaurant and cafés, a three-hundred-seat theater, boutiques selling souvenirs and three floors of panoramas. The top-floor panorama offered a departure from Marseilles to view the most interesting stops on the company's itineraries: Spain, Greece, Istanbul, Syria, Egypt, Ceylon, Cambodia, China and Japan. Downstairs, two levels featured such big cities as Rome, the Kremlin in Moscow under a snowfall, Amsterdam at night, New York and Sydney. In the foreground of the panoramas, however, were living people from the country represented, some doing dances, others engaged in craft-making; altogether the attraction employed more than one hundred such performers.[69] More performers and "cinematographic views" of the places

69. "Le tour du monde. panorama-diorama animé." Prospectus, BHVP, AA 103. There were numerous displays of "indigenous peoples" at the expositions, the most popular of which recreated a Cairo street, complete with cafés featuring belly dancers, "ethnic" food and a souk with cheap objects to purchase. On the Middle East as exhibit site see Timothy Mitchell, *Colonizing Egypt* (Berkeley: University of California Press, 1991); and Zeynep Celik, *Displaying the Orient* (Berkeley: University of California Press, 1992); and Sylviane Leprun, *Le théâtre des colonies* (Paris: Edition L'Harmattan, 1986).

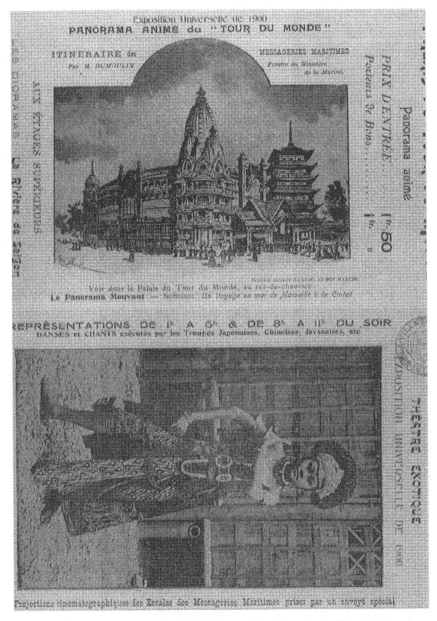

51. "Tour du monde," 1900. Bibliothèque historique de la ville de Paris.

represented in panorama form could be seen in the theater. This panorama to end all panoramas worked by juxtaposing multiple forms: painted panoramas, moving pictures, live performers—creating a realistic effect almost through sheer accumulation.

Panoramas and similar entertainments reproduced reality in a variety of ways: by relying on spectator-generated optical illusions, by echoing other realist genres such as the press and the wax museum, and by mechanically simulating motion. Rather than a technological march toward ever-more perfectly realistic reproduction and the invention of cinema, we find spectacles that technologically and discursively generated reality and its concomitant animation in a variety of ways between 1870 and 1900. What is interesting about the o-rama form is the way that it kept meeting the challenges from other forms of entertainment, such as the wax museum and film, by incorporating them. Panoramas such as the "Tour du monde" persisted in many ways in amusement parks, world's fairs and today at such places as the Epcot Center throughout this century. And wax museums (and the "animatronics" that followed them) remain a popular tourist attraction in most cities.

That said, few would contest the fact that cinema eventually overshadowed the popularity of panoramas and even wax museums in the early years of the twentieth century as the premier novelty attraction. The next chapter chronicles the emergence of film in the context of the visual culture of fin-de-siècle Paris detailed in this book thus far, and, in particular, at the Musée Grévin. Cinema's success resided neither in its originality nor in its innovative technology, but rather in the way it materialized the inherently cinematic culture of the Parisian fin de siècle.

CHAPTER 5

From *Journal plastique* to *Journal lumineux*

Early Cinema and Spectacular Reality

On June 21, 1916, the Musée Grévin's stockholders finally voted on an issue that they had begun discussing in March 1914, before the outbreak of war in August. They decided to transform the museum's ground floor into a palatial one-thousand-seat movie theater to be constructed by the celebrated architects the Perret brothers.[1] This decision had little to do with the war that raged not far from the museum's doors on the boulevard Montmartre. Rather, it came as a late recognition of what was already well known in Paris by 1916: cinema had eclipsed almost every form of technologically mediated entertainment and certainly competed with and was often incorporated into live entertainment, especially in music halls and café-concerts.[2] Less than a year after the stockholders' important decision, Gabriel Thomas informed them that the planned changes at the wax museum would not occur: "We asked the police prefect for the necessary permission to make the changes. It was much to my surprise that after a wait of several months, we met with a formal veto although all our contact with the appropriate offices had presaged approval."[3] The museum thus gave up

1. Because the Perret brothers designed the Théâtre des Champs-Elysées, they knew the museum's director, Gabriel Thomas. I acknowledge here the collaboration of Jean-Jacques Meusy (Centre national de la recherche scientifique, and Université de Paris VII), to whom I am indebted for much of my initial knowledge of early French cinema.
2. See Regina Sweeney, "Harmony and Disharmony: French Singing and Musical Entertainment during the Great War" (Ph.D. diss., University of California, Berkeley, 1992); and Abel, *Ciné Goes to Town*.
3. MGAG, March 28, 1917.

its hopes of becoming a movie theater and returned to what had been its main business for more than twenty-five years: representing current and historical events through wax tableaux, offering such scenes as "Life in the Trenches at Ablain-Saint-Nazaire" and "The Heroic Exodus from Serbia."

The year 1916 hardly marks the beginning of the museum's interest in projected moving images, however. Even before the Lumière brothers' *cinématographe* thrilled Parisians in late 1895, visitors to the Musée Grévin had been delighting for three years in Emile Reynaud's animated images, the *pantomimes lumineuses*. The Musée Grévin was, in fact, the first entertainment emporium in the world in which audiences paid to see projected moving images. From the early 1890s on, Gabriel Thomas attempted to use projected animation and later cinema, to keep the Musée Grévin on the cutting edge of realist entertainments in Paris, laying bare the centrality of novelty and profitability to the institution's existence.

This chapter delineates the history of projected moving images at the Musée Grévin because it provides a prism through which to see cinema's origins as part of a broader cultural climate that demanded "the real" as a spectacle. Rather than understand the history of cinema from the perspective of the technology of the cinematic apparatus—as an expression of a technological imperative—I frame cinematic spectatorship within its late nineteenth-century context. All cinema, and in this case, early cinema, is embedded in a variety of cultural forms and practices that producers and spectators alike bring to the cinematic experience. This assumption is particularly crucial for the study of cinema in its initial moments because spectators clearly did not bring conventions already learned by watching cinema, to the cinema.

To contextualize early cinema as part of a visual culture that included such phenomena as the mass press, the morgue, panoramas, dioramas and wax museums is not at all to detract from the specificity of film. Quite the contrary. It offers the means to explain why and how cinema marked an unprecedented crossroads of the culture of modernity. It arose from and existed in the intertwining of modernity's component parts: technology mediated by visual and cognitive stimulation; the re-presentation of reality enabled by technology; and an urban, commercial and mass-produced technique designed as the seizure of continuous movement. In providing a crucible for elements already evident in other aspects of modern culture, cinema accidentally outpaced these other forms, ending up as far more than just another novel gadget.[4]

Cinema histories that focus exclusively on film, whether on its reception or production, divorce it from other contemporaneous forms of cultural production with which it and its audiences were no doubt in dialogue. The cinematic "effect," like that of the panorama or wax museum, is not simply technologically generated. Viewers brought rich and complicated habits of viewing and comprehensions of reality and its representations, cultivated in other places, to the cinema. Despite the different relations created between spectator and spectacle among the numerous cultural forms discussed throughout this book, the history of early cinema suggests great continuities alongside the obvious differences. Cinema incorporated the mobilized gaze, used narrativity to sustain the realism of spectacle, offered a highly mediated and technological representation of reality, mastered novelty and rapid change. But the history of cinematic spectatorship cannot be recounted simply in terms of the connection between an individual spectator and a film. For it is necessarily among a crowd that we find the cinematic spectator.

From *Journal plastique* to *Journal lumineux*

In addition to its wax tableaux, the Musée Grévin, like most institutions of early mass culture, had always offered a series of attractions. The opening of each new attraction, the museum's directors argued, served as an occasion for publicity and helped renew public interest in the institution. The attractions thus promoted the museum's dedication to novelty. All revolved around a form of trompe l'oeil; visitors happily and willingly watched, knowing all along that what they saw was an illusion whose effect was often enhanced through its thematization of actual people and events.

Long before the Musée Grévin opened its doors, however, Parisians were familiar with optical devices in which fixed images could be given the illusion of movement. Joseph Plateau's Phénakistoscope (1832) and William George Horner's Zootrope (1834) were originally developed as

---

4. This is the argument of the joint introduction to Charney and Schwartz, ed., *Cinema and the Invention of Modern Life*, 10.

part of the scientific study of the persistence of visual images.[5] These technologies have been considered critical in the development of modern vision because they located vision in the subjectivity of the observer.[6] But persistence of vision also animated images and thus intersected with the public fascination with realistic representation because it could render images lifelike. What characterized the modernity of moving pictures is the technologically mediated reality that assembled individual observers in groups as members of an audience.

In technical histories of cinema, Emile Reynaud, inventor of the Praxinoscope, serves as a key figure. Through him the Musée Grévin was first linked to what became the cinema. Reynaud's device, designed for observation by several people at once, allowed images to remain before viewers' eyes at all times. He used mirrors to reflect his drawn images, which rotated on the inside of a drum, evincing a high degree of luminosity—eventually making projection possible. With the help of an "honorable mention" at the 1878 exposition, Reynaud sold many Praxinoscopes and patented another device in 1888, the *théâtre optique*. Mirrors still occupied this new machine's center, but the images now appeared, transparent and colored by hand, on a manually assembled band that could be of any length and was wound on feed and take-up bobbins instead of being fixed onto the borders of the drum. Reynaud perforated his band, which wound through the drum's teeth, assuring a stable image.[7] Finally, he used a projection lantern (the equivalent of a slide projector) to project the scene's backdrop for the drawn images. Unlike so many of the optical devices that preceded Reynaud's, these moving images could be projected for large groups of people. Reynaud's invention combined the century-long interest in synthesized motion with the late nineteenth-century emphasis on realist display for a wide audience.

Even before meeting Emile Reynaud, Gabriel Thomas had begun to explore the possibilities of showing projected moving images at the Musée Grévin. In August 1891 he wrote to Etienne-Jules Marey, whose

---

5. Alan Williams, *Republic of Images.* For the scientific interest in the persistence of visual images see Crary, *Techniques of the Observer;* and Lisa Cartwright, "'Experiments of Destruction': Cinematic Inscriptions of Physiology," *Representations* 40 (fall 1992): 129–52. For a technological archaelogy of film, see Laurent Mannoni, *Le grand art de la lumière et de l'ombre: archéologie du cinéma* (Paris: Nathan, 1985).

6. See Crary, *Techniques of the Observer.*

7. There was no flexible celluloid film yet.

work in motion studies led to the invention of the *chronophotographe*—what amounted to the first motion-picture camera of sorts—to inquire whether his images could be projected. Unfortunately, because Marey's system offered no exact means for registration (no perforations in the film creating a standard frame of reference), it offered no hope of projecting synthesized motion.

A year later Emile Reynaud contacted the Musée Grévin in the hope of finding a place to feature his *théâtre optique*. The two parties signed a contract on October 11, 1892, guaranteeing the museum a five-year monopoly on the use of Reynaud's machine and its bands, and paying Reynaud 500 francs a month and 10 percent of the revenue generated by the fifty centimes' additional admission charge for the show. The terms of the agreement specified that Reynaud would perform between three o'clock and six o'clock and then from eight o'clock to eleven o'clock, at least five times daily on weekdays and twelve times on Sundays and holidays, or more often if there were sufficient demand. Reynaud was to supply all the equipment necessary for the show and the museum to pay for the musical accompaniment by Gaston Paulin, the maintenance and lighting of the theater (the Cabinet fantastique, where the magician Carmelli had been performing) and all publicity costs. Reynaud was required to renew his show, which initially consisted of three bands: *Pauvre Pierrot, Clown et ses chiens* and *Un bon bock*, lasting approximately a half an hour, at least once annually.[8]

Days before the inauguration of the new show, the museum plastered the city with a colorful Jules Chéret poster advertising the *pantomimes lumineuses*, which premiered October 28, 1892. *Le Figaro* noted its opening in an article that most probably was paid copy:

The Musée Grévin has just opened a very interesting and absolutely unprecedented show. They are the *pantomimes lumineuses* of M. Emile Reynaud, inventor of the *théâtre optique*. By an ingenious method, M. Reynaud created characters with expressions and movements so perfect that they give the complete illusion of life. . . . The Musée Grévin has a winner here.[9]

Shortly after the show opened, the museum gave Reynaud permission to perform for one evening at a charity event in Rouen. A local news-

8. All material drawn from MGCA.
9. *Le Figaro,* October 29, 1892.

paper there, in what is far less likely a piece of paid advertising, also remarked on what it noted were the lifelike qualities of these hand-drawn animations: "On a screen, M. Reynaud projects life-size characters, who, through an ingenious contrivance seem endowed with life; [they] go, come, move, rush forward, change positions, pose, make proclamations, and so on, just like an actual mime and much more captivating because it is only an optical illusion."[10] In an article about the *pantomimes lumineuses,* the scientific writer Henri de Parville noted that the characters "played their roles as though they were flesh and blood."[11]

Aside from the striking reality that viewers attributed to the moving images, Reynaud's attraction also offered viewers a sustained narrative that bolstered its synthesizing effect. The journalist Max de Nansouty noted, "these are entire scenes that unravel before their eyes."[12] When it opened in 1892, two of the three strips offered narrative presentations, *Pauvre Pierrot,* a band of five hundred images and thirty-six meters long, lasting between ten and twelve minutes, recounted a classic pantomime in which Pierrot and Arlequin fight for Colombine's attention. The short that followed, *Le clown et ses chiens* (three hundred images and twenty-two meters long), included the standard "tricks" of other optical devices: dogs standing, jumping through hoops, and walking on balls. The third band, *Un bon bock* (700 images, 50 meters and twelve to fifteen minutes long), presented a seemingly more contemporary tale in which a restaurant kitchen boy drinks various customers' drinks while they are distracted by a series of antics.[13] Like the initial interest in panoramas, however, the reviewers' favorable comments reveal an interest in the technology's engagement in realistic illusion (in this case the synthesis of motion), rather than in the particular narratives recounted in the three strips.

The show was a great success. Thomas reported at the annual meeting of stockholders that "Emile Reynaud's *pantomimes lumineuses* have conquered our public. . . . This show, as charming as it is ingenious, is

---

10. December 3, 1892, cited in Cerham, *Anthologie du cinéma,* 240.

11. *Le Journal des débats,* April 3, 1895, cited in Maurice Noverre, *Emile Reynaud: sa vie et ses travaux* (Brest: Chez l'Auteur, 1926), 49.

12. *Le Petit Temps,* May 15, 1895, cited in ibid., 50.

13. That Reynaud's bands were narrative suggests that the spectacle of the illusion of synthesized motion, a sort of "cinema of attractions," as Tom Gunning has called early cinema, already combined with narrative practice as early as the *pantomimes lumineuses.* See Gunning, "The Cinema of Attractions: Early Film and Its Spectator and the Avant-Garde," in *Early Cinema: Space, Frame, Narrative,* ed. Thomas Elsaesser (London: British Film Institute, 1990), 56–63.

one of the museum's allures."[14] Visitors to the museum packed the theater to watch the bands and hear Gaston Paulin's musical accompaniment. Yet by April 1893 the museum directors began to complain that Reynaud had neither changed his show nor properly repaired the bands whose frequent use was simply wearing them out. Reynaud's illustrations, all of which were painted by hand, involved very time-consuming labor, for which his daily work at the museum simply did not allow. The museum decided to terminate Reynaud's contract, arguing that "the principal attraction of the *pantomimes lumineuses* was supposed to reside in their frequent renewal."[15] In March 1894 the museum rehired Carmelli the magician, and Reynaud took a leave from the museum to prepare new bands.

While Reynaud was busy hand-drawing a new band called *Autour d'une cabine*, Parisians gathered at 20, boulevard Poissonnière to marvel at the Kinetoscope, Thomas Edison's invention that arrived in France during the summer of 1894. For twenty-five centimes, spectators peeped into a box that stood over five feet tall and watched small animated photographs that lasted all of thirty seconds. Edison's images were viewed through a rotating slotted disc, which created dim images that could therefore not be projected. The Musée Grévin showed no interest in acquiring such a machine, in no small measure because its images could be viewed by only one person at a time.

Thomas pressed forward, however, more determined than ever before to find a way for the museum to project moving photographic images. In the minutes of a meeting on November 21, 1894, the directors remarked:

Given the success obtained by Edison's Kinetoscope, we expressed our interest, once again, to Emile Reynaud, about the possibility of adapting his *théâtre optique* with the use of projected snapshots. Having agreed on principle to study the problem, Thomas has been asked to put Reynaud in touch with M. Demeny, Marey's former assistant and member of the Institut [de France], whose work on snapshots has acquired universal renown.[16]

The idea of adapting Reynaud's *théâtre optique* by using snapshots taken with a *chronophotographe* had already been suggested two years earlier by a journalist, G. Tissandier, who wrote for the popular science magazine *La Nature*. "The *théâtre optique*," he noted, "seems to be the

14. MGAG, March 20, 1893.
15. MGCA, November 22, 1893.
16. Ibid., November 21, 1894.

ideal machine for the synthesis of a series of successive photographs."[17] But Reynaud believed that his drawings held greater artistic merit than photography ever would, and so he never tinkered with photography until the museum demanded that he do so.

Demeny was slow to respond to the museum's request for help. Six months after the initial request, the directors asked Thomas to "persist with Demeny to experiment with projected photographs, which would either perfect or replace the *théâtre optique*."[18] A month later Demeny met with the museum administration and explained his problem to them with great honesty, as the minutes of the meeting explain:

While sure of eventual success, given his prior research, he cannot continue his experiments using his own personal resources, and on the other hand, he cannot fix the sum the museum would have to advance him to construct the necessary machines needed to arrive at a definite success. Under these conditions, despite the advantages foreseen and the assured ownership of the invention, the administrators believe that they cannot undertake undetermined expenses.[19]

Relations between the museum and Demeny went no further.

By the second half of 1895, Gabriel Thomas became aware that the Lumière brothers, who made photographic plates in Lyons, possessed a machine that recorded and reproduced animated photographic images. They had demonstrated their *cinématographe* on March 22, 1895, at the Society for the Encouragement of National Industry and on July 11, 1895, at the offices of the *Revue des Sciences pures et appliquées*.[20] In November Thomas contacted Jules Carpentier, the Parisian machinist in charge of manufacturing the Lumières' machine:

The directors discussed the Lumière brothers' *cinématographe*. In response to their desire to see this machine used in the museum as soon as possible to project animated photographs, Gabriel Thomas reported his recent progress made in this matter, both with M. Carpentier and in his discussions with M. Reynaud. The directors are of the opinion that they should find a

17. *La Nature,* July 23, 1892. Reynaud himself imagined by 1880 that it would be possible to replace the Praxinoscope's drawings with photographs. See *Bulletin de la Société française de photographie* 26, no. 6 (June 1880).

18. MGCA, May 1, 1895.

19. Ibid., June 5, 1895.

20. The description of these events can be found in *La Revue générale des sciences,* July 30, 1895; *Le Moniteur de la photographie,* no. 13 (1895); and in the widely read *Nature,* August 31, 1895.

space specially constructed to facilitate the taking of the necessary snapshots for these projections and put it at these gentlemen's disposal.[21]

Carpentier could authorize nothing without the consent of the Lumières, and it was not, in all likelihood, until the celebrated showing on December 28, 1895, at the Salon Indien of the Grand Café that Thomas made contact with Antoine Lumière, their father, who directed this first public and commercial screening.

All cinema histories report that Gabriel Thomas attended this screening, along with Georges Méliès, the magician who directed the Théâtre Robert-Houdin, and the Isola brothers, all of whom offered to buy the machine.[22] Their proposals were in vain, as the Lumière father explained that he himself hoped to exploit the machine commercially. In fact, it was only a year later, in the face of a number of competing machines, that the Lumière family decided to offer their machine for sale on the market.

The success of the Lumière brothers' invention has been well documented. For a franc, viewers were treated to ten very short films—a program that in all lasted slightly under half an hour. Most of these films were simply shots of daily life such as the famous *Workers Leaving the Lumière Factory* and later in 1896 the *Arrival of a Train*. Although the technology was still very noisy and the image jumped a great deal, entrepreneurs such as Thomas foresaw great popularity and potential profitability.

He was thus pleased when early in 1896, Reynaud realized his first attempt at his *photo-peinture-animée* produced with a chronophotographe of his own design that he called the *photo-scénographe*.[23] He presented this to the museum at the end of March, and they decided to help him with costs in order to ready the technology for the public as quickly as possible.[24] The museum searched for a theme that was al-

21. MGCA, November 27, 1895.

22. See Meusy, *Paris-Palaces*, 24; Abel, *Ciné Goes to Town*; Alan Williams, *Republic of Images*; Charles Musser, *The Emergence of Cinema: The American Cinema to 1907* (New York: Scribner's, 1990), Jacques Deslandes, *Histoire comparée du cinéma* (Paris: Casterman, 1969); Emanuelle Toulet, *Cinématographe: l'invention du siècle* (Paris: Découvertes Gallimard, 1988), among others. The Isola brothers were magicians who later ran the Folies-Bergères and the Olympia music halls.

23. See Noverre, *Emile Reynaud;* and Pierre Bracquemond, "Emile Reynaud: peintre de films," *La Cinémathèque française* 12 (August 1986).

24. MGCA, March 30, 1896.

ready familiar to audiences and so convinced the popular clown stars of the Nouveau Cirque, Footit and Chocolat, to perform a comical scene, *William Tell,* in which Footit drenches Chocolat with a water pistol.[25] Reynaud's method of assembly remained the same as it had been with the *pantomimes lumineuses.* He selected various essential shots, enlarged and colored them and mounted them on the flexible and perforated band. The process seemed an improvement over drawing each image by hand in terms of the amount of labor required, but it remained essentially artisanal and a far more labor-intensive process than that used by the Lumière brothers.[26]

Given its overwhelming success, the museum put Reynaud to work on another film, *The First Cigar,* which featured the actor Félix Galipaux. Years later, the actor described the experience of making the film:

During the pantomime, a machine, of which all I could see was the copper box and the lens, was placed several meters in front of me, and a serious fellow regularly turned a handle with a steady hand: that was Emile Reynaud and his *photo-scénographe.* . . . A little while later, people were applauding me at the Musée Grévin. . . . I seemed alive, strikingly real.[27]

Galipaux's memory no doubt reflects what fascinated viewers about *The First Cigar:* his stage routine could be reanimated. In film, audiences would revel as they had in wax figures, in the lifelike and the real.

The museum added *The First Cigar* to its program in July 1897, yet despite its success, Reynaud's new bands and his use of photography did not really produce what Thomas and the museum's directors wanted: a show that could be rapidly changed, permitting the projection of current events with almost no delay, thereby complementing the wax tableaux that cost a great deal of time and money to prepare. This explains why Thomas continued to search for another projection machine.

In the meantime, the *cinématographe* enjoyed an enormous success. Police had to control the crowds on the boulevard des Capucines outside the Salon Indien, where each half-hour from ten in the morning to eleven at night, Parisians lined up to see the Lumière brothers' attrac-

---

25. Interestingly, the scene was shot against a black backdrop because Reynaud foresaw hand-drawing a garden in the background.

26. One advantage Reynaud had was that his bands lasted longer than the Lumière brothers' thirty-second to one-minute bands.

27. Noverre, *Emile Reynaud,* 57.

tion.[28] Not long after, in early 1896, people could see the *cinématographe* in a special room at the music hall the Olympia, at the café-concert the Eldorado, at the department store the Grands Magasins Dufayel and in a small space near the porte St-Martin at 6, boulevard St-Denis. A program from the Magasins Dufayel theater dated 1909 explained that the cinema was a great success: "because it captures the record of reality . . . it defies all competition, and important events are often represented the same day that they happen."[29] It not only reanimated life, it could and would be an important mediator in the representation of current events, that fundamentally nineteenth-century version of reality.

Antoine Lumière sent exhibitors all over the globe, but the Lumière monopoly on projected moving images was not to last long. In fact, in April 1896 "animated photographs" could be seen at the Théâtre Isola (although with what technology no one is quite sure) and at the Théâtre Robert-Houdin, where Méliès used a projector that he probably bought from William Paul in London, which he called a Kinétographe Robert-Houdin.[30] Soon different machines projected moving photographs all over the *grands boulevards:* at the Musée Oller, a wax museum in the basement of the Olympia, in the basement of the theater Le Petit Casino (next door to the Musée Grévin) and at the Grand Café de la Paix in the place de l'Opéra, most notably.[31] The quality of the projections varied tremendously, but these exhibitors capitalized on the fact that the Lumière brothers would not sell their machine.[32]

In September 1896 the directors of the Musée Grévin attended a demonstration of the *cinographoscope* by the Pipon brothers in a back room at the Olympia—a machine that they believed "offered no progress over the Lumière brothers' machine."[33] In early 1897 they met with a M. Leroy and Clément Maurice, a collaborator of the Lumières', when the machine was finally placed on the market for sale. By this

28. *Le Gaulois,* February 23, 1896. When things calmed down, showings were offered from 2 PM to 6 PM and from 8:30 PM to 11 PM.

29. Magasins Dufayel program, 1909. BHVP, AA.

30. Soon thereafter Méliès patented his own machine, the Kinétographe Robert-Houdin, which could register images as well as project them, and put it on the market in August or September.

31. For the definitive compilation of sites of cinematic exhibition, see Meusy, *Paris-Palaces.*

32. *Le Gaulois,* November 14, 1896. Demeny eventually perfected a machine to which Léon Gaumont bought the rights. See Alan Williams, *Republic of Images,* 22.

33. MGCA, September 23, 1896.

point, however, the novelty of projected moving photographs had begun to wear off (except among itinerant fairground exhibitors and audiences), and the museum hesitated to buy a Lumière projector. The museum scouted for technologies better than the *cinématographe,* most notably that of Paul Nadar, the son of the famous photographer Félix. His machine did not meet their satisfaction, however, because "the noise of the gears makes the projector . . . absolutely impractical."[34]

During that spring, on May 4, 1897, the fire caused by the *cinématographe* at the society charity event, the Bazar de la Charité, in which 120 aristocrats (mostly women) died, did not help the nascent film industry—or any institutions of commercial entertainment, for that matter. Thomas summarized in his annual report to the museum's stockholders that the fire at the Bazar de la Charité "was the cause of great worry for all in the entertainment business."[35]

In the meantime Reynaud continued his daily shows at the museum, which included both his hand-drawn projections and those featuring Footit and Chocolat and Galipaux. In June 1898 Léon Gaumont, who originally worked for Jules Carpentier, the manufacturer of the Lumière brothers' machine, presented the museum directors with projections using his Demeny machine.[36] Six months later, the museum directors forced Reynaud to include Gaumont's film *The Funeral of Félix Faure* as part of his *pantomimes lumineuses.* The museum catalog announced this addition to the program, promising that their show would now feature "the most remarkable and most recent cinematic products . . . gathering together the latest perfections of a wonderful art and joining the piquancy of fantasy with the attraction of current events."[37] In the face of film, the museum began to tout Reynaud's films as "fantasy" while Gaumont's film offered the "attraction of current events." By February of the following year, after 12,800 shows, the museum terminated Reynaud's contract.

As part of the decision to change their show, the museum directors

34. Ibid., May 17, 1897.

35. MGAG, March 29, 1898 for the year 1897. The fire's effect is still debated. According to Jacques Deslandes and Jacques Richard, *Histoire comparée du cinéma,* vol. 2 (Paris: Casterman, 1969), the fire at the Bazar de la Charité did not slow the projections by itinerant showmen working the fairgrounds of France.

36. Note that the Musée Grévin dealt with Gaumont, who was from a humble background but had bourgeois aspirations, rather than Charles Pathé, who was always considered a parvenu and a "Barnum" of sorts.

37. *Catalogue du musée Grévin,* 114th ed. (Paris, 1898).

decided to renovate the Cabinet fantastique and transform it into a three-hundred-seat theater, designed by the well-known artist Antoine Bourdelle, with a stage whose curtain was to be painted by Jules Chéret. In the meantime, the museum replaced cinema with other attractions, including a phonograph provided by Charles Pathé and a ventriloquist who performed on the stage of the newly renovated theater.

In the industry generally, 1900–1901 proved a great failure in terms of technological innovations in cinema, and there followed little institutional expansion. In particular, the unprofitability of cinematic exhibition at the universal exposition of 1900 suggested that interest in the attraction had significantly subsided. In fact, receipts for the various cinematic attractions were much lower than for other attractions such as panoramas, dioramas and recreated villages.[38] Paris still had almost no movie theaters per se—the principal sites of cinematic exhibition continued to be the Cinématographe-Lumière de la porte St-Martin, which was renamed Le Select that year, and the Grands Magasins Dufayel, whose films were supplied by Pathé and Méliès. Méliès showed his own films at the Théâtre Robert-Houdin, although a fire at the end of January 1901 kept his doors closed most of that year. Finally, cinema could still be seen, as at the Musée Grévin, among the attractions at places such as the wax museum, the Musée de la porte St-Denis at 8, boulevard Bonne Nouvelle, and at various cafés-concerts and music halls. Thus the institutional sites of cinematic exhibition remained those of 1896.

Although it emerged and eventually returned to the urban context, between the years 1896 and 1901 cinema probably witnessed its greatest popularity as an attraction at itinerant fairgrounds. The *forains* (fairground operators) became interested in moving pictures as a novel attraction; an advertisement for a Kinetoscope in the trade newspaper *Le Voyageur forain* promised: "*Forains!* if you want to earn money, hurryup and experience the benefits of this latest novelty."[39] The number of *forains* who bought the machine was small, but progress was nevertheless steady. They often added the attraction to their barracks, which might also feature a wax museum or a "freakish" display. One such *forain* interested in the novelty was Charles Pathé, who in 1894 began

38. See Emanuelle Toulet, "Le cinéma à l'exposition universelle de 1900," *La Revue d'histoire moderne et contemporaine* 33 (April–June 1986); and Meusy, "L'enigme du cinéorama."

39. *Le Voyageur forain*, October 16, 1895.

exploiting the Edison phonograph at fairgrounds all over France and eventually pirated a projector designed by Henri Joly and went into the business of projected moving images.[40]

Actualities and Reality

The *forains* envisioned film as a complement to their displays in much the same way that the Musée Grévin did: as a better way to represent current events. Most scholars of early cinema agree that coverage of actuality dominated initial cinematic production. Explanations for the predominance of actualities range from cinema's novelty as an attraction (the content did not matter), to the form's technological limitations, to its relation to photographic realism. Invariably categorized as nonfiction film, as "unmanipulated activity of more or less general interest," according to the film historian Raymond Fielding,[41] actualities are taken as the point of origin for the documentary tradition and as an example of cinema without its twin incisors: camerawork and editing.

In late nineteenth-century Paris, however, *actualités* did not denote nonfiction in any straightforward way. Simply put, they did not record commonplace reality—nor were they ever taken to do so. Nor could the term reality itself be explained in a merely negative sense as "nonfiction." As we have seen on multiple occasions, the cultural context for using the term reality was one in which life itself was framed—in which events were experienced as what could be represented.[42] Rather than record commonplace reality, early *actualités* built on a certain repertoire in which people were accustomed to a mediated and spectacularized version of reality. Indeed, the subjects of actuality films followed in the tradition of wax tableau subjects that imitated the mass press re-presentation of reality as a spectacle.[43]

40. For more on Pathé's background see Abel, *Ciné Goes to Town*, 14–15; and Alan Williams, *Republic of Images*.

41. Richard A. Barsam, *Nonfiction Film: A Critical History* (Bloomington: Indiana University Press, 1992), 17.

42. See Timothy Mitchell, *Colonizing Egypt*.

43. In *Before the Nickelodeon* (Berkeley, University of California Press, 1991), Charles Musser also makes the connection between the waxworks (at the Eden Musée in New York) and early cinema. The Eden Musée, which opened after the Musée Grévin, may

Thus, when early in 1901 the Musée Grévin recommitted itself to cinema, it opened a *Journal lumineux,* what Gabriel Thomas called a "magic lantern of current events."[44] Louis Morin, an artist known for his shadow theater at the Chat Noir, directed this show that projected both slides and films. Thomas noted that receipts for the theater were increasing and that they had great hopes for their newest attraction. The following year, the museum built a 130-seat theater designed especially for cinema in its basement.

Thomas marveled at the success of the *Journal lumineux.* He explained why cinema so perfectly matched the museum's conceptualization:

The museum could never be the plastic newspaper imagined by its founders; plastic art, unless compromised, cannot respond to the ephemeral and insatiable demands of current events. For too long we have been fighting this idea and as a result have created mediocre works. But, we have understood that our idea was not an idle fancy, and thanks to the *cinématographe,* we have substituted for the idea of a plastic newspaper that of a luminous [bright] newspaper, which is already a reality.[45]

The museum promoted this concept to its visitors in its catalog announcing the *Journal lumineux,* describing it as a "happy complement of the plastic newspaper."[46] A few years later, the *Phono-Ciné-Gazette* also noted the relation between cinema and newspapers: "The *cinématographe* is the newspaper of tomorrow, it's the definitive form of magazines and illustrated reviews. . . . Each night music-hall audiences in big cities can go watch an important event of the same day."[47] The museum dedicated its cinematic representations exclusively to actualities—becoming the first place to specialize in what would later be known as "newsreels." Supplied by Gaumont, the museum program during one week in March 1901 for example, included *The Parade of Mid-Lent, The Marriage of the Queen of Holland, William II on Parade* and the *Funeral of Queen Victoria.*[48] The museum also financed some of Gaumont's films. Gaumont proposed to go to Toulon to film the

---

have been founded by Charles Bal, one of the principal investors in the Musée Grévin and member of the initial board of directors. The Musée Grévin archives has material on the museum's "American" branch, to which the museum often sent was tableaux.

44. MGAG, March 28, 1901.

45. Ibid., March 26, 1904.

46. *Catalogue illustré du musée Grévin,* 7th ed. (Paris, n.d.).

47. *Phono-Ciné-Gazette,* October 15, 1905, cited in Deslandes and Richard, *Histoire comparée du cinéma,* 523.

48. *L'Intransigeant,* March 24, 1901.

reception of the Italian fleet. The museum paid 200 francs to help cover his costs on top of the usual price for the film, and Gaumont guaranteed the museum a monopoly on the film for three months.[49] Newsreels of *The Official Cortège, The Duke of Genoa* and *The Italian Fleet* could be seen at the Musée Grévin from April 14, 1901, only three days after the event, a more speedy representation than wax tableaux could hope to conjure.

Other newsreels reconstituted events. Rather than send camera crews around the globe, Georges Méliès, master of the genre, made films in his studio in Montreuil that reenacted important events, such as a volcanic eruption in Martinique. He also made what might be called "preconstitutions" as well. For the 1902 coronation of Edward VII, he constructed a set of Westminister Abbey and made the film before the actual ceremony had even taken place. Reconstitutions followed in the tradition of the wax museum and its imitation of the illustrated press. As one Pathé filmmaker explained concerning a reconstitution: "with the document in hand that had already impressed the public: the image from *Le Petit Journal illustré* in color, I reconstituted the alleged 'real' décor."[50] The reconstitution film was, however, labeled an actuality film. Actualities were not merely a naive and technologically unsophisticated early film genre, but rather they were part of a late nineteenth-century trope in which real life was packaged, labeled as "current events" and narrated and incessantly represented in a variety of forms, including film.[51]

While Méliès entertained with reconstitutions, Pathé, the great entrepreneur of early film, also turned to familiar forms of realism. Posters for Pathé and company promised a *scène vécue* (true-life scene), and their slogan boasted that Pathé was "à la conquête du monde." If the wax museum had drawn on Naturalism, so did early films, sometimes by explicitly offering film versions of wax tableaux. For example, the great Pathé director Ferdinand Zecca made his name with a 1901 title, *L'histoire d'un crime*. Zecca based his film on the well known "serial novel" at the Musée Grévin of the same name. The 140-meter film

49. MGCA, April 5, 1901.

50. Cited in Deslandes and Richard, *Histoire comparée du cinéma*, 316.

51. See Jacques Malthête, "Les actualités reconstituées de Georges Méliès," *Archives*, no. 21 (March 1989). Méliès is perhaps best known for his *trucage* films. See Abel, *Ciné Goes to Town;* Deslandes, *Histoire comparée du cinema;* and Paolo Cherchi Usai, ed., *A Trip to the Movies: Georges Méliès, Filmmaker and Magician* (Rochester: International Museum of Photography at the George Eastman House, 1991).

lasted five to six minutes and replicated the museum tableaux with one exception. Whereas in the wax scene the convict plays cards in his cell, in the film he is shown engaging in an activity that would later become the primary metaphor of the filmic experience; he is dreaming.[52]

The film, it seems, was never shown at the Musée Grévin, because its supplier was Gaumont and its machine could not project Pathé films. The subjects of the Gaumont films shown at the Musée Grévin, in fact, did not differ much from what could have been found in the wax tableaux over the years. The subjects of actuality films—a boat leaving a port, views of the exposition, the papal cortège, royal ceremonies, political meetings and celebrity performers—were also wax tableaux subjects ("Visit to the fleet," "A Cairo street, universal exhibition of 1889," "Papal cortège," "The coronation of the czar," "Hughes Leroux with King Ménélick of Ethiopia," "Loïe Fuller"). At times, the museum also featured a subject in wax and film. When the museum opened a tableau featuring a meeting with King Ménélick, the *Journal lumineux* featured scenes from Ethiopian life.[53]

Early actuality films were embedded in narratives that occurred off-screen in illustrated newspapers and at wax museums. Films often served as visual corollaries to the printed word, in a reversal of the way that the printed word in the newspaper offered a written digest of the *flâneur*'s mobile gaze. The culture that produced the first films and actualities happily and knowingly enjoyed a variety of contrived and faked representations of the real.

Cinema Endures, Wax Does Not

By 1902, Gabriel Thomas began pursuing additional novelties, fearful that cinema had run its course as an attraction. Gaumont, for example, suggested his own *chronophone,* which attempted to synchronize sound with the projected images. The museum directors declined his suggestion after two screenings, because "of the little interest the trials seemed to add to cinematographic representations."[54] But

52. The dream sequence puts people on a stage built above the sleeping figure of the criminal, to act out his happier days. The film is in the French cinema archives at the Bois d'Arcy.

53. MGCA, October 31, 1902.

54. Ibid., October 2, 1903.

Gaumont, determined to promote his invention to the public, offered to add *chronophone* showings to the regular *Journal lumineux* for two months, free of charge. Apparently, the small nasal voice produced by Gaumont's technology thrilled no one and was abandoned in November, after less than a month.

Thomas's fears concerning the durability of cinema were unfounded. The nascent industry witnessed a slow but steady growth between 1901 and 1905, with projections at cafés-concerts, music halls and on fairgrounds. The year 1905, in fact, brought great crowds to cinemas all over Paris. This popularity reverberated at the museum, where receipts increased steadily (and in fact, hit an all-time high), allowing the museum to expand the number of seats in the theater from 130 to 182 to accommodate their hundred thousand or so yearly cinema spectators.[55] Thomas's annual report for 1905 noted the rising interest in cinema:

The cinema, more and more appreciated by our visitors, is certainly today one of the strongest elements in our success. The room, often too small to contain the pressing crowd, had to be enlarged recently. It must be recognized that this is a marvelous show, of an inexhaustible interest on which we can count more and more. It allows us to keep current events on our posters and thereby give complete satisfaction to the most demanding tastes of the public.[56]

At the same time, he noted that "wax figures can no longer assure our success."

The Musée Grévin was not the only wax museum experiencing trouble in cinema's wake. In April 1896, projections on a *biograph français* began at the Musée Oller in order to save the wax museum in the basement of the Olympia Music Hall. The museum survived only until 1900 when a restaurant replaced it. In March 1897 the Musée St-Denis at 6, boulevard St-Denis replaced its wax museum with a *cinématographe*. In 1908 Pathé bought this location in order to open his Pathé-Journal. The Musée de la porte St-Denis, opened in 1892 and located at 8, boulevard Bonne-Nouvelle, offered cinema alongside its wax displays in 1900, all for one admission price of fifty centimes. By 1904, however, as an advertisement in *L'Industriel forain* indicated, the museum had

55. In 1901 the museum had decided to produce plays in the second-floor theater and in October moved the cinema to a small basement theater designed by Louis Morin, of Chat Noir fame (the room had held Grévin paraphenalia). For the number of seats see APP, sous-direction de la prévention, December 1905.

56. MGAG, March 29, 1906, for 1905.

given up on wax and presumably was going to dedicate itself to cinema: "Because of a complete transformation of the museum, the wax figures, the décors and accessories are for sale at an extremely cheap price."[57] Cinema was beginning, it appeared, to replace wax displays entirely. If one of the reasons for the popularity of wax museums had been their ability to represent current events realistically, certainly, as Thomas noted above, people believed that cinema was even more lifelike and had the advantage of representing life almost instantly.

By the end of 1906 and during all of 1907, "palaces" dedicated exclusively to film opened all over Paris. In December 1906 two new theaters opened on the *grands boulevards:* the Cinématographe-Pathé, which became the Omnia-Pathé, next to the Théâtre des Variétés and across from the Musée Grévin at 5, boulevard Montmartre; and the Gab-Ka, named for its owner, Gabriel Kaiser, at 27, boulevard des Italiens. The latter also specialized in actualities that resembled the Musée Grévin's *Journal lumineux*. The Cinématographe-Pathé's program promised that the cinema "showed all . . . had today become the mirror of life," and was "a seen and spoken newspaper."[58]

The arrival of these theaters seemed to signal that more of the same would follow. The *Phono-Ciné-Gazette,* a trade journal, commented on the invasion of cinema palaces on the boulevards: "The boulevards are big, there is room for everyone, so long as there is not a cinema at every door."[59] Less than six months later, the same publication noted that "Each day a new movie theater opens."[60]

This situation was not without consequences for the Musée Grévin. In his annual report for 1906, Thomas noted the drop in admissions to the museum's cinema. He explained,

Certainly the sun was an implacable competitor for a part of last year, but there is another that is at this moment the object of all of our vigilance; it's the *cinématographe,* whose wild success and whose easy exhibition has seen a multiplication in the number of places where it is shown. No theater, no music hall is without its *cinématographe,* without mentioning the movie theaters that at each step, solicit the passersby on the boulevard.[61]

57. *L'Industriel forain,* cited in Jacques Deslandes, *Le boulevard du cinéma à l'époque de Georges Méliès* (Paris: Editions du Cerf, 1963), 85.

58. Program from January 26 to February 1, 1907, BHVP, AA.

59. *Phono-Ciné-Gazette,* December 15, 1907, cited in Deslandes and Richard, *Histoire comparée du cinéma,* 494.

60. *Phono-Ciné-Gazette,* April 1, 1907, cited in ibid., 497.

61. MGAG, March 27, 1907.

In an effort to combat the competition from the new movie palaces, the museum directors looked for a novel attraction. They settled on the Palais des Illusions designed by a M. Henard, which had been one of few hits among the attractions at the exposition of 1900. Reborn as the Palais des Mirages, this "authentic staging of the *1,001 Nights*"[62] offered, for fifty centimes above the price of the museum admission, a light and mirror show that included the transformation of a forest into an Arab palace accomplished through the manipulation of electric lights, mirrors and various mechanical props.[63] Opened on December 6, 1908, it provided a much-needed boost in receipts.

For the next few years the museum intermittently adjusted the admission price for its cinema, hoping to improve its overall receipts in a frantic attempt to undercut the ever-increasing popularity of the movie palaces.[64] In 1911 its directors went so far as to make evening admission to the cinema free with admission to the museum and even hired a crier to announce this on the boulevard outside the museum.[65] Admissions did not improve. They reinstated the admission charge for the cinema and began to think about more fundamental institutional changes as they faced steady declines in admission to all their attractions between 1910 and 1913.

By 1914 the Musée Grévin had become the only wax museum left in Paris—a city that had seen probably a dozen wax museums come and go over the course of the 1880s and 1890s. In the face of cinema, wax tableaux were no longer the latest in realistic entertainment nor did they seem as realistic. Further, as cafés-concerts and music halls around the city were also to learn, the public seemed to prefer establishments that specialized in cinema and eventually seemed to prefer cinema to anything else. By 1914, in fact, cafés-concerts such as the Divan japonais, La Scala and the Eldorado all became cinemas.[66] The Musée Grévin's *Journal lumineux* also faced direct competition by the end of the century's first decade: the Pathé Journal, which replaced the Cinéma St-Denis in 1908, and the Gaumont Actualités, opened in 1910, both exclusively showed newsreels.[67]

---

62. *La Nature,* April 17, 1909, 312.
63. This exhibit can still be seen at the Musée Grévin today.
64. MGCA, November 27, 1908.
65. Ibid., June 16, 1911.
66. Romi, *Petite histoire des cafés-concerts* (1950), 57.
67. See Marcel Huret, *Ciné-actualités: histoire de la presse filmée (1895–1980)* (Paris:

Thus, in April 1914, the museum's directors began to discuss the possibility of transforming the entire first floor and a significant portion of the second into a large movie theater, which they intended to do with the help of Léon Gaumont.[68] Gaumont proved uninterested in the project, but Pierre Decourcelle and Eugène Gugenheim, the founders of the Société cinématographique des auteurs et gens de lettres, became very excited about running the theater, provided that it would hold at least one thousand spectators. The museum hired Auguste Perret to redesign the space on July 27, 1914, only days before the museum and all other entertainment venues closed their doors because of the outbreak of the First World War.

Despite the obvious financial losses that came with closing the museum's doors until December and then its gradual reopening for limited hours a few days a week, the war proved an important turning point for the faltering wax museum, although one that the museum directors did not exactly foresee. They halted their efforts to go forward with the transformation of the first floor. Thomas summarized the directors' plans at the annual meeting of stockholders held in March 1915 for the year 1914:

The growing number of cheap entertainments and the overall depression in business that preceded the war are the only causes of our losses. To remedy this, last July we were about to acquire good deals to turn the museum's ground floor into a big movie theater: this theater would hold a thousand seats and would respond completely to the public needs for its favorite show.

But the negotiations were halted by events [the war]. We will not hesitate to take them up again if the projects that are currently underway don't produce the results we expect.

We are talking about a museum of the war. It seems to us that the memories of the war will be a fertile source of patriotic emotions whose representation will have more of an impact than that of the movies, since our main competitor has not been authorized to follow the troops.[69]

Interestingly, when cinema was barred from the battlefield and thus from its instant representation of current events, wax tableaux could attract visitors again. The "museum of the war" opened with a tableau representing the burning of the Cathedral at Reims accompanied by

---

Henri Veyrier, 1984), 28–29. Incidentally, the original name of the Pathé-Journal was Pathé faits divers.

68. MGCA, April 24, 1914.

69. MGAG, March 24, 1915.

figures of French Marshal Joffre and the British General French. The basement movie theater was replaced with a tableau of the battle of the Marne. The museum, however, continued to show films, first in the salle de la Coupole on the ground floor and later in the theater on the second floor where they were paired with live comedic theater. Interest appeared only moderate, so the museum rehired Carmelli, the magician who had been featured as part of the museum's attractions in the mid-1880s.[70]

The directors appeared pleased with an increase in visitors beginning in the fall of 1915, which they attributed to their new war tableaux and to the free admission they offered soldiers. They concluded, however, that their future was far from stable:

But this is still not sufficient to guarantee our future, above all because of the slowness of our production. We must take under serious consideration the proposals that have only been superficially considered concerning the transformation of a part of the museum into a movie theater.

The ever-increasing popularity of this engaging spectacle, is as we have noted any number of times, our forbidding competition.

Thanks to the celebrity of the Musée Grévin and our exceptional location on the boulevards, we believe that despite the already considerable number of cinemas, the one we will open could not help but succeed.[71]

In ten years' time, cinema had gone from "one of the greatest elements of our success" to "our main competitor." In essence, the museum could not beat them, so they proposed to join them and limit wax tableaux to the museum's basement.

During the summer of 1916 architectural plans were submitted to the police prefect, who sent an agent to inspect the museum. The theater would have two seating areas: a first floor with 690 seats and a balcony with 257 seats. The police insisted that they limit the theater to the ground floor for safety reasons, but even then, the smaller theater still seemed a worthwhile project to the museum's directors. In fact, Thomas had begun negotiations with M. Sandberg, an important owner of several movie theaters in Paris, to run the theater and reported that Sandberg did not feel the reduction in the number of seats should halt the project.[72]

The museum was poised for its transformation. Thomas and com-

70. MGCA, July 18, 1915.
71. MGAG, April 3, 1916.
72. MGCA, September 4, 1916.

pany had not counted, however, on the negative report of the fire bureau's police chief. He said that the museum was already a firetrap and was "tolerated because of its 'antiquity.'" He believed that adding the theater would significantly increase the number of visitors to the museum at any one time, which would cause unwarranted risk should a fire break out.[73] With its transformation abruptly forbidden, the museum continued to show films in its theater after the magician's performances during the day; in the evenings, only the cinema and the Palais des Mirages operated at the Musée Grévin.

Business improved steadily in 1917, thanks to the presence of American troops who "have contributed much to the success of spectacles in Paris."[74] And, as Thomas duly noted, "we must recognize that the war, in supplying our industry with a new subject, has given wax figures a boost in popularity." The museum's cinematic shows, however, did not produce sufficient results; the museum abandoned them entirely in February 1917, having neither beaten nor joined the rage for cinema. For the duration of the war, even after cameras reached the battlefields, the museum's wax tableaux of war-related events drew increasing numbers of patrons.

The Musée Grévin survived as a wax museum and did not become a movie theater by virtue of an arbitrary decision made by the fire inspector. Waxworks enthusiasts for whom the Musée Grévin is the only extant waxworks in Paris might, in a rare moment, feel grateful to Parisian bureaucracy. That said, this detailed look at the institutional connection between the wax museum and film—and the cultural connections viewers made as they consumed what appeared at last to be the actual representation of boulevard life itself—provides a context in which we can locate cinema's emergence in and from the broader fin-de-siècle visual culture that has been delineated in this book. In fact, without that context, cinema might have been simply another gadget and not the emblem of modern life that it became.

73. APP, sous-direction de la prévention, 8e bureau.
74. MGAG, March 20, 1918.

Conclusion

This book ends with a discussion of film because film and the cinematic experience together marked both a juncture and a rupture. As an unprecedented crossroads of key elements associated with modern life, cinema combined a technological attempt to transform reality into spectacle with an audience of spectators gathered as an undifferentiated and constantly changing mass audience. But if cinema epitomized the broader fin-de-siècle culture elaborated in this book, it also more successfully transcended the period of its initial emergence. Both as an entertainment for a new kind of crowd—referred to as the "audience" or "the public"—convened by the cultural forms discussed here, and as an object of great debate as well as economic investment, cinema became the "muse of the twentieth century."[1]

As a vital element in this short century that most historians do not even begin until 1914, the culture of cinema moved from Paris, "the capital of the nineteenth century," to Hollywood—a clear contender for "capital" of the twentieth century. The difference, in fact, between being the capital of this century and the last is embodied in the sense of place associated with the two cities. Paris is "someplace"—a city that has never lost its center; one whose culture seems to rely on its con-

---

1. See Miriam Hansen, "America, Paris, the Alps: Kracauer (and Benjamin) on Cinema and Modernity," in *Cinema and the Invention of Modern Life,* ed. Leo Charney and Vanessa R. Schwartz (Berkeley: University of California Press, 1995), for an elaboration of cinema's twentieth-century trajectory. Susanna Barrows suggested the view of cinema as the "muse of the twentieth century."

sumption *en place*. Hollywood is "no place"—founded precisely for its vast and empty spaces as part of the sprawl that has made Los Angeles both famous and infamous; as the "dream factory" that does not urge people to join together in an urban mix. Culture in Hollywood is made for export.

I do not sentimentalize Paris or the late nineteenth century. Rather, I draw this distinction in order to signal both the significance and specificity of fin-de-siècle Parisian culture. As a site rich in artistic cultural invention—Realism, Impressionism, Naturalism and the Modernism emergent from and against these movements—Paris has already received more than its fair share of attention from scholars. This book, however, drew a parallel universe of technological mastery, of energetic crowd-pleasing and of multisensory modern amusements that apprehended and re-presented mundane and familiar real-life as sensation both in words and in images. In addition, it delineated a universe as small or large as the city of Paris, with phenomena generated from and expressing the important transformations in city life there over the course of the nineteenth century.

Capitalism and industrialization, along with their allied technologies such as trains, electrical lighting and telegraphs, made or remade urban cultures everywhere; Paris is in that way but one modern city. The press, wax museums, department stores, even film were not exclusively Parisian, even if the morgue and the number and importance of the expositions were. The extreme political and economic centralization of the city that coincided with Napoleon III's plans to glorify himself by transforming and "modernizing" the city no doubt lent Paris some of the specificity that has drawn scholars to it as the great case study of the transformations in the nineteenth-century city. Although this book explored a unique juxtaposition of various cultural phenomena in the 1880s and 1890s in Paris, the issue was not so much whether the institutions were exclusively Parisian. Rather, regardless of the fact that New York or Berlin or London, for example, had train stations, department stores, and entertainment culture, these phenomena and the urban crowd that attended them were rhetorically constructed in different ways there than they were in Paris. If depictions of the new crowd elsewhere seem heavily invested in gender or class differentiation, I have been advancing a distinctive construction of the Parisian crowd—one whose heterogeneity constituted its collectivity and one celebrated for that quality.

Although other cities had their riots, rebellions and protests, no city rivaled Paris for the changes wrought by urban populations acting collectively, from the French Revolution until the Paris Commune. The revolutionary crowd has, in fact, become so associated with Parisian life that scholars make conceptual links between the crowd and revolution, implying that without revolutions there is no crowd, in a strange inversion of what is more likely the case: that without a crowd, there is no revolution. This formulation virtually erases the presence of crowds in a nonrevolutionary city context. In order to explain the lack of revolution and violence, we must describe the crowd as alienated individuals, disconnected from those with whom they are gathered. Parisians interested in maintaining the status quo thus seem to be engaged in constructing a variety of means to keep other urban dwellers disconnected and nonrevolutionary. The creation of leisure and mass culture in Paris often appears in this light.

This book suggested that mass culture, and in particular, the apprehension of urban experience and modern life through visual re-presentation, was a means of forming a new kind of crowd. These re-presentations did not efface class and gender except in their conceit that diverse consumers should, could and would have similar access to them. They offered a mass cultural equivalent to universal education in that they believed that everyone might consume the same product. It is not mere happenstance that these phenomena coincided temporally, since they shared a democratizing conception of culture. How limited or successful their creation was and continues to be is a subject for further research.

Each of the five chapters described a different kind of spectacle, paying attention to how its audience was constituted and described. The first examined the visuality of a modern boulevard culture and its connection to the way the mass press used sensationalism to frame and re-present the everyday as spectacle. If through boulevard culture, *flânerie* became a Parisian activity, the newspaper served as a printed digest of the *flâneur*'s roving eye.

The second chapter about the popularity of public visits to the Paris Morgue suggested that municipal and national authorities also cultivated *flânerie*, transforming the serious business of identifying bodies into free theater for the masses. In particular, the morgue fit into a modern Parisian landscape that expressed the banal and the everyday in sensational narratives. If the first two chapters elaborated the way that modern urban life was experienced as spectacle, the next three chapters focused on actual spectacles that aimed at the greatest realism in form and content.

Chapter three introduced the phenomena of wax museums, and the Musée Grévin, in particular. It looked specifically at the relation between the museum's conceptualization as both a museum and a "plastic newspaper," and argued that aside from its reproductive aesthetics and the accumulation of objects and details in its tableaux, the museum's realism resided in its depiction of familiar real-life narratives. Close analysis of the tableaux at the Musée Grévin revealed what appeal the actual displays might have had for visitors. The content of the dioramas and the way they situated spectators helped turn museum visitors into *flâneurs* of sorts. Through *flânerie*, spectators commanded the spectacle: they participated in it at the same time that they believed it was constructed for them. They also occupied a variety of viewing positions: both individual and socially determined. Visitors inhabited multiple perspectives—panoramic views—at the same time that the displays often offered privileged access: peepholes into Paris.

Chapter four examined the "o-rama" craze of the 1880s and 1890s— the proliferation of panoramas and dioramas and other entertainments that technologically represented and eventually simulated reality. By looking at this phenomenon over the entire century, this chapter highlighted changing definitions of the real. In some ways, panoramas replicated the techniques of the wax museum in attempting to capture and re-present an already familiar version of reality. Yet by the century's end, the panorama's realism, both technologically and discursively produced, hinged on the notion that to capture life a display had to reproduce it as a multisensory experience. Simulation superseded representation.

The last chapter detailed the history of early cinema in Paris by focusing on film at the Musée Grévin. The history of projected moving images at the wax museum suggested that cinema emerged as a part of a broader visual culture yet found its audience ready-made by virtue of their previous experience as patrons of and participants in those other activities. After all, it is in and among a crowd that we find the cinematic spectator.

Although there are interesting parallels to be drawn from that fin de siècle to this one, especially in realist spectacles and the consumption of the everyday as news,[2] the intervening century has witnessed impor-

2. See my study "Understanding the Public Taste for Reality: The Morgue and the Musée Grévin," in *Spectacles of Realism*, ed. Margaret Cohen and Christopher Prendergast (Minneapolis: University of Minnesota Press, 1995), which discusses this material in the context of postmodernism and contemporary phenomena such as Reality TV.

tant changes. The profusion of new media such as television, video and the internet has facilitated the unprecedented physical transportability of entertainment as well as the possibilities of imagining *niche* audiences. The experience of the "couch potato" is a far cry from that of the movie-goer. The mall, as many cultural critics have noted, has replaced the downtown.[3] This book described the emergence of a nineteenth-century fin-de-siècle urban culture of spectatorship; one through which Paris became synonymous with the visual pleasures of a new kind of crowd. The crowd, its transformations and even its happiness over the course of this century remain at the heart of definitions of modern mass societies. And with it, visual pleasure remains a powerful device of modern crowd-pleasing.

3. For a thorough discussion of this transformation see Friedberg, *Window Shopping*.

Bibliography

Archival Sources

PARIS

Musée Grévin (MGA)

Rapports du Conseil d'administration (MGCA); rapports à l'Assemblée générale (MGAG); photos, catalogues

Bibliothèque historique de la ville de Paris (BHVP)

Actualités anciennes (AA): series 35, 38, boulevards, théâtres, jardin d'acclimatation; 101, music-halls; 102, attractions foraines; 103, attractions diverses; 120, Magasins Dufayel; 122, exposition 1900; 146, morgue; 157, guillotine, exécutions

Archives de la Prefecture de police (APP)

BA 81, affaire Billoir; BA 82, assassinations; BA 83, affaire Pranzini; BA 85, affaire Gouffé; BA 887, exécution des arrêts criminels (1872–1899); BA 1612, assassins; DA 27, grand panorama national; DA 32, morgue—statistique; DA 129, panorama patriotique; DB 100–101, théâtres, concerts et autres spectacles; DB 105, théâtres, concerts et autres spectacles publics; DB 107, cinématographe; DB 141, peine de mort; DB 142, exécutions capitales; DB 185, expositions; DB 198, kiosques de marchands de journaux; DB 202, fêtes foraines; DB 210, morgue; DB 440, médecine-légale; DB 802, Don Tristan Rémy; EB 26, 9e arrondissement; EB 95, panoramas; EB 100, musée Grévin

Archives de Paris

D2N1, procès-verbaux du Conseil général de la Seine; D8N4(1) and D8N4(2), morgue

Bibliothèque de l'arsenal

Collection Rondel

Bibliothèque nationale

Cabinet des estampes; manuscrits, correspondance Zola-Grévin

Bibliothèque administrative

Rapports, Conseil général de la Seine, Conseil municipal de la Seine

Musée Carnavalet

Collection iconographique—topographie, moeurs

LONDON

Guildhall Library

Ephemera collection

Madame Tussaud's

Tussaud archive

Museum of London

Periodical Sources

(Focus on 1876, 1882, 1886, and 1907; not all entries exist for 1870–1910. * = weekly.)
L'Audience*
La Caricature*
Le Charivari*
La Chronique parisienne
Le Clairon
Coemedia*
Le Constitutionnel

Le Contemporain
Le Courrier du Soir
Le Cri du Peuple
Le XIXe Siècle
L'Echo de Paris
L'Eclair
L'Eclat de Rire
L'Estafette *
L'Evènement
L'Evènement parisien illustré
L'Excelsior
L'Express
Le Figaro
Le Français
La France
La France nouvelle
Le Gaulois
La Gazette de France
La Gazette des Tribunaux
Le Gil Blas
The Graphic
Le Grelot *
L'Illustration *
L'Indépendance belge
L'Indépendant
L'Intransigeant
Le Journal
Le Journal amusant
Le Journal des Débats
Le Journal illustré *
La Justice
La Lanterne
La Liberté
Le Magasin pittoresque *
Le Matin
Le Monde illustré *
Le Monde parisien *
Le Moniteur universel
Le Nain jaune
La Paix
Le Paris
Le Paris-Journal
Le Parlement
La Patrie
Le Pays
Le Petit Journal
Le Petit Journal, supplément illustré *

*Le Petit Journal pour Rire**
Le Petit Moniteur universel
Le Petit Parisien
*Le Petit Parisien, supplément illustré**
*Le Petit Populaire illustré**
La Petite Presse
*Plaisirs et Bureaux de Paris**
La Presse
Le Rappel
La République française
*La République illustrée**
*La Revue de Paris**
Le Siècle
Le Soir
Le Soleil
Le Télégraphe
Le Temps
L'Union
*L'Univers illustré**
La Vérité
*La Vie moderne**
*La Vie parisienne**
*La Ville de Paris**
*Le Voleur illustré**
Le Voltaire

Primary Sources

ABC de Paris. Paris: Vermot, 1897.

Amicis, Edmond d'. *Souvenirs de Paris et Londres*. Paris: Hachette, 1880.

Annesley, Maude. *My Parisian Year*. London: Mills and Boon, 1912.

Annuaire almanach du commerce. Paris: Bottin, 1880–1900.

Arlaud, R. M. *Cinéma-bouffe*. Paris: Jacques Melot, n.d.

Armengaud, Jules. *Nettoyons Paris*. Paris: M. Bauche, 1907.

Astruc, Gabriel. *Le pavillon des fantômes*. Paris, 1929.

Avenel, Henri. *Histoire de la presse française depuis 1789 à nos jours*. Paris: Flammarion, 1900.

Bapst, Germaine. *Essai sur l'histoire des panoramas et des dioramas*. Paris: Imprimerie nationale, 1889.

Baudelaire, Charles. *The Painter of Modern Life and Other Essays*. Translated and edited by J. Mayne. London: Phaidon Press, 1964.

Beaulieu, Henri. *Les théâtres du boulevard du crime*. Paris: H. Daragon, 1905.

Bell, Lilian. *As Seen by Me*. New York: Harper and Brothers, 1901.

Benjamin, Edmond, and P. Desachy. *Le boulevard: croquis parisien*. Paris: Flammarion, 1893.

Beraldi, Henri. *Les graveurs du XIXe siècle*. 7 vols. Paris: Librairie Conquet, 1886.

Bluysen, P. *Paris en 1889*. Paris: P. Arnould, 1890.

Boutet, Henri. *Almanach pour 1899: les heures de la parisienne*. Paris: Melet, 1899.

Bradshaw's Illustrated Handbook to Paris. London: W. J. Adams, 1896.

Brissot, Adolphe. *Portraits intimes*. Paris: Armand Colin, 1901.

Brochin, H. "La morgue." In *Paris pittoresque*, edited by G. Sarrut and B. Saint-Edmé. Vol. 2. Paris: D'Uturbie, 1837.

Campardon, Emile. *Les spectacles de la foire*. Geneva: Slatkine Reprints, 1970.

Castellani, Charles. *Les confidences d'un panoramiste*. Paris: Maurice Dreyfous, n.d.

Cherbuliez, Ernest. "La morgue." *Revue des deux mondes* (January 1891): 344–81.

Chevassu, Francis. *Les parisiens*. Paris: Alphonse Lemerre, 1892.

Claretie, Jules. *La vie à Paris*. Paris: Victor Havard, 1883.

Claretie, Léo. *Les coins de Paris*. Tours: Alfred Mame et fils, 1887.

———. *Histoire de la littérature française*. 4 vols. Paris: Société d'Editions littéraires et artistiques, 1909.

Coquiot, Gustave. *Dimanches d'été*. Paris: Librairie de l'art, 1897.

Darzens, R. *Nuits à Paris*. Paris: Dentu, 1889.

Dausset, Louis, and Georges Lemarchand. *Rapport sur la reconstruction de la morgue et la création d'un institut médico-légal*. Conseil général de la Seine. Paris: Imprimerie municipale, 1908.

Delvau, Alfred. *Les plaisirs de Paris*. Paris, 1867.

Deschaumes, Edmond. *Pour bien voir Paris*. Paris: Maurice Dreyfous, 1889.

Desraimes, Maria. *L'épidémie naturaliste*. Paris: Dentu, 1888.

Détournelle, Athanase. *Aux armes et aux arts! Journal de la société républicaine des arts*. Paris: Détournelle, 1794.

Devergie, Alphonse. *Notions générales sur la morgue de Paris*. Paris: Félix Malteste, 1877.

———. "La morgue de Paris: sa description, son service, son système hygiènique—de l'autopsie judiciaire, comparée à l'autopsie pathologique." *Annnales d'hygiène publique et de médecine légale*, 2d s., 4 (1878): 44–79.

de Donville, F. *Guide de l'étranger dans Paris*. Paris: Garnier Frères, 1884.

Dubief, Eugène. *Le journalisme*. Paris: Hachette, 1892.

Du Camp, Maxime. *Paris, ses organes, ses fonctions et sa vie*. Vol. 1. Paris: Hachette, 1869.

Edwards, H. Sutherland. *Old and New Paris*. London: Cassell, 1893.

Eméry, Rose. *Une année à Paris*. Paris: Chez l'auteur, 1886.

Encyclopédie du siècle: l'exposition de Paris 1900. Paris: Montgredien, 1900.

L'exposition universelle de 1889. Paris: Dentu, 1890.

Flameng. Léopold. *Paris qui s'en va et qui vient*. 1860. Paris: Editions de Paris, 1985.

Fournel, Victor. *Ce qu'on voit dans les rues de Paris*. Paris, 1858.

———. *Le vieux Paris: fêtes, jeux et spectacles*. Tours: Alfred Mame et fils, 1887.

Fraipont, Gustave. *Paris, à vol d'oiseau.* Paris: Librairie illustrée, 1889.

Galignani. *Illustrated Paris Guide.* London: Galignani, 1884.

———. *Paris Guide.* Paris: Galignani, 1884, 1889, 1888.

Gavinzel, J. C. *Etude sur la morgue au point de vue administratif et médical.* Paris: Baillière et fils, 1882.

Gaze, W. Edwin. *Paris and How to See It.* London: Gaze and Son, 1884.

Goudeau, Emile. *Paris qui consomme.* Paris: Henri Beraldi, 1883.

Gourdon de Genouillac, H. *Paris, à travers les siècles.* 7 vols. Paris: Roy, 1882–89.

Gozlan, Léon. "La morgue." In *Le livre des cent et un.* Vol. 1. Paris: Chez Ladvocat, 1831.

Le Grand Dictionnaire universel. Paris, 1867.

Grison, Georges. *Paris horrible et Paris original.* Paris: Dentu, 1882.

Guide des plaisirs à Paris. Paris: Edition photographique, 1900.

Guide to Paris. London: Cook, 1885.

Guillot, Adolphe. *Paris qui souffre: la basse-geôle du Grand-Châtelet et les morgues modernes.* 2d ed. Paris: Chez Rouquette, 1888.

Haussmann, Georges. *Mémoires.* 2 vols. 1890–93. Paris: Guy Durier, 1979.

Henriot. *L'année parisienne.* Paris: Librairie Conquet, 1894.

Herboso, F. J. *Reminiscencias de viajes.* 2 vols. Caracas: J. M. Herrera Irigoyen, 1905.

Hittorf. "Description de la rotonde des panoramas." *Revue générale de l'architecture* 2 (1841).

Huret, J. *La catastrophe du bazar de la Charité.* Paris: F. Juven, 1897.

Illustrated Guide to Paris. London: Cassell, 1884.

Lafond de Saint-Mir, Baron. *Impressions de voyages dans Paris.* Paris: Nouvelle Librairie parisienne, 1893.

Larousse du XXe siècle. Paris, 1931.

Le Breton, Gaston. *Essai historique sur la sculpture en cire.* Rouen: Cagniard, 1894.

Lemaître, Jules. *Impressions de théâtre.* 1887. 8th ed., second series. Paris: Société française de l'Imprimerie, 1897.

Leroux, Hughes. *L'enfer parisien.* Paris: Victor Havard, 1888.

———. *Les jeux du cirque et de la vie foraine.* Paris: Plon, 1889.

Livre d'or de l'exposition de 1900. Paris: Editions Cornély, 1900.

Livret descriptif et raisonné du musée anatomique de J. Talrich. Paris, 1876.

Lucas, E. V. *A Wanderer in Paris.* London: Methuen, 1909.

Macé, Gustave. *Mon premier crime.* Paris: Charpentier, 1885.

———. *Mon musée criminel.* Paris: Charpentier, 1890.

Maillard, Firmin. *Recherches historiques et critiques sur la morgue.* Paris: Delahays, 1860.

Maindron, Ernest. *Les affiches illustrées (1886–1895).* Paris, 1896.

Marlet, Jean-Henri. *Le nouveau tableau de Paris.* Paris, 1821–24.

de Marot, Gaston, et al. *Casse-Museau.* Paris: Tresse, 1882.

Martin, Alexis. *Paris: promenades des 20 arrondissements.* Paris, 1890.

Marx, Adrien. *Les petites mémoires de Paris.* Paris: Calmann Lévy, 1888.

Mauclair, Camille. *Jules Chéret*. Paris: Maurice Le Garrec, 1930.

Mercier, Louis-Sébastien. *Le tableau de Paris*. Paris, 1783.

Mermet. *Annuaire de la presse française*. Paris, 1883.

Meyer, Arthur. *Soyons pratiques*. Paris: Lucotte, 1888.

———. *Ce que mes yeux ont vu*. Preface by Emile Faguet. 3d ed. Paris: Plon, 1911.

Montorgueil, Georges. *La vie des boulevards*. Paris: Librairies Imprimeries réunies, 1896.

———. *Les parisiennes d'à présent*. Paris: H. Floury, 1897.

Mourey, Gabriel. *Les fêtes foraines de Paris*. Paris, 1906.

Narjoux, Félix. *Monuments élevés par la ville (1850–1880)*. Paris: A. Morel, 1880–83.

Paris-Diamant: guide Joanne. Paris: Hachette, 1881, 1883.

Paris en poche: guide Conty. Paris, Maison Conty, 1883.

Paris Express: guide illustré et pratique du journal "Le Matin". Paris: Le Matin, 1889.

Paris-Guide. Paris: A. Lacroix, 1867.

Paris: guide Joanne. Paris: Hachette, 1889.

Paris illustré: guide Joanne. Paris: Hachette, 1885.

Paris in Four Days. Paris: Charles Moonen, 1886.

Passy, Frédéric. *Les fêtes foraines et les administrations municipales*. Paris: Picard, 1883.

Petit Paris: guide illustré. Paris: Marpon, 1889.

Pierre, Clovis. *Les gaietés de la morgue*. Paris: Gallimard, 1895.

Platel, Félix. *Paris-secret*. Paris: Victor Havard, 1889.

Pleasure Guide to Paris for Bachelors. London: Nilsson, n.d.

Prudhomme, L. *Miroir historique, politique et critique de l'ancien et du nouveau Paris*. Vol. 2. Paris, 1807.

Reynolds-Ball, E. A. *Paris in Its Splendours*. 2 vols. London: Gay and Bird, 1901.

Robida, A. *L'île de Lutèce: enlaidissements et embellissements de la cité*. Paris: Daragon, 1905.

du Roure, Henry. *La presse aujourd'hui et la presse de demain*. Paris: Au Sillon, 1908.

Ruelle, Angelin. *Les chansons de la morgue*. Paris: Léon Varnier, 1890.

Saint-Mir, Laffond de. *Impressions de voyage dans Paris*. Paris, 1893.

Sala, G. A. *Catalogue of Madame Tussaud's Exhibition*. London, 1892.

Scholl, Aurélien. *L'esprit du boulevard*. Paris: Victor Havard, 1886.

Strauss, Paul. *Paris ignoré*. Paris: Librairies Imprimeries réunies, 1892.

Talmeyr, Maurice. "Le roman-feuilleton et l'esprit populaire." *Revue des deux mondes* 17 (September 1903): 203–27.

Tardieu, Ambroise. "La morgue." In *Paris-Guide de 1867*. 2 vols. Paris: A. Lacroix, 1867.

Tcheng-Ki-Tong, Général. *Les parisiens peints par un chinois*. Paris: Charpentier, 1891.

Texier, Edmond. *Tableau de Paris*. 2 vols. Paris: Paulin et Chevalier, 1852.

Tyssandier, Léon. *Figures parisiennes.* Paris: Ollendorff, 1887.

Vallès, Jules. *Le tableau de Paris.* 1882. Paris: Messidor, 1989.

Véron, Pierre. "La morgue." *Le Magasin pittoresque,* March 1907, 171–72.

Virmaître, Charles. *Les curiosités de Paris.* Paris: Lebigre-Duquesne, 1868.

Whiteing, Richard. *The Life of Paris.* Leipzig: Tauchnitz, 1901.

Williams, Elizabeth. *Sojourning, Shopping, and Studying in Paris.* Chicago: McClung, 1907.

Zola, Emile. *Thérèse Raquin.* 1867. Paris: Flammarion, 1970.

Secondary Sources

Abel, Richard. *The Ciné Goes to Town.* Berkeley: University of California Press, 1994.

Abelson, Elaine. *When Ladies Go A-Thieving: Middle-Class Shoplifters and the Victorian Department Store.* New York: Oxford University Press, 1989.

Allen, James Smith. *In the Public Eye: A History of Reading in Modern France, 1800–1940.* Princeton: Princeton University Press, 1991.

Altick, Richard. *The Shows of London.* Cambridge, Mass.: Harvard University Press, 1978.

Anderson, Benedict. *Imagined Communities.* 2d ed. London: Verso, 1991.

Anderson, Patricia. *The Transformation of Popular Culture.* Oxford: Oxford University Press, 1991.

Ariès, Philippe. *The Hour of Our Death.* Translated by Helen Weaver. New York: Vintage Books, 1982.

Auclair, Georges. *Le mana quotidien.* 1970. Paris: Editions Anthropos, 1982.

Auerbach, Eric. *Mimesis.* Translated by Willard Trask. Princeton: Princeton University Press, 1974.

Bailey, Peter. *Leisure and Class in Victorian England.* London: Methuen, 1987.

Bann, Stephen. *The Clothing of Clio.* New York: Cambridge University Press, 1984.

Bardèche, Maurice, and Robert Brasillach. *Histoire du cinéma.* Paris: Editions André Martel, 1948.

Barrows, Susanna. *Distorting Mirrors.* New Haven: Yale University Press, 1981.

———. "Nineteenth-Century Cafés: Arenas of Everyday Life." In *Pleasures of Paris: Daumier to Picasso,* edited by Barbara Stern Shapiro, 17–26. Boston: Museum of Fine Arts, 1991.

Barsam, Richard. *Nonfiction Film: A Critical History.* Bloomington: Indiana University Press, 1992.

Barthes, Roland. *The Rustle of Language.* Translated by Richard Howard. New York: Hill and Wang, 1986.

Baschet, Roger. *Le monde fantastique du musée Grévin.* Paris: Tallandier, 1982.

Baudrillard, Jean. *Simulations.* Translated by Paul Foss et al. New York: Semiotext(e), 1983.

Becker, Colette. *Lire le réalisme et le naturalisme.* Paris: Dunod, 1992.

Bellanger, Claude. *Histoire générale de la presse française.* Vol. 3. Paris: Presses universitaires de France, 1972.

Bellet, Roger. *Presse et journalisme sous le Second Empire.* Paris: Armand Colin, 1967.

Benjamin, Walter. *Illuminations.* Introduction by Hannah Arendt. New York: Schocken, 1969.

———. *Charles Baudelaire.* Translated by Harry Zohn. 3d ed. London: Verso, 1989.

———. *Paris, capitale du XIXe siècle.* Edited by Rolf Tiedmann, translated by Jean Lacoste. Paris: Editions du Cerf, 1989.

Bennett, Tony. *The Birth of the Museum: History, Theory, Politics.* New York: Routledge, 1995.

Berenson, Edward. *The Trial of Madame Caillaux.* Berkeley: University of California Press, 1992.

Berlanstein, Lenard R. *The Working People of Paris, 1871–1914.* Baltimore: Johns Hopkins University Press, 1984.

Berman, Marshall. *All That Is Solid Melts Into Air.* New York: Penguin Books, 1982.

Bernheimer, Charles. *Figures of Ill Repute.* Cambridge, Mass.: Harvard University Press, 1989.

Bertaut, Jules. *Le boulevard.* 1924. Paris: Tallendier, 1957.

Bertherat, Bruno. "La morgue et la visite de la morgue à Paris au XIXe siècle, 1804–1907." Master's thesis, Université de Paris, I, 1990.

Betts, Raymond. *Tricouleur.* London: Gordon and Cremonesi, 1978.

Bowlby, Rachel. *Just Looking: Consumer Culture in Dreiser, Gissing, and Zola.* New York: Methuen, 1985.

Braun, Marta. *Picturing Time: The Work of Etienne-Jules Marey.* Chicago: University of Chicago Press, 1993.

Bronfen, Elizabeth. *Over Her Dead Body.* London: Routledge, 1993.

Bruno, Giuliana. *Street-Walking on a Ruined Map.* Princeton: Princeton University Press, 1993.

Bruynogher, M. *Cires anatomiques du XIXe siècle: collection du docteur Spitzner.* Brussels: Centre culturel de la communauté française de Belgique, 1980.

Buck-Morss, Susan. *The Dialectics of Seeing.* Cambridge, Mass.: MIT Press, 1989.

Burns, Stanley. *Sleeping Beauty: Memorial Photography in America.* Altadena: Twelvetree Press, 1990.

Castelnau, Jacques. *En remontant les grands boulevards.* Paris: Le Livre contemporain, 1960.

Çelik, Zeynep. *Displaying the Orient.* Berkeley: University of California Press, 1992.

Certeau, Michel de. *The Practice of Everyday Life.* Translated by Steven Rendall. Berkeley: University of California Press, 1984.

Cézan, Claude. *Le musée Grévin.* Paris: Editions Rombaldi, 1947.

———. *Le musée Grévin.* Toulouse: Editions Privat, 1961.

———. *Gabriel Thomas.* Paris: private printing, n.d.

Chapman, Lady Pauline. *Madame Tussaud's Chamber of Horrors.* London: Constable, 1984.

———. *The French Revolution as Seen by Madame Tussaud, Witness Extraordinary.* London: Quiller Press, 1989.

Chapuis, A., and Edouard Gélis. *Le monde des automates: études historiques et techniques.* Paris, 1928.

Charney, Leo, and Vanessa R. Schwartz, eds. *Cinema and the Invention of Modern Life.* Berkeley: University of California Press, 1995.

Chartier, Roger. *Cultural History.* Translated by Lydia Cochrane. Ithaca: Cornell University Press, 1988.

Chartier, Roger, and Henri-Jean Martin, eds. *Histoire de l'édition française.* Vol.3. Paris: Fayard, 1990.

Clark, T. J. *The Painting of Modern Life.* Princeton: Princeton University Press, 1984.

Clayson, S. Hollis. *Painted Love.* New Haven: Yale University Press, 1991.

Clifford, James. *The Predicament of Culture.* Cambridge, Mass.: Harvard University Press, 1986.

Cobb, Richard. *Death in Paris.* Oxford: Oxford University Press, 1978.

Cohen, Margaret, and Christopher Prendergast, eds. *Spectacles of Realism: Gender, Body, Genre.* Minneapolis: University of Minnesota Press, 1995.

Comment, Bernard. *Le XIXe siècle des panoramas.* Paris: Adam Biro, 1993.

Condemi, Concetta. *Les cafés-concerts.* Paris: Quai Voltaire, 1992.

Corbin, Alain. *Les filles de noce.* Paris: Aubier Montaigne, 1978.

———. *The Foul and the Fragrant.* Cambridge, Mass.: Harvard University Press, 1985.

———. "Le sang dans Paris, réflexions sur la généalogie de l'image de la capitale." In *Ecrire Paris,* edited by Daniel Oster and Jean-Marie Goulemot. Paris: Editions Seesam, 1990.

———. *Le village des cannibales.* Paris: Aubier, 1990.

Cottrell, Leonard. *Madame Tussaud.* London: Evans Brothers, 1981.

Courtine, Robert. *La vie parisienne: cafés et restaurants des boulevards, 1814–1914.* Paris: Perrin, 1984.

Crary, Jonathan. *Techniques of the Observer.* Cambridge, Mass.: MIT Press, 1990.

Cvetkovich, Ann. *Mixed Feelings: Feminism, Mass Culture, and Victorian Sensationalism.* New Brunswick: Rutgers University Press, 1992.

Darmon, Pierre. *Médecins et assassins à la Belle Epoque.* Paris: Seuil, 1989.

Debord, Guy. *Society of the Spectacle.* Detroit: Black and Red, 1983.

De Grazia, Victoria. "Mass Culture and Sovereignty: The American Challenge to European Cinemas, 1920–1960." *Journal of Modern History* 61 (March 1989): 53–87.

Deslandes, Jacques. *Le boulevard du cinéma à l'époque de Georges Méliès.* Paris: Editions du Cerf, 1963.

———. *Histoire comparée du cinéma.* Vol. 1. Paris: Casterman, 1969.

Deslandes, Jacques, and Jacques Richard. *Histoire comparée du cinéma.* Vol. 2. Paris: Casterman, 1969.

Drachline, Pierre. *Le fait divers au XIXe siècle.* Paris: Editions Hermé, 1991.

Dumur. *Histoire des spectacles.* Paris: Pléiades, 1965.

Eco, Umberto. *Travels in Hyppereality.* Translated by William Weaver. New York: Harcourt Brace, 1986.

El Nouty, Hassan. *Théâtre et pré-cinéma.* Paris: Editions Nizet, 1978.

Elsaesser, Thomas, ed. *Early Cinema: Space, Frame, Narrative.* London: British Film Institute, 1990.

English, Donald. *The Political Uses of Photography in the Third Republic.* Ann Arbor: UMI Research Press, 1984.

Faure, Alain. *Paris. Carême-prenant: du carnaval à Paris au XIXe siècle.* Paris: Hachette, 1978.

Ferguson, Priscilla Parkhurst. *Paris as Revolution: Writing the Nineteenth-Century City.* Berkeley: University of California Press, 1994.

Fleury, Michel, and Jean Tulard. *Almanach de Paris.* 2 vols. Paris: Encycloadia Universalis, 1990.

Foucault, Michel. *Discipline and Punish: The Birth of the Prison.* Translated by Alan Sheridan. New York: Vintage Books, 1979.

Fox, Richard Wrightman, and T. J. Jackson Lears, eds. *The Culture of Consumption: Critical Essays in American History, 1880–1980.* New York: Pantheon, 1983.

Fremigacci, Isabelle. "L'incendie de la bazar de la Charité." Master's thesis, Université de Paris I, 1989.

Freund, Gisèle. *Photographie et société.* Paris: Seuil, 1974.

Fried, Michael. *Absorption and Theatricality.* Berkeley: University of California Press, 1980.

———. *Courbet's Realism.* Chicago, University of Chicago Press, 1990.

Friedberg, Anne. *Window Shopping.* Berkeley: University of California Press, 1993.

Fritzsche, Peter. *Reading Berlin 1900.* Cambridge, Mass.: Harvard University Press, 1996.

Friutema, Evelyn, and Paul Zoetmulder, eds. *The Panorama Phenomenon.* The Hague: Mesdag Panorama Foundation, 1981.

Gernsheim, H., and A. Gernsheim. *LJM Daguerre: The History of the Diorama and the Daguerrotype.* London: Secker and Warburg, 1956.

Grand-Carteret, John. *L'histoire de la vie, les moeurs et la curiosité.* Vol. 5. Paris: Librairie de la Curiosité, 1928.

Les grands boulevards. Paris: Réunion des musées de Paris, 1987.

Green, Nicholas. *The Spectacle of Nature.* Manchester: Manchester University Press, 1990.

Greenhalgh, Paul. *Ephemeral Vistas.* Manchester: Manchester University Press, 1988.

Gunning, Tom. "An Aesthetic of Astonishment: Early Film and the (In)-Credulous Spectator." *Art and Text,* no. 34 (spring 1989).

Hamon, Philippe. *Texte et idéologie.* Paris: Presses universitaires de France, 1984.

———. *Expositions.* Translated by Katia Sainson-Franck and Lisa Maguire. Berkeley: University of California Press, 1992.

Hansen, Miriam. *Babel and Babylon: Spectatorship in American Silent Film.* Cambridge, Mass.: Harvard University Press, 1991.

———. America, Paris, the Alps: Kracauer (and Benjamin) on Cinema and

Modernity." In *Cinema and the Invention of Modern Life,* edited by Leo Charney and Vanessa R. Schwartz. Berkeley: University of California Press, 1995.

Haraway, Donna. "Teddy Bear Patriarchy: Taxidermy in the Garden of Eden, New York City, 1908–1936." *Social Text* (winter 1985): 20–63.

Harris, Neil. *Humbug: The Art of P. T. Barnum.* Boston: Little Brown, 1973.

———. *Cultural Excursions.* Chicago: University of Chicago Press, 1990.

Harris, Ruth. *Murders and Madness: Medicine, Law, and Society in the Fin de Siècle.* Oxford: Clarendon Press, 1989.

Harvey, David. *The Condition of Postmodernity.* Cambridge: Basil Blackwell, 1989.

———. *Consciousness and the Urban Experience.* Baltimore: Johns Hopkins University Press, 1989.

Herbert, Robert. *Impressionism.* New Haven: Yale University Press, 1988.

Hughes, Helen. *News and the Human Interest Story.* New York: Greenwood Press 1968.

Hunt, Lynn, ed. *The New Cultural History.* Berkeley: University of California Press, 1989.

Huret, Marcel. *Ciné-actualités: histoire de la presse filmée, 1895–1980.* Paris: Henri Veyrier, 1984.

Hyde, Ralph. *Panoramania: The Art and Entertainment of the 'All-Embracing View.'* London: Trefoil Publications, 1988.

L'invention d'un regard (1839–1918). Paris: Réunion des musées nationaux, 1989.

Isherwood, Robert. *Farce and Fantasy: Popular Entertainment in Eighteenth-Century Paris.* New York: Oxford University Press, 1986.

Jameson, Fredric. *The Political Unconscious.* Ithaca: Cornell University Press, 1981.

———. *Signatures of the Visible.* New York: Routledge, 1990.

Jay, Martin. *Downcast Eyes: The Denigration of Vision in Twentieth-Century French Thought.* Berkeley: University of California Press, 1993.

Jordanova, Ludmilla. *Sexual Visions.* Madison: University of Wisconsin Press, 1989.

Journal universel: l'illustration. Paris: Réunion des musées de Paris, 1987.

Kasson, John. *Amusing the Millions.* New York: Hill and Wang, 1978.

Kendrick, Walter. *The Thrill of Fear.* New York: Grove Weidenfeld, 1991.

Kern, Stephen. *The Culture of Time and Space.* Cambridge, Mass.: Harvard University Press, 1983.

Kracauer, S. *Jacques Offenbach ou le secret du Second Empire.* Translated by Lucienne Astruc. Paris: Grasset, 1937.

Kselman, Thomas. *Death and the Afterlife in Modern France.* Princeton: Princeton University Press, 1993.

Kuisel, Richard. *Seducing the French.* Berkeley: University of California Press, 1993.

Laqueur, Thomas. "Bodies, Details, and the Humanitarian Narrative." In *The New Cultural History,* edited by Lynn Hunt. Berkeley: University of California Press, 1989.

Leach, William R. *Land of Desire: Merchants, Power, and the Rise of a New American Culture*. New York: Pantheon, 1993.

Lemire, Michel. *Artistes et mortels*. Paris: Chabaud, 1990.

Lemoine, Bernard. *Les passages couverts en France*. Paris: Délégation de l'Action artistique, 1989.

Leprun, Sylviane. *Le théâtre des colonies*. Paris: Edition L'Harmattan, 1986.

Leps, Marie-Christine. *Apprehending the Criminal: The Production of Deviance in Nineteenth-Century Discourse*. Durham: Duke University Press, 1992.

Lethève, Jacques, *La caricature et la presses sous la IIIe République*. Paris: Armand Colin, 1961.

Levine, George, ed. *Realism and Representation*. Madison: University of Wisconsin Press, 1993.

Livois, René. *L'histoire de la presse française*. 2 vols. Paris: Les Temps de la Presse, 1965.

Lukács, Georg. *Studies in European Realism*. Introduction by Alfred Kazin. New York: Grosset and Dunlop, 1964.

Mainardi, Patricia. *Art and Politics of the Second Empire*. New Haven, 1989.

Manévy, Raymond. *La presse de la Troisième République*. Paris: J. Forêt, 1955.

Matlock, Jann. *Scenes of Seduction: Prostitution, Hysteria, and Reading Difference in Nineteenth-Century France*. New York: Columbia University Press, 1993.

Max, Stéphane. *Les métamorphoses de la grande ville dans les Rougon-Macquart*. Paris: A. Nizet, 1966.

McLellan, Andrew. *Inventing the Louvre: Art, Politics, and the Origins of the Modern Museum in Eighteenth-Century Paris*. Cambridge: Cambridge University Press, 1994.

Meisel, Martin. *Realizations: Narrative, Pictorial, and Theatrical Arts in Nineteenth-Century England*. Princeton: Princeton University, 1983.

Metz, Christian. *The Imaginary Signifier*. Bloomington: University of Indiana Press, 1981.

Meusy, Jean-Jacques. "L'énigme du cinéorama de l'exposition universelle de 1900." *Archives,* no. 3 (January 1991).

———. *Paris-Palaces, ou le temps des cinémas (1894–1918)*. Paris: Centre national de la recherche scientifique, 1995.

Meyer, Jean, et al. *Histoire de la France coloniale: des origines à 1914*. Paris: Armand Colin, 1991.

Miller, Michael. *The Bon Marché: Bourgeois Culture and the Department Store, 1869–1920*. Princeton: Princeton University Press, 1981.

Mitchell, Alan. "The Paris Morgue as a Social Institution in the Nineteenth Century." *Francia* 4 (1976): 581–96.

Mitchell, Timothy. *Colonizing Egypt*. Berkeley: University of California Press, 1991.

Mitterand, Henri. *Le regard et la signe: poétique du roman réaliste et naturaliste*. Paris: Presses universitaires de France, 1987.

Monestier, Alain. *Le fait divers*. Paris: Editions de la Réunion des musées nationaux, 1982.

———. *Les grandes affaires criminelles*. Paris: Bordas, 1988.

Morin, Edgar. *Le cinéma, ou l'homme imaginaire.* Paris: Editions de Minuit, 1958.

Mukerji, Chandra, and Michael Schudson. *Rethinking Popular Culture,* Berkeley: University of California Press, 1991.

Mulvey, Laura. *Visual and Other Pleasures.* Bloomington: University of Indiana Press, 1989.

Musser, Charles. *The Emergence of Cinema: The American Screen to 1907.* New York: Scribner's, 1990.

———. *Before the Nickelodeon.* Berkeley: University of California, 1991.

Naremore, James, and Patrick Brantlinger. *Modernity and Mass Culture.* Bloomington: Indiana University Press, 1991.

Nasaw, David. *Going Out: The Rise and Fall of Public Amusement.* New York: Basic Books, 1993.

Nesbitt, Molly. "In the absence of the parisienne . . . " In *Sexuality and Space,* edited by Beatriz Colomina. New York: Princeton Architectural Press, 1992.

1913: le théâtre des Champs-Elysées. Paris: Editions de la Réunion des musées nationaux, 1987.

Nochlin, Linda. *Realism.* London: Penguin, 1971.

Nora, Pierre, ed. *Les lieux de mémoire.* Paris: Gallimard, 1984.

Nord, Philip. *Paris Shopkeepers and the Politics of Resentment.* Princeton: Princeton University Press, 1986.

Noverre, Maurice. *Emile Reynaud: sa vie et ses travaux.* Brest, 1926.

Nye, Robert. *Crime, Madness, and Politics in Modern France.* Princeton: Princeton University Press, 1984.

O'Doherty, Brian. *Museums in Crisis.* New York: Braziller, 1972.

Olsen, Donald J. *The City as a Work of Art.* New Haven: Yale University Press, 1986.

Orvell, Miles. *The Real Thing.* Chapel Hill: University of North Carolina Press, 1989.

Ory, Pascal. *L'expo universelle.* Paris: Editions Complexe, 1989.

Oster, Daniel, and Jean-Marie Goulemot, eds. *Ecrire Paris.* Paris: Editions Seesam, 1990.

Osterwelder, Marcus. *Dictionnaire des illustrateurs: 1800–1914.* Paris: Husschmidt et Barret, 1983.

Palmer, Michael. *Des petits journaux aux grandes agences.* Paris: Aubier, 1983.

Park, Robert. "The Natural History of the Newspaper." *Journal of Sociology* 29 (November 1923): 273–89.

Parkenham, Thomas. *The Scramble for Africa.* New York, Random House, 1991.

Peiss, Kathy. *Cheap Amusements.* Philadelphia: Temple University Press, 1986.

Perrot, Michelle. "L'affaire Troppman." *L'Histoire,* January 30, 1981.

———. "Fait divers et histoire au XIXe siècle: note critique (deux expositions)." *Annales: économies, sociétés, civilisations* 38, no. 4 (July–August 1983): 911–19.

Petrey, Sandy. *Realism and Revolution.* Ithaca: Cornell University Press, 1988.

Pinkney, David. *Napoleon III and the Rebuilding of Paris.* Princeton: Princeton University Press, 1958.

Poulot, Dominique. "L'invention de la bonne volonté culturelle: l'image du musée au XIXe siècle." *Le Mouvement social,* no. 131 (April–June 1985): 35–64.

Prendergast, Christopher. *Paris and the Nineteenth Century.* Manchester: Basil Blackwell, 1992.

Prochasson, Christophe. *Les années électriques.* Paris: Editions de la Découverte, 1991.

Py, Christiane, and Cécile Ferenczi. *La fête foraine d'autrefois: les années 1900.* Lyons: La Manufacture, 1987.

Ragon, Michel. *The Space of Death.* Translated by Alan Sheridan. Charlottesville: University of Virginia Press, 1983.

Rearick, Charles. *Pleasures of the Belle Epoque.* New Haven: Yale University Press, 1985.

Rioux, Jean-Pierre. *Frissons fin-de-siècle.* Paris: Le Monde, 1990.

Roberts-Jones, Philippe, *De Daumier à Lautrec: essai sur l'histoire de la caricature française entre 1860 et 1890.* Paris: Beaux-Arts, 1960.

Robichon, François. "Les panoramas en France au 19e siècle." Thèse de IIIe cycle, Université de Paris, Nanterre, 1982.

———. "Le panorama, spectacle d'histoire." *Le Mouvement social* (April–June 1985): 65–86.

Romi. *Petite histoire des cafés-concerts.* 1950.

Roncayolo, Marie-Florence. "Recherches sur la topographie des loisirs populaires dans Paris au XIXe siècle." Master's thesis, Université de Paris, I, 1977.

Root-Bernstein, Michelle. *Boulevard Theater and Revolution in Eighteenth-Century Paris.* Ann Arbor: UMI Research Press, 1984.

Ross, Kristin. *Fast Cars, Clean Bodies.* Cambridge, Mass.: MIT Press, 1995.

Ruby, Jay. *Secure the Shadow: Death and Photography in America.* Cambridge, Mass.: MIT Press, 1995.

Sadoul, Georges. *Histoire générale du cinéma.* Vol. 2. Paris: Denoël, 1948.

Sallée, André, and Philippe Chauveau. *Music-hall et café-concert.* Paris: Bordas, 1985.

Sandberg, Mark. "Missing Persons: Spectacle and Narrative in Late Nineteenth-Century Scandinavia." Ph.D. dissertation, University of California, Berkeley, 1991.

———. "Effigy and Narrative: Looking into the Nineteenth-Century Folk Museum." In *Cinema and the Invention of Modern Life,* edited by Leo Charney and Vanessa R. Schwartz. Berkeley: University of California Press, 1995.

Schivelbusch, Wolfgang. *The Railway Journey.* Berkeley, University of California Press, 1977.

Schneider, William. *An Empire for the Masses.* Westport, Conn.: Greenwood Press, 1982.

Schor, Naomi. *Reading in Detail.* New York: Methuen, 1987.

Schudson, Michael. *Discovering the News: A Social History of American News-papers.* New York: Basic Books, 1978.

Séguin, Jean-Pierre. *Nouvelles à sensation.* Paris: Armand Colin, 1959.

Shapiro, Barbara Stern, ed. *Pleasures of Paris: Daumier to Picasso.* Boston: Museum of Fine Arts, 1991.

Sharpe, William, and Leonard Wallock, eds. *Visions of the Modern City.* Baltimore: Johns Hopkins University Press, 1987.

Sherman, Daniel. *Worthy Monuments.* Cambridge, Mass.: Harvard University Press, 1989.

Silverman, Debora L. *Art Nouveau in Fin-de-Siècle France: Politics, Psychology, and Style.* Berkeley: University of California Press, 1989.

Simon, Robert. "Cézanne and the Subject of Violence." *Art in America,* May 1991.

Sonn, Richard D. *Anarchism and Cultural Politics in Fin-de-Siècle France.* Lincoln: University of Nebraska Press, 1989.

Sontag, Susan. *On Photography.* 1977. New York: Doubleday, 1989.

Sternberger, Dolf. "Panorama of the Nineteenth Century." *October* 4 (fall 1987).

Stewart, Susan. *On Longing.* Baltimore: Johns Hopkins University Press, 1984.

Sweeney, Regina. "Harmony and Disharmony: French Singing and Musical Entertainment during the Great War." Ph.D. dissertation, University of California, Berkeley, 1992.

Taylor, Katherine Fischer. *In the Theater of Criminal Justice: The Palais de Justice in the Second Empire.* Princeton: Princeton University Press, 1993.

Terdiman, Richard. *Discourse / Counter-Discourse.* Ithaca: Cornell University Press, 1985.

Tester, Keith, ed. *The Flâneur.* New York: Routledge, 1994.

Thiesse, Anne-Marie. *Le roman du quotidien.* Paris: Le Chemin Vert, 1984.

Toulet, Emanuelle. *Cinématographe: l'invention du siècle.* Paris: Découvertes Gallimard, 1988.

Veeser, H. Aram, ed. *The New Historicism.* New York: Routledge, 1989.

Verhagen, Marcus. "Refigurations of Carnival: The Comic Performer in Fin-de-Siècle Parisian Art." Ph.D. dissertation, University of California, Berkeley, 1994.

Veyriras, Paul. "Visiteurs britanniques à la morgue de Paris au dix-neuvième siècle." *Cahiers victoriens et édouardiens,* no. 15 (April 1982): 51–61.

Walkowitz, Judith. *City of Dreadful Delight: Narratives of Sexual Danger in Late Victorian London.* Chicago: University of Chicago Press, 1992.

Weber, Eugen. *France: Fin-de-Siècle.* Cambridge, Mass.: Belknap Press, 1989.

Wilcox, Scott. "The Panorama and Related Exhibitions in London." Master's thesis, University of Edinburgh, 1976.

Williams, Alan. *Republic of Images.* Cambridge, Mass.: Harvard University Press, 1992.

Williams, Linda. *Viewing Positions.* New Brunswick: Rutgers University Press, 1994.

Williams, Rosalind. *Dream Worlds: Mass Consumption in Late Nineteenth-Century France*. Berkeley: University of California Press, 1982.

Wilson, Elizabeth. *The Sphinx in the City: Urban Life, The Control of Disorder and Women*. Berkeley: University of California Press, 1991.

Wittkop-Menardeau, Gabrielle. *Madame Tussaud*. Paris: France-Empire, 1976.

Wolff, Janet. *Feminine Sentences*. Berkeley: University of California Press, 1990.

Wolgensinger, Jacques. *L'histoire à la une: la grande aventure de la presse*. Paris: Découvertes Gallimard, 1989.

Zeldin, Theodore. *France, 1848–1945*. 2 vols. Oxford: Clarendon Press, 1977.

Index